QUINNTESSENTIAL
FEARGAL

Feargal Quinn is perhaps best known as the founder of the Superquinn supermarket chain, which he sold in 2005. He wrote the best-selling books *Crowning the Customer*, which has been translated into ten languages, and *Mind Your Own Business* and presented the television series *Feargal Quinn's Retail Therapy* and Local Heroes: *A Town Fights Back*. He has received a Fellowship, five Honorary Doctorates, the French Ordre national du Mérite and a Papal Knighthood. He is Adjunct Professor at the National University of Galway and a past President of Euro Commerce.

Feargal was an independent Senator for twenty-three years. He lives in Dublin with his wife Denise; they have five children.

QUINNTESSENTIAL
FEARGAL

A Memoir
FEARGAL QUINN

THE O'BRIEN PRESS
DUBLIN

First published 2016 by
The O'Brien Press Ltd,
12 Terenure Road East, Rathgar,
Dublin 6, D06 HD27 Ireland.
Tel: +353 1 4923333; Fax: +353 1 4922777
E-mail: books@obrien.ie
Website: www.obrien.ie

The O'Brien Press is a member of Publishing Ireland.

ISBN: 978-1-84717-842-8

Front cover photograph © Fiona Brophy.
Back cover photograph © Hannah Levy.

1 3 5 7 8 6 4 2
16 18 20 19 17

Printed and bound by ScandBook AB, Sweden

The paper in this book is produced using pulp from managed forests

Published in:

DUBLIN
UNESCO
City of Literature

Quinntessential
FEARGAL

CONTENTS

A BRIEF NOTE
OF THANKS

I can't even begin to thank all the colleagues, customers, friends and family members who have helped me over the years. In fact, if I were to attempt to do so, I would probably need another book just to fit everyone in. So I won't do that here! But a memoir does not write itself; and with this in mind there are a number of people who have provided me with help, encouragement and advice in bringing this most personal of projects to fruition.

Denise and my children Eamonn, Giliane, Stephen, Zoe and Donal as well as my sister Eilagh were always at hand to lend their support and provide context throughout the writing and editing process. This is deeply appreciated.

Vincent O'Doherty, Damien Carolan, Pat Byrne and Jim Treacy provided a watchful eye and helped to proofread relevant sections.

I also owe a very special thanks to John Downes, Bairbre Murray and Anne O'Broin, who researched and compiled the interviews that form the basis of this book.

Finally, to Michael O'Brien and all at O'Brien Press, and Brendan O'Brien (freelance editor): I (literally) could not have done it without you.

SELLING SUPERQUINN

I will always remember the day I sold the company that bore my name. As I sat in the offices of William Fry, Solicitors, just off Dublin's Fitzwilliam Square, there was an unmistakable sense of celebration in the air. Champagne bottles were on ice; those present in the room were in a happy, positive mood.

This surprised me: I had expected the day to be a dull affair, filled with legal formalities.

My sons Eamonn, Stephen and Donal and my daughter Gilliane, as well as the former Executive Chairman of Superquinn, Vincent O'Doherty, had accompanied me to the meeting where we finalised the signing over of the company. After that day, it would no longer be directly run by me or my family. Even saying those words now, at more than a decade's remove, seems a little strange.

Earlier that morning, I kissed my wife Denise goodbye as I left our home on the hill of Howth, where we have lived for forty years. She muttered a brief few words of encouragement and reminded me that this would be a happy day for us, as a family. Onwards and upwards to the next chapter.

As always, the thirty-minute car journey to Dublin's city centre took me through Sutton Cross, past the Superquinn store, my base as a retailer for decades.

During the drive into the city, I couldn't help remembering the many great times we had over the years at Superquinn. It all started in 1960 when we opened our very first shop, Quinn's Supermarket, in Dundalk.

The fun times ranged from madcap publicity ideas involving soap stars, elephants and tractors to general election candidates taking part in hustings off the back of a truck in one of our car parks. They included price wars, public speaking engagements and much more besides.

The many brilliant people who worked alongside me in Superquinn truly made it what it was. They helped to generate a lifetime of memories.

And yet on 25 August 2005, as I prepared to sell up, I was more convinced than ever that it was the right decision for me, for my family, and to secure the future of the company and its staff. In truth, that day in the solicitors' office represented the culmination of a conversation within my family that had been taking place for some time.

The reasons for selling when we did were many and varied. The advent of increased competition, both from German retailers Aldi and Lidl and the response of other larger competitors with much deeper pockets, was a definite factor.

At Superquinn, we had always insisted where possible that we would own our own sites. But in boom-time Ireland, such sites were becoming increasingly hard to find at rates that made any kind of financial sense. This meant that the scope to continue our company mantra of sustainable expansion was becoming seriously curtailed.

Also, others valued our land at multiples of what we could make from running a grocery business there. I remember one developer saying to me, 'I can't believe you don't put eight floors on top of that shop and two levels of car parking underneath. You could make much more money.'

It was a way of looking at the Superquinn sites that was alien to me. At heart I was a grocer, not a property developer. Also I was keenly aware that all good family-owned companies need to have a well-formulated succession plan, allowing the founder to exit the company in a controlled fashion.

The perils of failing to prepare properly are plain to see in the ruins of many such family companies around the world. As I will talk about later, this is something that directly affected a previous generation within my own family.

I was anxious to learn from these experiences.

Fundamental to any such succession planning is whether there are members of the family who wish to take on the mantle, to build on whatever success the company has enjoyed to date. So I went to my five children and outlined the lie of the land. Some, like my sons Eamonn and Stephen, were already involved in the company on a day-to-day level and were well aware of the pressures we faced.

'Others value this company highly, and I'm getting to the stage that I'm not going to start getting into construction and building,' I told them. 'Do you want to?'

Quite rightly, particularly with the hindsight that the collapse of the Celtic Tiger allows, they said 'We don't know anything about property development. It's not for us.'

It was abundantly clear to me that all five of my children's interests lay elsewhere. As parents, Denise and I had always tried to encourage them to follow their passions. It just so happened that these did not lie with property development.

Amid potential interest from some of the biggest players on the scene, one offer stood out. The successful bidder, Select Retail Holdings, would go on to be fronted by an experienced and dynamic young Dublin-born retailer, Simon Burke.

As I sat in the lawyers' offices there was an undoubted element of sadness at signing over a company that had meant so much to my family for almost half a century. A business that had started with me and just seven others working in one small shop had grown, almost fifty years later, to employ about 3500 people.

But this sadness was tinged with relief – and celebration – that the day I had been anticipating for some time had finally arrived.

I was ready to sell the company, to wish the new owners well, and to start a new chapter.

This is my story.

SECTION I

TO BEGIN AT THE BEGINNING

1

THE MAKING
OF ME!

To say that I have retailing in my blood is something of an understatement. I am a third-generation grocer. And it all started with my grandfather John Quinn, who was born in 1865 in Atticall, Co. Down, a small village in the middle of the Mourne Mountains.

Grandfather Quinn was the early business pioneer in our family. He left home at an early age and went to Liverpool, where he worked in a grocery shop called Hughes (which still exists). It was along the lines of the well-known Findlater's grocery stores in Ireland. To the best of my knowledge, that is the first family link to the grocery business.

By dint of sheer hard work, and more than a little flair for the business, he rose to General Manager at Hughes, a prestigious position in this most Irish of English cities.

He travelled home to a wedding in Saul, Co. Down, where he met the love of his life, my grandmother Mary Fitzsimons. They were married on 2 June 1898 at Saul Church, Downpatrick, and went on to have ten children. The first six (!) in a row were boys: Seán, Padraig, Eamonn (my father), Malachy (father of my cousins, the former Labour Minister Ruairí and Lochlann of Glen Dimplex fame), Brian and Kevin. And, as luck would have it, their last four children were girls: Una, Joan, Sheila and Máire.

In 1909, my grandparents decided to move home from England, along with their ever-expanding brood. Later that year, Grandfather Quinn opened his first shop in Newry. He called it 'Quinn's of the Milestone', after a milestone on the building that signalled it was fifty old Irish miles to Dublin.

A black and white photo of that shop – which is now owned by Dunnes Stores – hangs proudly on the wall of my office at the end of my garden at home in Howth. It paints a picture of a very different era. You can see the proud staff lined up in their crisp uniforms outside what was quite a large store, with sides of bacon hanging beside them. The idea of taking photos of staff members, displaying pride in their work so publicly, was something I would apply in Superquinn many years later.

Grandfather Quinn was known in the area as a canny businessman, introducing innovations like the first slicing machine for rashers. In 1910, he introduced tomatoes to his store for the first time – a delicacy that was unheard of in the town.

He built the company up over the years, opening a number of other shops. Within a decade he owned between eight and ten such shops in what would become Northern Ireland, in places like Warrenpoint and Banbridge.

When Irish Independence came in 1922, the next big move was to have a shop in Dublin. So he did just that, eventually opening three shops – in Dún Laoghaire, Moore Street and the Phibsborough/Drumcondra area.

By this time my father, Eamonn, born in 1902, had joined the family trade. But before settling into his own business career, my father did something quite extraordinary and completely in tune with his natural curiosity.

Not many people realise this, but I come from a family with deep Republican ties. Grandfather Quinn was an ardent supporter of the Irish Republican movement, and in particular Sinn Féin. In fact, just two years after the 1916 Easter Rising, he acted as the proposer for future Taoiseach Éamon de Valera in the 1918 general election. At this time the political climate in Ireland was extremely unsettled.

Shortly afterwards, perhaps in an attempt to keep my father out of trouble, he sent him to Liverpool to stay with his cousins. My father was just seventeen years of age.

The relative proximity of Liverpool to Ireland was never going to suffice for my father, who was known to have an adventurous spirit. Even at that relatively tender age, he had always wanted to have a first-hand look at what he called 'the other side of the hill': the USA.

One day he met a sailor in a Liverpool pub, who was going to America the following day. The sailor said 'For £10 I'll get you on board, but you are on your own from then on.' The story goes that the pair just walked on board, bold as brass, with a sack thrown over my father's shoulder! And with that, he stowed away on a boat to the New World.

As a youngster I didn't hear much about his time in the USA from my father; he wouldn't have talked about it for fear it might give me ideas to go gallivanting too! But years later, I heard more about how he got on. Apparently he made a pal on board the ship. He and his new pal agreed that when they got to New York they would go their separate ways and then meet the following day. The only building they knew of was the famous Woolworth building.

They said 'I'll see you at the front door of Woolworths.' At 11 a.m. the following day, my father dutifully turned up to Woolworths, but he never saw his new friend again! The other young man may have been standing at another door: in their naivety, neither had realised that because Woolworths was so big, it covered the full block and there were at least four front doors.

So there he was, just seventeen years of age and completely alone in New York. He managed to survive, working his passage around the USA. All the while, he was honing the spirit of enterprise and innovation that so character-ised him in later years.

He ended up in Canada, working in a variety of jobs. At one stage, these included a job in forestry in a small town called Sioux Lookout, in Northwest-ern Ontario. By this point he had been away from Ireland for about four years without having once contacted home to tell his family how he was getting on.

Almost the entire time he was in the USA and Canada, his family had little or no idea where he was, or even that he had crossed the Atlantic. A far cry from the Skype generation of today!

While he was working in Sioux Lookout, he had an accident where he injured a finger. The nurse assigned to him in hospital asked him if he had been in touch with home. His response shocked her! This kindly nurse encouraged my father to write home, which he did. I gather that Grandfather Quinn told all the family to write back to him, with the aim of coaxing him back to Ireland.

I still have one of those letters, dating from around 1923, written by his brother Kevin, who was at school in Newry at the time. One sentence in the letter paints a vivid picture of the political climate of the time in Ireland. Kevin advises his older brother that 'The Free State is falling apart at the seams, nobody gives it any more than 6 months.'

Ultimately, the familial entreaties worked, and after five or six years away he went home. Ireland had changed almost beyond recognition. His country of birth had just come to the end of a bitter Civil War, which claimed the life of his own brother.

A year previously Seán and Pádraig, his brothers, had been fighting with the IRA under the command of Frank Aiken in the fourth northern division. They were surrounded by Treaty forces in a safe-house near Ardee in Co. Louth.

They made a break for it, but were shot as they climbed over a wall. They were taken to the Curragh; sadly, Seán died there some weeks later. He would have been around twenty-five years of age. Pádraig lost a leg in the same incident. He would go on to train as a doctor and raise a family of his own with his wife Marcy.

Many years afterwards, on my wedding day, we introduced my wife Denise's father, Commandant Ned Prendergast, to my Uncle Pádraig. To our amazement, it emerged that Ned had been the officer in charge at the Curragh army camp where Pádraig and Seán had been jailed. The pair had not met since. I remember them shaking hands. So, our wedding at the Lucan Spa Hotel in Dublin was the site of an impromptu reunion between my uncle and his jailer.

Ned himself had fought with the IRA during the War of Independence. I remember asking him 'Was it a big decision of yours as to which side in the Civil War to join?' He replied 'Not really; it was just Mick Collins [the great Irish Free State leader Michael Collins] picked up the phone and said "I need you on Tuesday." So I went with him.'

* * *

So, my father found himself back in Ireland in his early twenties, full of the 'can-do' American spirit of enterprise. He took a job working in the Dún Laoghaire branch of Quinn's of the Milestone, but soon found his opportunities to innovate quite limited.

Grandfather Quinn was a traditional grocer and believed it was not right to cut the price on goods in order to woo customers. In other words, you had to compete on service and quality, not on offering better prices than your competitors. That would be considered 'unethical'.

Looked at through a modern lens, this seems utterly bizarre. But it was the way business was conducted in Ireland at the time. In fact, a Government policy called 'resale price maintenance' was in force right until the mid-1960s, meaning it was actually against the law to compete on price for certain 'controlled' items.

So, if Jacob's said the price for one of their goods was to be a shilling, they wouldn't supply you if you sold it for eleven pence. If Cadbury's said 'That's a sixpenny bar of chocolate', you couldn't sell it for fivepence ha'penny. The approach was very much 'If you do, we won't supply you.'

I can well understand how frustrating this must have been for my father. He had come back from America, where simply everybody competed for business. By 1936, the year I was born, he had been working for over ten years at Quinn's of the Milestone in Dublin. Now in his mid-thirties, he decided that words alone would never convince his father of the need for innovation.

So he did the unthinkable. He opened a new shop in Kilmainham that year in order to show his father exactly how such a model could work.

Unknown to my grandfather, he asked Tom Barry, a man who had worked for Quinn's of the Milestone, to manage the shop for him. The name he chose for the new venture was Payantake. Apparently, such was the secrecy of this new enterprise that my father would visit the shop wearing a fake pair of glasses so that nobody would recognise him!

It is difficult to overstate just how different the retail climate was in those days. Up until that time traditional grocery businesses had been trading under the old style of 'credit and delivery'. My father's big idea was to ask customers to pay for their goods and take them away with them, there and then.

The way it worked was that when you went into the shop there were four or five departments, and you had to pay cash at each department. So you went to the fruit & veg department, you went to the bacon department, etc., and paid in full at each counter. The shock and horror of it all!

My father cut prices but he also had very tight controls on stock. There were a limited number of products. They didn't sell meat, apart from bacon, but you would have had a whole side of bacon. Other staples on sale included eggs and butter, which came in on a big slab. You had to cut it up into fifty-six 1 lb portions and then wrap it for the customer to take home.

It is hard to imagine nowadays, but back in those days the Payantake way of conducting retailing was a huge innovation in the grocery trade. At that time, Quinn's of the Milestone would have employed horses, carts and bicycles and would have delivered the goods alongside offering credit. This meant they often didn't get paid for weeks or months.

Payantake had no vans, no transport, no bicycles and no delivery. And it only sold for cash, rather than offering credit to its customers.

The new venture was a big success from its opening day, leading to queues outside the store as word got around that household staples were cheaper there than anywhere else. It was then that tensions within the wider Quinn family reached boiling point.

Grandfather, who by this stage was fairly wealthy and travelling abroad on holiday a lot, was also spending most of his time in Newry. So he was perhaps not as aware of the goings-on in Dublin as he might have been.

Meanwhile my father lived in Dublin, helping to run all three Quinn's of the Milestone shops, as well as his new venture. He always saw Payantake as a

way of illustrating to Grandfather Quinn just how important it was to innovate. He maintained it was never his intention to compete with the established
shops, but rather to show the way forward for the company as a whole.

When grandfather came back from holiday he was met at the boat and told
that 'Eamonn has opened up a shop in Kilmainham in competition with you.'
There was a huge row, with much misunderstanding, and Grandfather Quinn
and Eamonn fell out badly.

Eventually, in order to resolve the impasse, it was agreed that they would
close Quinn's of the Milestone in Dublin and change them all over to the
Payantake brand in 1936. Meanwhile the Quinn's of the Milestone shops
north of the border would remain as they were, with my father playing no role
in the operation of these stores.

But he would now own 45% of the new company formed to operate Payantake in Dublin. His father and the rest of the family would own 45% and two
managers, Tom Barry and Hugh Boyle, would each own 5%.

The business continued to prosper in the following years. By 1946 my father,
having run Payantake during a period that included the Second World War,
when it was extremely hard to prosper in any line of business, had opened
eight shops. He was quite well off, and had bought a lovely house on Vernon
Avenue in Clontarf three years earlier.

Payantake was doing very well, and was a successful business. But, unfortunately, tensions in the family erupted again. They must have been bubbling for
the previous 10 years or so, and the dispute ended up in court in 1946.

I know this upset my father hugely, and no doubt my grandfather also. On
one side were grandfather and all of his other children in the business. On the
other side was my father, pretty much on his own against his family apart from
the support of one of his Payantake managers, Tom Barry.

So what was it all about? Well, I know part of the reason was that a number of the family had jobs in Payantake but it was felt that they weren't pulling their weight. In truth, I think some members of the family also felt, probably unfairly, that my father wasn't sharing the proceeds of the business equally with them.

Matters got so bad that the rowing parties ended up in court three times. The third time, the story made it into the papers. Unfortunately for him, my father got the blame and was embarrassed over the fact that people would say 'It's terrible that there's a family feud and it is getting into the papers', and 'Why did you take them to court?'

Eventually this most bitter of disputes was settled, essentially by the less than scientific method of tossing a coin! Whoever won the toss would place a value on the company. Whoever lost could either buy out the winner or sell their shareholding to the winner based on that valuation.

My father must have won the toss, as he placed quite a high value on the company. This was because he felt he could make the business pay and the other family members would automatically sell to him. But, to his surprise, they called his bluff and bought him out of the business.

In 1946 this left him, at the age of just 44, with a considerable sum of money but no real job anymore. There was no question of him not working: it was simply not in the DNA of this energetic, driven entrepreneur.

But under the terms of the deal, he could not go back to the grocery business in Dublin for a long period. This would have huge implications for my entire family, and ultimately the success of my own business career.

It meant that, for the first time, we would be entering the world of entertainment.

Based on the simple flick of a coin!

2

AN ENTERTAINING
CHILDHOOD

She has smoothed out the ruts which at times came in my path and by her sweet
personality has cheered me when I most needed cheering. I thank God for placing
me in her way ... Any success or good I have done in life I owe to her.
(Excerpt from the Last Will and Testament of Eamonn Quinn, June 1933)

It is fair to say that my mother, Maureen Donnelly, made a huge impact on my father from the very first moment they encountered one another, in the not-so-romantic setting of Dún Laoghaire Post Office, Co. Dublin.

My mother, known as 'Daisy', was one of six children born to her mother, Mary Corr, and her father, Simon Donnelly, who lived to be 85. She grew up on a farm in North Armagh. Her family were Catholics in a Protestant area, so they farmed the less fertile land on the banks of Lough Neagh. Their income would have come partly from eel fishing.

I remember driving out from Portadown to their home one day. One of their neighbours had painted the roof of his barn green, the walls white and the doors orange. So you could see this green, white and orange Irish tricolour from a distance. It was a move aimed at goading the Unionist members of the community who lived nearby. It was that kind of place.

Within her family, Daisy was regarded as a bright, intelligent young girl. She left school at about the age of sixteen in 1918. She got a job in the post office, which was still the Royal Mail in those days as Ireland was part of the United Kingdom. She was sent immediately to Aberystwyth in North Wales. She often talked about it because she loved Aberystwyth. There was a university there and there were a lot of students around her age.

After a while she applied to be transferred closer to home. She went first to a post office in Clones before she was moved to Dún Laoghaire. That was when fate, and a few phone calls, intervened.

Back in those days, when you wanted to phone home – as my father regularly did to Newry – first you had to ring through to the local post office. My father discovered that the telephonist who took his call had a nice Northern accent, like his own. After speaking to her a couple of times, he was quite taken by her and said 'We must meet.'

But then he got a little apprehensive. What had he done, organising a date with a woman he had never set eyes upon? He decided to investigate surreptitiously.

He went along to Dún Laoghaire Post Office; there were three women behind the counter. He recounted that 'There was one auld one, one plain-looking one and one smasher!' He bought a penny stamp from the 'auld one': she had a Cork accent. He went out, entered again and bought a penny stamp from the 'plain-looking' lady. She had a Dublin accent.

To his eternal relief, by a process of elimination he knew the 'smasher' must have been the one with the Northern accent. From that moment, he was smitten.

I told this story at an event in Dún Laoghaire Post Office not long after I took up the Chairmanship of An Post. The postmaster brought up a big book, about the size of a table. We opened it and there, to my surprise, in my mother's handwriting was how much she earned in the different jobs she had. It said 'Left upon marriage' in May 1931, when she was twenty-nine.

My parents got married on 17 June in Maghery in North Armagh, on the banks of Lough Neagh. While my father was still young, he was the son of John Quinn, a very successful businessman. He was seen as an 'up and coming' person, so to a certain extent she got a 'catch' as a husband. At the same time he was lucky to marry a smart, intelligent woman who was fiercely loyal to him.

I don't remember hearing my parents talking much about their courtship or relationship, but I do know they loved each other deeply.

Some years after my father died in 1972 (of which, more later), I got a call from Newry to say they had opened a safe and found an envelope inside. It was the Quinn's of the Milestone safe, and the letter in the envelope was from Eamonn Quinn. It said on it 'Not to be opened until after my death.' I went up and got it.

It is dated 3 June 1933, and is described as his last will and testament (see Appendix 1). But in truth, it is also the most wonderful love letter to my mother. I brought it down to Dublin and showed it to her and to my sister Eilagh. My mother burst into tears as we read it together.

I would love to be able to write a letter like that. It had lain unopened in that safe for over 40 years.

My parents had one of those relationships where everything is debated. In fact, some people would get into the car with them and say afterwards, 'Your mother and father are always arguing.' But we never saw it as that; rather we knew they got a real enjoyment out of debate and discussion.

My mother would have been the more 'religious' of the two, although my father would never have suggested that he wasn't religious. I remember when Eilagh and I were young, he would kneel beside the bed to say prayers with us. We had to say the rosary every night, with all the trimmings. But I always suspected he was doing it as much to set an example to us both as anything else.

My father was a tickler, a talker and a fun man. He was a far less austere father than Grandfather Quinn. He would come home in the evening and tell me all about what had happened in the office that day.

It is something I continued with our own children years later. I remember our youngest son Donal would ask as I came in from work, 'Dad, Dad, what happened today?' I always had to have a story, just as my father would have had stories. He was running Payantake and there was always something happening. Some of the stories I heard, particularly the excitement of drumming up extra business and that sort of thing, sounded like great fun.

My mother had come from a different background. Her brothers were very astute and became successful fruit farmers in Co. Dublin. She wasn't a fun person as my father was, and most certainly was the disciplinarian in the family; she ensured that we learned our manners. But she was absolutely devoted to us both. As a couple, they complemented each other brilliantly.

I was born in November 1936, three years before the Second World War started in September 1939. Overall I have very happy memories of my childhood. My sister, Eilagh, is two and a half years older than me. We are extremely close to this day. Her real name is Sheila Mary, but she has been known as Eilagh because as a child I could not pronounce her name properly, and it stuck. So she has me to thank for that!

That is not to say that growing up we always agreed on everything. We were always having rows. I would come running into the house in tears saying 'She did this' or 'She did that', like any other brother and sister.

One of my earliest memories of the war years is of when I was about four, and we went on a day trip to Rush in north Co. Dublin in my father's car. I had a great time going up and down the sand dunes on the beach there. I was at school the following day when everybody was talking about the German attack on Russia.

Now this didn't make any sense to me at all. Somewhat indignantly, I told the class this could not be true as we had been there the day before, in the sand dunes. When I got home my father had to tell me that that we had not in fact been to a different country, and that Rush was not Russia!

One of the things my father would often ask, if anybody came to the house, was 'What do you do if the bombers come?' Eilagh and I would answer immediately: 'You run under the table or run under the bed and put your hands over your ears, that's what you do.'

We never saw German bombers overhead, but at midday on a Saturday the air-raid sirens went off to remind you what they sounded like. So the threat of war was always present.

Then one night, we were at home in Blackrock and the air-raid sirens went off for real. We could hear the sound of planes overhead and shots being fired at them. Then we heard the sound of bombs being dropped on Dublin's North Strand.

That was 31 May 1941, and I was five years old. I don't remember being scared: it was all a bit of a game to us children. But twenty-eight people were killed that night, a further ninety were injured and around 300 homes were damaged or destroyed.

Two years later, in a fit of patriotic fervour, I got it into my head that I could stop any more bombings of Irish territory. We had just moved to our house in Clontarf, so it would have been around May 1943. The reason my parents chose to live in Clontarf was that my mother's brothers and sister had moved to Oldtown in north County Dublin, and she wanted to be closer to them.

I had transferred to the Holy Faith Convent in Clontarf, which taught boys up until their First Holy Communion. Our new house was on a good five acres of land, and you can imagine my excitement at seeing the size of the fields for us to play in. There was even a fish pond with a fountain in it. Marilyn, my cousin, came to live with us for a number of years as her mother had died. I remember exploring the house with her and Eilagh.

I was upstairs when they came across the fish pond with the fountain. The girls figured out how to turn the fountain on, and I was very excited running down to look at it, along with all the different fish in the pond.

But looking at the field, I was most taken by the huge number of daisies and buttercups. German warplanes would pass overhead on their way to bombing missions in Britain. So I had a bright idea: a way to tell the planes that they were over Ireland and not to bomb us. I mapped out a huge area of the field – it must have been around 100 metres by 200 metres – and divided it in three.

I decided that if I picked all the daisies and the buttercups in the first section it would be green. Then if I picked all the buttercups in the middle, that section would be white. Finally, if I picked all the daisies the last part, it would be gold. I knew the Irish tricolour was technically meant to be green, white and orange, but I figured I was close enough. I diligently set to work.

Unfortunately, I was a little too ambitious in choosing such a large area! I got the green bit done, but by the time I picked the buttercups in the 'white' section, the daisies and buttercups were being blown all over the 'green' section, and when I moved on to the 'gold' section … well, let's just say I never actually finished my Irish Garden Tricolour Initiative!

I maintain to this day that the concept was good: to save Ireland from the war; to protect us from any planes coming over to bomb us by mistake!

Overall, they were very happy days, with lots of fun and plenty of freedom to explore. In many ways it was very different to the type of upbringing young children have today.

For example, I remember vividly that a few months earlier, when we were still living on Newtownpark Avenue in Blackrock, my father decided to teach me a lesson about being independent.

At this stage he had offices in the city centre. Mummy would put me on the tram in Temple Hill, Blackrock, and Daddy would wait for me at Nelson's Pillar on O'Connell Street. His office was on Chapel Lane, off Parnell Street, but you could approach it from Moore Street.

This one time, he asked 'If I wasn't there some day, would you know your way?' Full of chutzpah, despite being just six years old, I replied with absolute confidence that I would.

I was preparing for my Holy Communion at the time, and I travelled in to visit Danny McDevitt, the tailor who was making my suit.

When I got off the tram on O'Connell Street, my father wasn't there to meet me. I wasn't too worried. I headed down Henry Street and counted out the streets. But there's a little lane which I counted as a street, so I found myself on Moore Street instead of Liffey Street.

And suddenly I didn't know where I was. The tears started to flow. There I was, standing in the middle of Moore Street, alone in the world and bawling crying. Out of nowhere a man from my father's office came up to me to ask if I was all right. Of course, he had been sent by my father to watch me all along.

It's interesting now, looking back, that my mother didn't have any worry about regularly putting her six-year-old son on to the tram. And my father, ostensibly, didn't have any worry about me getting off the tram and heading down to his office on my own. How times have changed!

* * *

I made my First Holy Communion in May 1943 at the Holy Faith School in Clontarf. I was small for my age: in fact, I'm by far the smallest in the Holy Communion photograph. I then left Holy Faith and went to the local private school, Kostka College. It's named in honour of a Polish saint, St Stanislaus Kostka. I loved that I could cycle to the school on Seafield Road, Clontarf, as we lived just down the road on Vernon Avenue.

By the time I was nine years of age, I had made my first firm plans to become an entrepreneur. A section of our field at home was cordoned off for growing vegetables, and I was helping to grow lettuce there. It got me thinking: 'Could I sell these lettuces?' So off I went down to Madden's store, now called Nolan's, on Vernon Avenue with two of my finest heads of lettuce.

They were glorious, big heads of lettuce! Clearly impressed, Mr Madden said 'You probably picked the best of the lot, did you?' And I said 'Yes, well, I wasn't going to pick the worst!' He said 'They are very good lettuce; I'll happily buy them. I'll pay you three pence a head, three shillings a dozen. And I'll take two dozen.'

This meant I had to pick out two dozen every day or every second day. He wanted to get them before I went to school, too. I was growing them in the big field, and there was no shortage of lettuces to meet demand. But supplying them could prove a logistical challenge!

I had a bicycle, but was not sure how I was going to get two dozen down to Madden's to fill the order. So I roped in a school pal, Liam (Bill) Thompson, who now lives near me in Howth, and we struck a deal.

Liam would come up in the morning. We cut the lettuce together and put them in the boxes. He put a dozen on the back of his bike and I put a dozen on the back of mine. And off we cycled down to Mr Madden.

But the perils of the fluctuating lettuce market intervened. Mr Madden decided that 'I'm afraid the lettuce isn't selling all that well and I can only pay you 2/6.' In other words, 2 and a ha'penny per head of lettuce, which was a big hit on our 'margins'!

At nine, I was too shy to argue. After all, I was still getting a decent price, although I had to share it with Liam. I got my deal, but I wasn't tough enough to negotiate. Looking back, I probably could have got 2/9 instead of 2/6. And, of course, to this day a part of me still smarts at the fact I didn't get the best deal possible!

As a nation, we owe a huge debt of gratitude to the former Irish rugby captain, Brian O'Driscoll, or BOD as he is known to many. I have spent many an afternoon in the Lansdowne Road stadium marvelling at his exploits on the playing field. But not many people know that I have a much more personal reason to be thankful to the O'Driscoll family. In fact, if it wasn't for them I would not be here today.

If you ask my sister Eilagh to describe me as a child growing up, one thing she would say is that I was accident-prone, constantly getting cuts and scrapes. One incident in particular stands out.

I was nine years of age, and was playing in a loft at home when I fell and hit my head on the stone floor beneath. I remember being brought up to bed and my father being sent for. He came home and ran up the stairs to me. I don't remember much else after the accident, but apparently I was talking nonsense at the time.

My father immediately phoned our local doctor, a certain Dr O'Driscoll, aka BOD's grandfather, who lived on Mount Prospect Avenue. Dr O'Driscoll insisted that I be brought to hospital, rather than 'sleeping it off' at home, as he feared I might have fractured my skull. He was proved right!

He knew a skilled head surgeon who had just returned from the USA and was working at the Richmond Hospital in Dublin. Luckily for me, he was able to get the surgeon to examine me. I was very ill, and was in a coma for three days. But with time, and thanks to Dr O'Driscoll's quick intervention, my life was saved.

I was in hospital for a few weeks and missed a whole term at school. I went up North and my mother, who refused to leave my side, stayed in the guest room of my Aunt Kathleen and Uncle Jim Joe's house while I recuperated.

Many years later, Dr O'Driscoll met my father and told him: 'Do you know, I've been a doctor all my life and if there's one life I know that I have saved, it's your son Feargal's.'

In the early 1980s I got a chance to thank him personally. I was working in our Sutton shop on a very wet, dark night. The place was packed with queues of people at the checkout and this older man, who was about 80, came up to me with a big box of chocolates that he wanted to buy. It was for 10/6, so it was an expensive box of chocolates.

He had only a pound note on him and he said 'Do I have to queue up at the checkouts, young man?' Never one to inconvenience a customer, I said 'I'm sure we'll get you through somehow; you've only the one item.' As I was trying to find out where I could get change for his one pound note, he looked at me and said 'You know, I saved your boss's life.'

I looked at him and said 'You must be Dr O'Driscoll so!' And the man nearly burst into tears. He did not realise who I was. I tried to cover my tracks by saying something like 'Sure everybody in Superquinn is told the story about how Dr O'Driscoll saved Feargal's life.'

I said 'Dr O'Driscoll, there's no way you are paying for those chocolates' and I walked out to the car with him. I had to decide 'Will I tell him who I am?', as I was on the point of letting him believe that every member of staff in Superquinn knew he had saved my life forty years earlier. But as I put him in the car I introduced myself.

It was a really lovely moment, and explains just why I hold the entire O'Driscoll family in such high esteem.

I mentioned previously that we grew up in a family with strong Republican ties. I have a vivid memory of being on my father's shoulders in O'Connell Street in 1945 when Seán T. O'Kelly was inaugurated as President, as well as being taken at a very early age to the Mansion House to a public meeting featuring a man representing the Mau Mau secret society in Kenya. At the time, the Mau Mau would have been regarded as similar to the IRA; the British would have seen them as killers. But my father clearly sympathised with their cause.

Later my father became Chairman of the Dublin Green Cross Committee, an organisation that existed mainly up North. It was established to help the families of Republican prisoners who were interned. It still exists.

I remember that I came home from school one day during the war, in 1943, and there was a strange man sitting there. I had no idea who he was – all I knew was that he was put up and sheltered in our home.

Later I learned that there had been a jailbreak in Derry and a number of prisoners had escaped. When my father went to his office he was told there was a man who wanted to see him. The man was one of the escapees, and he said 'Your cousin was in prison with me.' This was John (Seán) Quinn. Apparently Seán had said to him 'If you ever go to Dublin look up my cousin Eamonn; he'll look after you.'

Without batting an eyelid, and despite being in a room with an escaper who was being hunted by the authorities, my father asked 'What do you do for a living?'

'I'm a roofer, a tiler,' was the reply.

My father responded, 'Well, you can come home with me because we have some tiles that need repair.' So this man came home and stayed while he did the work. When it was finished after a few days, he said 'I'm going back for the cause.' My father tried to counsel him against such a move, but he was resolute.

As soon as he crossed the border on the bus he was arrested and interned again.

3

RED ISLAND DAYS

I was around ten at the time of the sale of my father's share in Payantake. There was simply no question of him not working. He was an incredibly energetic, enthusiastic man, with a lust for life and a real passion to innovate. Also he was still quite a young man, aged only forty-four, with a sum of money to invest.

Precluded from entering the grocery business, he looked at his options. He travelled to the UK, where he noticed that there was a lot of publicity for a man called Billy Butlin: a well-known tourism entrepreneur who had opened a chain of Butlin's Holiday Camps from 1936 onwards. And that's where the idea to build a holiday camp started.

My father had no experience whatsoever of the travel trade, but he was not the type to let this stop him. He went to Filey in North Yorkshire for a week to see what a Butlin's camp was like. I remember him recalling that it was raining and he was staying in a chalet. He said 'I could do a much better job. Instead of building chalets I'll put it all under one roof.'

There must have been a fair amount of trauma for my parents – my father in particular – while the family drama around Payantake played itself out in the courts. But at my age it didn't really mean anything to me. I was just told that my father was building a holiday camp!

And he did just that. In 1947 he opened Red Island Holiday Camp – a first in Ireland – at Skerries, Co. Dublin, targeted exclusively at British tourists. The Irish didn't take holidays or, if we did, it was to the cousins down the country!

The story of how my father built Red Island tells a lot about how he operated. Actually he bought two sites: one in Red Island and one in Bray. He was planning to open a chain of holiday camps. He had formed a company called Irish Holidays Ltd, and had brought investors in to supplement his money from Payantake.

His early investors included my mother's brothers and friends, as well as business contacts he had made over the years. But he was having difficulty with the architect. My father was saying 'I had in mind that people coming over from England would love to get a view of the sea' whereas the architect was saying that only some of them would have a view of the sea. My father's response was 'No, no, there must be a better way than that.'

One day, around that time, he was getting the bus out to Blackrock and he noticed a tall young man with glasses, in his early to mid-twenties, screwing a nameplate onto the office door at 4 Merrion Square – exactly where the bus stop was. Daddy got chatting to the man and said 'What are you doing?' and was told 'Well, I've just qualified as an architect and I'm just opening up my business here. I'm screwing my nameplate to the door so people know where to find me.'

His name was Vincent Gallagher. My father went home that evening and told my mother all about it. A short while afterwards he went back to Vincent and said 'You're an architect. I'm building a holiday camp in Skerries. Could you talk to me about whether I should consider giving the job to you?'

Now this was Vincent Gallagher's first job and it was a big job, building a 252-bedroom resort. He outlined his vision of how best to maximise the sea views. Straight away my father realised 'I could work with this guy. He's listening to me. He's not telling me what I can't do.' So he gave him the job and they built Red Island together.

Red Island was very different to the traditional Irish seaside hotel; it had 252 bedrooms on an eight-acre site and was built at a cost of £150,000. It gained a first-class reputation for providing the very best in low-cost holiday accommodation. One of the big innovations was that everything was under one roof rather than in chalets, as with Butlin's. Every room had hot and cold water and central heating – real luxuries at the time. The dining-cum-function room accommodated up to 500 guests.

When the holidaymaker booked a week or a fortnight at Red Island, they paid a bill that included everything: travel, meals, accommodation and entertainment. From the moment they arrived, they didn't have to put their hand in their pocket. There were literally no extras.

In those days in particular, just after the Second World War when there wasn't much money around, that all-in price was a tremendous attraction. Customers knew exactly where they stood. No matter how hard we worked to give them a good time, we would not increase our profit from their stay; that was already 'fixed'.

Originally our mainly adult guests came by boat and stayed from Saturday to Saturday; later they would arrive by plane to Dublin airport. They paid on the day they arrived, along with a five-shilling deposit for their key. When they returned the key on the day they left, they had five shillings for the journey home. The challenge was that we wanted them to go away so satisfied with their experience at Red Island that they would be certain to come back the following year. Every single thing we did was centred on that one overriding aim.

We had a ready benchmark by which to judge our success – the number of repeat bookings. Before many of the guests left the holiday camp, they paid a deposit for the next year's holiday. Week by week, we had immediate feedback as to how well we had done.

If it was a good week, we might get fifty bookings for the next year. If it wasn't a good week, we might get only twelve. At the end of each week, we were able to say: 'It went well [or not so well] this week.' We mightn't know exactly why, but we would know how we had done. We had an instant barometer of how we had performed in satisfying customers.

Also my father took it upon himself to remain open and accessible to his guests from day one. Each evening, during the four-month holiday season, he took his meal in the main dining-room where the 500 guests were eating. This didn't take him away from his family, because we all ate there too!

But it did mean that every one of our meals was interrupted again and again by guests who would see him and come over to have a word. My mother didn't particularly like these interruptions, but they were exactly what my father wanted.

In fact, he positioned our table to encourage them. We were not hidden away in a corner, but placed near the entrance to the dining-room where nobody could fail to see him. He was not just trying to show that he and his family ate the same food as the guests; it went beyond that. He wanted to make it easy for guests to approach him.

Of course, he was around the holiday camp all the time during the day. If people had a serious problem he was not difficult to find. But he was particularly anxious to elicit informal contact about things that were not 'serious' but could be important to the customer's satisfaction.

It was a smashing example of listening to your customers, and it worked a treat. Again and again, people came up to him in the dining-room and talked to him about things that they would never have gone to his office to talk about. It was easy for them to do, and they knew he would be there every evening. His feel for his customers was greatly enhanced by making himself available in this way.

All of this would form how I did business in Superquinn, many years later. When I opened my first shop in Dundalk in 1960, I was influenced strongly by the objective of getting our 'guests' to return. I had obviously inherited this from the years spent working side by side with my father.

What's more, I discovered that my competitors' prime objective was simply to see how much profit they could make from the customer on that particular visit. Our view was this was secondary to getting the customer to come back. We called this the boomerang principle. Of which, more, later …

* * *

The ballroom in Red Island was the very definition of a multi-purpose room. In fact it was the hardest-working room in showbiz! In the mornings it was used as a breakfast room. In the evenings it was a dining room, with 500–600 guests served at tables of four.

As soon as the meal was over at 7 p.m. we cleared the tables, stacked them away, swept the ballroom, rearranged the chairs and transformed it into a theatre. Twice a week we would show films, and on other nights there was a show with entertainment from fixed entertainers like the great Hal Roach, Syl Fox and Ben Bono.

As soon as that entertainment was over, the guests left and it was transformed again into a ballroom. At 1 a.m., when the dancing was over, we swept it and set up the tables for the following morning.

Now Ireland in the 1940s was still very much a Catholic country, and the Catholic hierarchy was part and parcel of setting the social mores of the time. The difficulty was that Butlin's in Britain had built a name for sexual misbehaviour. This was because you could go away and share a chalet with somebody who was not your spouse. So the suggestion was that holiday camps were places of intrigue.

In order to combat this potential threat to the moral reputation of Red Island (!), we agreed that there would be no married quarters. All the men would be on the ground floor and all the women on the first floor! There were 125 rooms downstairs and 125 rooms upstairs. Mr Sheridan, the former Garda Sergeant in Skerries, was in charge of maintaining order.

Every night he would stay at the bottom of the stairs as the ladies and girls went upstairs and the men and boys downstairs. Within a couple of years, as the business grew, we added married quarters, but initially it was definitely a question of 'never the twain shall meet'!

Of course, we did not always get it quite right. Some years later, I became friends with a very glamorous Aer Lingus hostess who would come to Red Island regularly as it was quite near Dublin Airport. She would ask 'Have you a room for the night?' and we would always do our best to accommodate her. We would typically say 'Yes, sure, we'll squeeze you in somewhere but you'll have to share.' And she would reply 'Ah, that's OK.'

On one occasion an older brother and sister came to stay from England. He went downstairs to the men's quarters and she was sent upstairs. But they decided her legs weren't good on the stairs and they switched, without telling us.

So this older lady went to room 10 and her brother went up to room 128, on the first floor. My friend the air hostess, who was out dancing and enjoying herself, went up to bed at 2 a.m. She didn't want to wake the lady who was already fast asleep. So she undressed, got into bed and nodded off. You can imagine her shock when she woke up the following morning to discover an auld fellow in the bed opposite!

One of the big attractions for British people coming to Red Island was the food. The war had just ended and – unlike in Britain, where they had rationing until the mid-1950s – we had no rationing. So our guests could get as much food as they wanted.

Miners and other working people coming to the resort simply couldn't believe they were getting bacon, egg and sausage for breakfast, with as many extra helpings as they liked. It was something they couldn't get at all in Britain.

One of the other things my father really enjoyed was the trips we ran for the guests; the fact that he could have a direct input into promoting Ireland. Eilagh says our father did more for Irish–English relations than any Irish Government ever did!

He was very proud of Ireland and wanted people to see his country. In fact, I remember the opening day of Red Island and my father's frustration that he was not able to get the Irish Tourist Board to provide a minister to open the resort. Remember this was a big investment that employed 110 people for four months of the year, bringing in 500 guests from England every week.

He always felt that the failure to back the new holiday camp so publicly was because there was a little bit of a snobby 'hunting, shooting, fishing, golfing' mentality in the Irish Tourist Board at the time, and Red Island was too downmarket for their liking. In later years he was passionate about creating trouble for the people who wouldn't support tourism!

He used to print a pretend newspaper, *Irish Holiday Guide*, and send it to the guests along with the brochure for Red Island. The headline he had one year was 'Britain invades Ireland'. His joke was that the British had discovered what a wonderful holiday they could have in Red Island, and were coming over in huge numbers.

Several years later he made his peace with the Irish Tourist Board after they agreed to give us £2000 to advertise on television. We then had to consider how we would advertise on Granada Television.

The decision was that I would be the 'frontman' for the campaign. I was only eighteen or nineteen when I went on television to promote Red Island, showing the views from Skerries and talking it up. The 15–20-second advert aired only on Granada, around Liverpool and Manchester, where much of our clientele was based. Of course this made me famous, at least among the guests!

In 1948 my father bought a 16 mm cine camera. I still have it. He used it to entertain the guests and would go over to the working men's clubs to show them what Red Island was like. They are a real snapshot in time.

I would also travel to England to drum up trade quite regularly. My first visit to England was probably when I was in my late teens, and I went to Manchester. I visited travel agents and working men's clubs and showed the cine footage that my father had taken. We would give the brochures away and generally sell the place to them.

One of the brochures included Mixer Reed, a dwarf. He, Noel Purcell and others were part of our entertainment crew. Mixer dressed up as a leprechaun and we went over and grabbed our guests coming off the planes. At one stage our little publicity ploy even got us onto the front page of the papers.

The Monday excursion at Red Island might have been a trip to Dublin and the Guinness factory. Tuesday was a trip to the Mourne Mountains: really the Cooley Mountains, but you could see the Mournes. Another of the trips was to go over the border to Warrenpoint, where our guests could post things home to England, thereby avoiding customs. Items were available here that you couldn't get there – butter, nylons, etc. The tours also went to Bray or on a shopping trip to 'the Algiers of the North' – Drogheda!

We employed 110 during the peak season of July and August. At one stage we considered stretching the season and opening Red Island for Easter, but you really couldn't get the guests to come until May. It opened in May at a very low rate. I still have some of the brochures, with ads saying 'Liverpool back to Liverpool for £7'! And that included a week's accommodation with food and everything else.

We also tried to stretch the season until October, but it usually finished in September. Then the place would only be used over the winter for local dances on Sunday nights.

The same half dozen people would return to work there every year; the gardener was the same gardener, the chefs were pretty much the same, Mr Sheridan was on security. The rest of the staff were mainly seasonal.

We had great fun working there. Unlike most employers, my father had a policy of trying to hire people with no experience: he believed he could mould them into what he wanted. They would all come to Red Island at the beginning of the season and, of course, the place wouldn't have been looked after all that well during the winter. We would all move in. Everybody was given a paint pot and we painted everything.

Sometimes we would look to see where we could get a whole team of people who would work there, as schools didn't finish until June and you really wanted staff to start in May. One year a shirt factory closed in Derry and a factory closed in Co. Cork; of the 110 staff, there were about forty from Derry and forty from Co Cork. They couldn't understand one another because of the accents! They hadn't a clue what the others were saying!

The late 1940s and early 1950s were a really great time to be running a holiday camp in Skerries. There was a real sense of change; that we were coming out of the post-war years.

My father always loved seeing youngsters coming up from the country: many had never been to a hairdresser, never had a penny to spend on clothes, wearing the clothes handed down from their family.

Within two weeks of getting wages, the style of the hair and the clothes had changed. You could really see the difference that having a few pounds brought. It was just a joy! I remember my father saying 'Look at her: I remember her coming in and she was wearing her mother's hand-me-downs, and look at her now!'

* * *

I literally grew up in a summer holiday camp. The family moved lock, stock and barrel to Skerries for the summer. We were away from June right through to September.

It was a magical place in which to grow up. It was also a business that covered many different areas. It was expected that Eilagh and I would work in the family business even though we were still quite young.

I had a mike in my hand from an early age, acting as compère or calling out the bingo numbers. I was a waiter in the restaurant; I worked in the kitchen; I worked as a lounge boy; I worked in the office: I worked almost everywhere, but my very first job in Red Island was as a shoe-shine boy. One of the services we offered the guests was that they could have their shoes polished. As they came downstairs, I was there with a 'nugget spot' and I polished their shoes for free. I often got tips from grateful guests, which of course I loved.

The second job I had was selling the newspapers. And boy, did people love their newspapers in those days, particularly the Sunday newspapers! Our English guests would often look for the *News of the World*, but I could not oblige as it was banned by the censors in Ireland.

I was at the centre of everything at Red Island. It was all about entertaining our guests, making sure they had a brilliant time from the moment they set foot in Ireland.

My colleague John O'Halloran and I would wear a dress suit on the Saturday evening when the guests arrived so people could see that we were staff. One of the gags we used to play was when someone would come up to ask 'Excuse me, could you tell me where the men's room is, please?' and we would say 'We don't actually have one in the building, but a lot of people go down there behind that tree.' You could see them turning around towards the tree in amazement, before we confessed that we were only pulling their leg!

One of the most enjoyable years I had was when I worked as 'official' Red Island photographer. I discovered very early that the photographs that sold best were those of people smiling. Therefore, one of the photographer's key jobs was to get people to laugh. I discovered that I enjoyed getting people to laugh, even if I had to use the same routine over and over again, because, like a comedian, it was a different audience each time.

We had beautiful gardens in Red Island, but my father was certainly no expert on gardening. When the guests asked him about the plants he gave them the names of diseases – hepatitis, appendicitis. It was only when he got to influenza that they knew he was teasing them!

My mother was also a huge part of Red Island's success. She ran the main shop and a jewellery shop. She did a bit of everything. There was a hairdressing salon and she selected whoever was going to run that. She also looked after the housekeepers.

In today's parlance that would have been a senior managerial role, but in those days it was just part of everyone 'chipping in' to help the family business.

The staff were all young, and it had to be organised for everyone to get Mass on Sundays and Confession on Saturdays. Staff never really spent a penny when they were there because everything was included, and there was no alcohol to talk of.

Accommodation and food were all looked after. At the end of the summer they would have saved most or all of their money, which was a huge bonus in those days.

The guests who came to Red Island were generally older people, but every now and then there would be a reasonable number of young people. And if there were young women and no men, what would we do?

We would get in touch with Gormanstown camp and invite the Irish army reserve (or FCA) to send a group of guys. The only condition was they would have to wear jackets and ties. They were told there was no jitterbugging and no jiving: none of that modern stuff!

We would lay on transport to bring them down if we needed to make up for a surplus of girls staying there.

I remember a few girls came along that caught my eye. It was all very innocent in those days. But I would have been known as the boss's son, which probably helped!

Also, I learned to dance when I was in Red Island, which was a big asset. A lot of the dancing originally was not ballroom dancing but old-time waltzing. The Gay Gordons was a favourite old-time dance.

I was good at table tennis and there was a competition every week. I would enter, but it was expected that if by chance I won, the prize would go to the guests. I still have a cup from that time. There was a cup for table tennis, for tennis, for golf, etc. They weren't very expensive, but you got your name engraved on it.

It's now a family tradition that all the Quinns and the McCabes (Eilagh's family) compete at table tennis for the Maureen Quinn cup, called after my mother: it's a little Red Island cup, and the competition is hosted in a different house each summer. We play doubles, so it's a different team each time. It's great fun.

Being in Red Island meant I really did grow up entertaining people. My father loved company; he loved entertaining people and he had no problem getting on the microphone on occasion. But he wouldn't normally do it. That would be my job.

One of the things I remember was getting requests from older boys at school – 'What are the chances of getting a job in Red Island for the summer?' – and being able to fix it for them. That was socially useful from my point of view.

We worked hard. Although I enjoyed every minute, as I got older I was working outrageous hours. At one stage I was co-managing Red island, along-side John O'Halloran, based on 24-hour shifts. He would do from midday to midday, and I would do the following day to allow him to catch some sleep.

This meant I was up until 2 or 3 in the morning, then up again at 6 or 7. I had that afternoon and the following morning off, so it worked out.

One day, however, I was driving the minibus from a Leinster Hurling Final between Kilkenny and Wexford, and was so exhausted that I fell asleep on the way home just outside Skerries. Seven of us ended up in the Mater Hospital. Two of the girls were from Manchester – Moira and Brenda. A photograph appeared in the paper of the minibus on its side. Somebody was trying to fix it. They had got underneath the minibus, but the photograph looked as if it was on top of their legs! Moira broke her leg, and I have a scar on my eyebrow from the accident to this day.

Pretty much everybody from Red Island came to visit us in the Mater, including Eddie McGrath, who afterwards called a son after me: Feargal McGrath. Eddie came into my ward and I remember he said 'Oh gosh, Feargal, that was a terrible accident! Did you see the car, and did you see the van? Gosh, it was terrible.' Then he said 'I better go now to see the others.'

I remember thinking, 'If I ever visit somebody in hospital, I'm not going to go in there without planning it.' And now when I visit somebody in hospital, I stand outside and wonder what story I will tell, what news I will give. So I entertain them, rather than they having to entertain me.

Sometimes I can take it a bit too far! I went to visit someone a couple of years ago who was a friend of my father's and had been involved with Red Island: he was a lot older than me. I sat outside in the car before I went to see him: he wasn't in hospital; he was at home and had been ill for some time. I thought 'Oh, he'll be interested in that, and interested in this.'

I went in; he said 'Feargal, good to see you!' and I said 'I must tell you about this, and I must tell you about that!' I had about five things that would entertain him and help take his mind off himself. Eventually he said 'Will you ever shut up for a minute and let me tell you about what's wrong with me!'

Despite its success in attracting thousands of tourists to Ireland every summer, Red Island was not a huge money-spinner. It paid its way, it gave my father a good income and allowed my parents to take time off in the winter months for a holiday. The company paid dividends every year and he enjoyed the work too.

But it was not a business that had a long-term future in terms of expansion. My father realised this, and eventually shelved his plans to build another holiday camp along the same lines as Red Island in the seaside holiday town of Bray, Co. Wicklow.

As I mentioned earlier, he had already bought the site in question. It fronted onto the railway line before the line entered Bray proper from Greystones. High above this property, on Bray Head, was the Eagle's Nest Restaurant and Ballroom and some surrounding land, and he bought that property too. Ultimately he decided to run it as a going concern.

However, there was a problem in connecting the parcel of land below with the Eagle's Nest above. Although a 'right of way' footpath existed up to the Eagle's Nest, the incline in places was so steep and the terrain so rough that only hardy walkers would venture up.

My father's solution?

To commission and build Ireland and Britain's very first passenger-carrying chairlift. This would open up Bray Head (and the Eagle's Nest Restaurant and Ballroom) to greater numbers of people. It was a hugely ambitious plan.

A similar type of lift for quarried limestone (but not passengers) had been in operation for some years at the Drogheda Cement Factory. Its system involved metal containers permanently locked onto a moving steel rope, and was obviously not suitable to carry people safely.

So my father called in British Ropeway Engineering Co., specialists in this type of construction. He asked them to design and construct the project at Bray – under the strict regulations of our insurance company.

They came up with a design that involved a base station and a top station on the Eagle's Nest property. A large horizontal steel wheel was located at each station and an endless steel rope, powered electrically and supported on seven intervening pylons, would carry chairs and passengers at a gentle pace up and down again as required.

On arriving at its destination each double chair would disengage from the rope automatically and glide to a halt on a steel track, allowing the passengers to disembark. In the event of a power failure the movement of the rope could be operated by hand, though this was a somewhat slower process.

My father transferred one of his key employees at Red Island out to Bray to oversee the operation and maintenance of the installation. Obviously, safety was paramount. Jimmy Coleman, a young Tyrone man from Coalisland, had a special aptitude and understanding of the machinery involved.

But more than this, Jimmy knew the vagaries of the weather because winds of a certain strength and direction on Bray Head could mean a temporary shutdown of operations.

The chairlift was a huge attraction for Bray's visitors. I remember queues forming at the bottom station on summer mornings, awaiting the 10.00 a.m. opening to ride up to the Eagle's Nest for morning coffee. They would then continue to the Holy Year Cross and further afield. Perhaps they might inspect the 'roadway' on the towpath that was built specially for Queen Victoria as a viewing point. Lunch was available at the Eagle's Nest, if required, on the way down.

Tuesday was always a busy day for Jimmy and his staff, since Red Island operated a full day tour for its guests (sometimes up to 100 persons) to Bray (for shopping). They would take the chairlift to the Eagle's Nest for lunch before continuing to explore the Wicklow Mountains. It cost 1/6 to go up, and only a shilling to get back down.

But apart altogether from Red Island, the Eagle's Nest and Ballroom built a successful trade in catering and dancing over the years: all the while assisted, of course, by the convenience of the chairlift.

Unfortunately, for a number of reasons, in the 1960s the tourist traffic into

Bray and elsewhere began to decline. The advent of car ferries meant that a lot of incoming tourists to Dún Laoghaire came in their cars and tended to bypass Bray. In addition, holidays in Spain by air from the UK came strongly onto the market. The Northern Irish Troubles had a further dramatic impact on tourism in Ireland generally.

Early in the 1960s, my father felt obliged to sell about half of the Church Field in Bray to other commercial interests for building purposes, and thus the Raheen Park housing estate came into being. The portion that remained was laid out as a pitch & putt course.

The chairlift ran successfully from 1950 to 1970 before my father sold the remaining portion of land associated with the Bray site.

Throughout those years there was never a serious incident, which is a tribute to the dedication of its overseer. Jimmy died in 1984, but I am happy to say that Jimmy's family live nearby in Raheen Park to this day.

4

A PROPER
SCHOOLING

I was thirteen when I went to Newbridge College as a boarder in 1950. By then, Red Island had been open almost three years and I was spending all of my summers there.

I don't know why my parents chose Newbridge, but I remember Eilagh was going off to school in France that year too.

It was a Catholic school with Catholic traditions, including prayers at mealtimes and regular attendance at Mass. There were lots of priests working in the school in those days, and I always remember how they wore those majestic white robes.

I recall my father leaving me into school on my first day. Father Kiely, the headmaster, asked 'Is there any particular thing you would like us to concentrate on? I'm sure you want him to get his exams?' Now my father was a man who had travelled to America on his own at the age of just seventeen. He never went to university. So it is fair to say he wouldn't have regarded success in exams as important. His reply was quite simple: 'No, just make a man of him.'

I absolutely loved the rough and tumble of boarding school. I had been living at home with no brothers in a big house, a bit removed from my pals at school. Suddenly I was in a boarding school with loads of 'brothers'.

Anyone who has ever met me may find it hard to believe now (!), but during my schooldays I was actually quite a shy person. Part of the reason for this was that I couldn't pronounce the letter 'r'.

I remember a guest teacher coming to visit the school one day. I couldn't say 'Around the rugged rocks the ragged rascal ran.' He got me to try to say it in front of the class, and I was very embarrassed. Even today I still have some little difficulty with the letter, but I just ignore it now.

I was teased a bit about being small, but it was never in a bullying way. One of the games we played was where the smaller boys would get on the shoulders of the bigger boys and try to knock their opponents off. I remember my mother was not at all happy with this: that her son was being knocked off the bigger lads' shoulders! But it was great fun.

I was a bit of a swot at school. In 1952, the year of the centenary of Newbridge, I got first place in the class and President Seán T. O'Kelly himself came to the school. I still have the book at home that I received to mark the occasion.

I stayed in Newbridge for most of the term, including weekends. The one exception was if you made it onto one of the rugby teams: then you got to go up to Dublin to play matches there. What's more, you got the afternoon off. This was a major prize in itself.

But first of all you had to get a place on the team. I set my mind to it from the get-go. My initial ambition was to make it onto the second rugby team, which I managed to do quite quickly. Around the same time, one of my pals, Hugh Cummiskey – an auctioneer in Balbriggan now – came up with me to one of our first matches in Dublin.

I said 'You must come out to the house.' So we went to my home but my parents weren't there. It was a Saturday afternoon in Clontarf and we found we couldn't get in. I said 'There's a small window at the back. Let's try to get in there.' I broke the window, got my hand in and opened the window.

We scrambled in, but poor Hugh cut himself on the glass. Luckily he had a handkerchief and he wrapped it around the cut. When my parents came back that night, they had no idea we had been there until, of course, they found a handkerchief with 'Hugh Cummiskey' written on it. They did not think much of our ability as burglars!

I worked so hard at rugby that I made it onto the first team for my age group, playing at second centre. I had grown up playing GAA until I went to Newbridge, and in Gaelic football you just dived for the ball. It would not be unfair to say I essentially played Gaelic when I was playing rugby, insofar as when somebody was kicking the ball I would jump in front just to stop it, even if the ball hit me hard in the chest.

Fr Hegarty, our coach, was very impressed by this and talked about it at training. We were gathered around him in Newbridge, in the field across the road. He was talking about the attacking team and the defending team. I interrupted to say 'Does that mean where the ball is? I mean, how do you tell which is the attacking team and which is the defending team?' He thought about it and he said 'No, no, the attacking team is the one in possession of the ball, even on your own backline.'

I use that analogy quite a lot in speeches. My very first speech in An Post many years later was at the postmasters' conference in Bundoran. I remember finishing with that. 'You know, we may be on the backline now against Telecom; they are the big sexy crowd with all this new technology. But we are in possession of the ball, we have a great team and we are going to win.'

So I quoted Fr Hegarty.

One of my first proper rugby matches for Newbridge was at Clontarf rugby grounds, against Mountjoy. My lovely spotless Newbridge jersey and shorts had been washed specially for the occasion.

I didn't get sight of the ball for the entire match. Towards the end of the game my jersey and shorts were still spotless! I was fourteen at this stage, and very embarrassed. So when no one was looking I lay down in the muck. I didn't want to come back to Newbridge to have people discover the ball had never even got to me!

A couple of years later, when I was sixteen, I made it onto the Senior Cup team, again playing for the firsts. You were seen as a bit of hero in school if you achieved that. What's more, you got even more scope to enjoy the trips away.

I remember one big match against Presentation Cork, where we travelled to Cork for two nights and stayed in the Metropole Hotel. I was the only one of the whole twenty of us who could dance, thanks to my time in Red Island.

Now we wouldn't have had 'hops' or dances with other schools when I was at Newbridge, and I was far too much of a 'goody-goody' to sneak out or mitch off.

We went out on the Saturday night, to the Arcadia Ballroom. There was a big problem: all of the girls there were eighteen or nineteen years of age, much older than us. We didn't get on very well, as the 'auld ones' looked down on us because of our age!

Then we heard on the grapevine that on Sunday night there was another dance run by the nuns. It was in the local school, and was for the girls attending the local oratory. This seemed to have much more potential.

It took place in the building that was used as a chapel during the week; they closed off the altar section. Of course they left the holy pictures, the Stations of the Cross and the statues around, and the nuns were there to keep a beady eye out for any misbehaviour!

One of my pals, Eric, had been chatting up a girl who was happy for him to 'leave her home'. But she had two friends with her, and he asked me and another of my team-mates, Dermot from Fethard, if we would escort them too.

Now at this stage we had absolutely no experience of girls. So, being ever the gentlemen, we shook hands with them when it came time to say goodbye. Eric meanwhile took his girl around the corner for a kiss and a cuddle.

This left us with a huge conundrum. Everybody back at the hotel knew we had left three girls home, yet we had not got so much as a peck on the cheek! I came up with a plan: we bought a packet of Smarties, took out the red ones, put them onto a handkerchief and rubbed them on our faces to make it look like we had lipstick on us. Well, to say we were the envy of everybody in the hotel would be an understatement! I couldn't be sure, but I think that included our Dean, Fr O'Riordan, who I suspected was secretly rather proud of us!

After I made it onto the first team, we won the first and second rounds of the Senior Cup and were into the quarter final. This was a seriously big deal for the school. Unfortunately, we were up against Belvedere College. Belvedere had one famous player in particular, a seventeen-year-old who went by the name of Tony O'Reilly. He was so good that he went on to gain his first cap for Ireland later that year. He was a great opera singer, he was a great raconteur – basically he could do everything!

Unluckily for me, I was given the task of marking him as we were both playing as centres. He was a big red-haired guy, handsome, strong and fast. And I am most certainly not known for my height! I remember my school pals teasing me: 'Oh God, what chance have we?' Well, I figured the only chance we had was if the ball never got to Tony O'Reilly. If it did, I had no chance of stopping him!

So we cheated. We did a Novena: nine days of prayer for bad weather. And it worked. It was March 1954 and it turned out to be the filthiest day. The mud was awful. The paper the following day said 'This match should not have been played.' But our plan was executed perfectly, as the ball only got to O'Reilly twice!

Unfortunately, on both occasions he scored a try. This was back in the days when you got only three points for a try, so they beat us 6–0. Tony, who went on to be a hugely successful international businessman and media baron, would always tease me in later years: 'Ah, sure, you only need one leg to get on the Newbridge team!'

I really loved playing rugby at school, but I also threw myself into all the other activities available to us. Sunday night was cinema night at Newbridge. I joined the stamp collecting club, the arts and crafts and the cinematographic club. I remember being asked why I joined it and saying 'Well, my father has a cine camera and I want to learn as much as I can about it.'

I also took part in the school operas. I have a photograph of the first of these: *The Mikado*. I was chuffed to get a role in it, but not quite as chuffed to hear that as no girls were allowed, I was going to have to dress up as one of the schoolgirls!

* * *

After I did my Leaving Certificate at Newbridge, I went on to study Commerce in UCD. Now I use the word 'study' loosely! Many years later, I was fortunate enough to be awarded five different honorary doctorates from various educational institutions, as recognition for my work in business and public life. But back in those days, I was so busy with Red Island, and working in various day jobs, that I was not the most committed fresher on campus!

Even during my breaks from UCD, there was no question as to how I would be spending the summer. I was a member of the Pearse Battalion of the FCA. I have photographs of myself in uniform as a teenager. But I never got to go to any of their camps, as I couldn't go swanning off for two weeks in the middle of the Red Island summer season!

I was somewhat active in the Commerce Society in UCD but was never brave enough to speak at the L&H Society there, which has been the venue of many famous Irish orators over the years. I would go in there on a Saturday night and watch in awe as these guys would stand up and hold the room. They also knew how to put up with interruptions and heckles. They were marvellous.

I remember attending one or two Sinn Féin meetings while I was a student at UCD. I had given them my address when signing in. This was the 1950s, and the cause of Irish republicanism was very much 'in the ether' politically. While I never got involved actively in the 'cause', I would have automatically been Republican due in no small part to my father's views.

Then one day there was a knock on our door in Clontarf. I opened the door, and standing in front of me was a man who would only speak to me *as Gaeilge*. I believe he had taken the bus from town and walked up our long driveway.

He told me 'You signed in and gave your address, and I would like to involve you in the Republican movement because we may be attempting to attack the North and save the Six Counties.'

Now being part of the IRA certainly wasn't in my plans. I had obviously been somewhat sympathetic to Sinn Féin by attending the meeting in UCD, as was anybody who went and gave their address. When I told my father what had happened, and despite his own political leanings, his advice was simple: 'Steer clear of them.'

In truth I wasn't tempted at all. Even though I had joined the FCA when I was at school, it was a big leap to suggest that I would be in any way interested in getting involved in the 'armed struggle'. Quite simply, I wasn't.

I was never very politically engaged during my time at UCD, but I had an interest in how politics worked even in those days. Quite early on, I discovered that one of the cheapest forms of entertainment was to attend debates in the Dáil chamber.

To get into the public gallery, all I had to do was go to the gate at Kildare Street and ask for our local TD. Eamonn Rooney, a friend of my father's, was a Fine Gael politician who hailed from North County Dublin. Paddy Burke was the other local TD, who would also have been a friend of my father's. So I would ask for one or the other. Now, I didn't want to see them: invariably they would come all the way down and I would say 'Ah, I didn't want to see you; I just wanted to get in!'

I remember feeling a huge sense of prestige attending the Irish Houses of Parliament. If there was a good row going on, it was like being at a really great debating society. There was no television in those days, so being able to see the faces of the politicians whom I would read about in the newspapers was just brilliant.

At the time, to go to university you didn't have to get 'points' in your Leaving Certificate. Nobody had told me that university was different to school. I found it strange that there was no-one examining my homework in college. As far as I could see, this meant I didn't have anything to do while I was there!

There was maybe a lecture on Monday morning at 9.00, another lecture at 10.00, and that was the end of it for the day.

Meanwhile, I was also working at the Co-Op store on George's Street in Dún Laoghaire, in which my father had an interest. I worked in the grocery shop behind the various counters such as bacon or fruit & veg. Also I would be asked to help with early morning deliveries. So I never fully participated in college life, other than to play a bit of table tennis.

My UCD student days were definitely quite different to most. The van belonging to the Co-Op picked me up at, say, 7 a.m. at our house in Blackrock (we had moved back to Blackrock in 1957). We went in to the market, I'd buy the vegetables and fruit, get them out to the van, and the van would then drop me off at Earlsfort Terrace or Leeson Street for a lecture. I went to my 9 a.m. and 10 a.m. lectures and headed out to work again.

I actually enjoyed working in the shop so much that I failed my first year! In truth, I don't think getting my degree at UCD was that important to me; I wanted to get finished and out into the 'real' world.

Given my background in Red Island, I sort of assumed I would go into the hotel business when I finished university. And I felt the Continent was where the hotel business was most interesting.

In fact, the day after I finished my final exam in UCD in September 1958, I got the boat from Cobh to Le Havre in France. Red Island had closed for the season and my parents came along on the ferry. I remember leaving them at the port, and heading to Paris. From there, I went alone to the World Fair in Brussels. When that finished, I decided I wanted to go back to France. I went to the train station and in my best school French said: 'Je veux acheter un billet pour la France, s'il vous plait', and the man said 'Quelle partie de la France?'

I hadn't actually thought that far ahead! I just knew I wanted to go to France. I had my rucksack with me, but that was pretty much all the preparation I had done. So I replied, 'La première gare après la frontière.'

I arrived in Metz in Alsace-Lorraine, a big industrial city. I stepped off the train and there was a sign in the window of the 'Buffet de la Gare' restaurant saying 'Help wanted'. I went in and the man said 'Can you start immediately?', to which I replied 'Oui!'

I stayed in the local youth hostel at first, but it was due to close at the end of the season, so I needed somewhere new to stay. I asked the woman in the local tourist office if she could help. It was late September or October by now, and she said 'Well, they are looking for somebody in the school: the College de St Clement, a Dominican school, I think. You should try there.'

So I went to the school administrator and asked for a job, again chancing my arm with my best school French. I didn't quite understand him. He said 'Yes', he could give me a job. 'We have accommodation and you can get your food here', he added. I stayed overnight, was given a room and came down to start work the first day.

The only problem was that I had no idea what I had been hired to do! It was a big school, a college, in the middle of the town. And I thought 'Gosh, how will I manage this, what will I teach, will it be English?' He had asked me what I was working at in the town already. And I went down to discover I was working in the kitchen! Obviously he thought my experience at the Buffet de la Gare made me an expert!

I ended up working as a waiter, serving the senior school teachers and the priests. I stayed in France for the winter and I didn't know one person when I started. I suppose I was not unlike my father and his father before him in wanting a bit of an adventure, to see another part of the world on my own.

I returned to Ireland the following March. I had failed my accountancy exams, so I had to retake them. This meant I didn't graduate from UCD until the following year. I've always claimed that that's why I'm anti-accountants!

When I came home, my father asked me (quite rightly) 'What are you going to do for a living?' The honest answer was that I wasn't sure what I wanted to do. Then I got talking with him and I said 'Do you know, there's a smashing thing in France called self-service?'

In the 1950s, when you went to buy a magazine in Ireland, you said to the person behind the counter, 'Could I have that magazine please, the third one from the left; no, not that one, the one beside it.' You couldn't touch them because there was a counter blocking your way.

In France it was very different. The magazines were laid out on tables. You could pick them up, look at them and decide which you wanted, and then pay for it at the cash desk.

My father said 'You know, that self-service thing sounds great. But people might not always want to read books or magazines. They will always want to eat food.'

Now, don't forget he had been in the grocery business until 1946, and this was 1958. He said 'You should consider learning more about the grocery business.' We had both read a lot about a new type of self-service supermarket opening in America. Closer to home, H Williams had opened a few of this type of shop in Dublin.

My father's words really got me thinking.

That winter I took a plane to Newcastle upon Tyne and again went looking for work, specifically to learn about self-service in the grocery trade. I went to Lipton's in York to ask for a job.

The manager said 'What age are you now?' (I was twenty-one or twenty-two), and asked 'What have you been doing up until now?' I didn't want to say I had been to university, because I thought they would think a university graduate was over-qualified to work in the shop.

But I didn't explain the gap in my CV very cleverly. I must have waffled! I didn't get the job because I could have been in jail during the previous years for all he knew.

So I headed to London and tried to get a job in Sainsbury's, to no avail. Eventually I got a job in Lipton's. But as soon as I landed the job, which was in their self-service shop, they transferred me to a counter-service shop. This was most definitely not part of my grand plan!

I ended up working in different shops, all the while not really learning anything about self-service. But it was all part of the adventure. I stayed for a winter and then returned to Red Island, with my father's words ringing in my ears: 'People might not always want to read books … They will always want to eat food.'

* * *

There was another pressing reason why I wanted to return to Ireland. I didn't know it at the time, but a chance meeting with a girl in a pillbox hat some time earlier had changed my life forever.

In 1958, the local priest, Monsignor Casey, asked my father to look after a couple, Ned and Grace Prendergast, whose marriage ceremony he had performed some years earlier.

They brought their sixteen-year-old daughter, Denise, on a trip to Red Island one Sunday. I was around twenty-one years of age at the time and Denise was working in Skerries that year as an au pair with a local family.

The job of collecting them and bringing them to Red Island was 'outsourced' to me by my father, as was so often the case! I showed them around, they had a meal and Denise's mother and father went home. Denise stayed on for the dance. I thought nothing of it at the time, other than she seemed like a very nice girl.

The next time I saw young Denise Prendergast was the following year. I will always remember walking up the stairs in Fleet Street where my father's office was located, and seeing this very attractive young woman dressed in a blue suit and pillbox hat.

She had applied for a job in Red Island and was waiting for an interview. I saw her and said 'Oh, hi, how are you? Are you being looked after?' And she said 'I'm waiting for Mr Quinn.' I asked her name and she said 'Denise Prendergast'. I clocked who she was: 'Sure, we met last year. Come in, come in. Don't be sitting out here in the corridor.' I sat listening intently as my father interviewed her. I was probably trying not to make it clear just how attractive I thought she was!

My father had explained to me that when you are interviewing somebody you ought to make them relaxed, so talk to them about their family: how many in the family, brothers and sisters, etc. He chatted away to her and she answered back very well. When she left he said 'That's great, that's the receptionist job filled. She'll be perfect.' And that solved that.

Now, remember, she was only seventeen. Her birthday was in February and this interview was in March. He was only interviewing people for the senior positions – a head waiter or a chef (although the chef came back every year), somebody to be in charge of the shop, or somebody to be in charge of reception or housekeeping. But he was clearly very impressed by her, as was I.

There were two receptionists, and they took turns. It was an important job. Denise came down to Red Island for the week or two before the resort opened, for the annual big pre-season 'clean up'. Willie Murphy, the permanent care-taker down there, organised everybody. They were all 'new starters' and she was given a paintbrush and pot.

She just loved it, and grabbed hold of everything with real gusto. She ended up with a nickname – 'Flash' – because she moved so fast. She never walked, she ran. I think my father fell in love with her. He thought she was great. And I did too!

Denise worked in Red Island for only one summer, in 1959. Luckily for me, we started dating that summer.

On our first official date outside of Red Island, I 'treated' my new girlfriend to a céilí on Parnell Square as I had been given a pair of free tickets! It turned out that she was not exactly enamoured with Irish dancing. It was Saturday night and there was a photographer there from the *Sunday Press*. He photographed the two of us and the following day we appeared in a social column under the banner 'In town last night'.

On Monday morning the parish priest who had introduced us, Msgr Casey, was on the phone, thrilled to see the photo and asking if he could 'be of any help now!' But poor Denise was disgusted because her friends were much more sophisticated than just going to a céilí.

She was big into horse racing, as her family had friends who were well known in that industry, the Hartys in Chapelizod. She used to go to the Phoenix Park Races and she and her sister Nuala would get their photograph taken there for the paper.

It turned out that one of the jobs she had as receptionist was to act on behalf of the local bookmaker. She was regarded as a great tipster. She would take bets and became known as the 'tipster' in Red Island.

That winter of '59 I went to England again, but I kept in touch with her throughout the time I was away. I came back from the UK at Christmas and I bought her a present of a pair of gloves, not knowing that her mother had said

'Ah, that's the sign of a broken friendship.' This I had never heard, but it had me a little worried!

By this stage Eilagh had been married since the age of nineteen to a brilliant man, Jack McCabe, and we were very close. Both he and my father were most anxious that I not lose Denise!

But the actual engagement took Denise by surprise. We went for a coffee on 9 May 1962, on Baggot Street. We just sat at the table and I said 'I would love to get married, would you marry me?' Luckily she agreed.

I said 'I better ask your father's permission.' We drove out to Chapelizod and I asked her to leave the room when we went in. Then I asked her mother and father for permission to get married. So I kind of did things in reverse!

We went together to get the ring the following day. The beautiful girl in the blue suit and the pillbox hat was twenty and I was twenty-five when we married on 6 October 1962. That was more than fifty years ago, and I have loved every minute of my life with her since.

BUILDING A SUPERMARKET FROM SCRATCH

5

A GROCER'S LIFE
FOR ME

P ut simply, without my father's guidance, I might never have become
a grocer.

While he strongly encouraged me to run with the self-service idea I had
witnessed first-hand in French newsagents, his suggestion was that I find a
way to apply it to the grocery trade.

It is the best advice I have ever received. Without his wise counsel there
might well have been no Quinn's supermarket, and ultimately no Superquinn.

In fact, I originally fully intended to open a bookshop and newsagents in
Dublin. There was even a shop vacant near the Gaiety Theatre in the city
centre. I looked into it at one stage but the sums didn't work out.

Instead, after returning home from my little 'research trip' to England, I was
even more convinced that a self-service grocery model was the way forward in
Ireland. But it had to be done right.

Spurred on by my father's enthusiasm, we trawled the papers regularly looking for a suitable site for our first store. Eventually we identified a site up
for auction at 3 and 4 Clanbrassil Street in Dundalk. My father went to the

auction on my behalf, along with one of his most trusted lieutenants, Kevin Kernan. I stayed in Red Island, anxiously awaiting news.

The site in question had been a shoe and furniture shop, which had burned down ten years previously. It had since been rebuilt. It was in very good shape when the people who owned it, the Eakins, decided to sell. We won it at auction for £10,100 after a brief bidding war with a rival.

Then we went to the bank manager to look for the money to follow through on the sale! Luckily I had done my sums well, and the bank gave me the overdraft of £14,000 that I needed to get up and running. This was solely based on my father's reputation, which he had nurtured with the bank over many years.

It was a large sum of money. Call it the enthusiasm of youth, but I didn't let that bother me. All I cared about was that we were in business!

Quinn's Supermarket opened its doors for the very first time on 25 November 1960. It was a relatively large premises, with around 2000 square feet and no parking. It was very much a case of 'suck it and see', but I knew I wasn't simply going to copy what everyone else was doing.

In a previous chapter, I told how H Williams had already opened a few self-service shops. John Quinn, the boss of H Williams (and no relation), had actually opened one on Henry Street in 1947. He inherited the business at a very early age from his uncle and was made Chairman of the company when he was still in his twenties. He decided to try 'self-service' but it didn't quite work at that time.

I looked at the H Williams self-service shop with my mother. The way it worked was that the retailer put the goods on the shelves and people took what they wanted, weighed it and put it into bags. Marietta Biscuits, for example, were sold at that stage from large boxes rather than in individual packets, as is the case nowadays. Everything came loose, not in packets. Think of it as a bit like the way 'Pick n Mix' candy arrangements work in cinemas.

But John made the mistake of innovating with self-service too soon. He was forced to close his store down because he couldn't get any pre-packed products. For example, sugar didn't come in a bag: you had to weigh it first and then put it into a bag. Butter had to be cut individually.

This made the whole shopping experience far too cumbersome and inconvenient. So he ended up closing the store in Henry Street. Ten years later, when more suppliers were producing products in convenient packaging, he opened again.

For my part, I had seen first-hand how self-service could work, and had done my best to study the models used by the likes of Sainsbury's and Lipton's in London. I also knew the competition we faced in Dundalk town.

There were already two small self-service grocery shops, both called McCourt's, when we opened there. My store, although quite small by today's standards, was much larger than theirs.

Meanwhile all the bigger shops in Dundalk were offering a more traditional 'counter service', with a delivery and credit system in place. Our shop would have none of these 'luxuries'. I saw these outdated bigger shops as my primary targets. I was convinced that there was real scope to win their business.

We advertised for staff, and my father helped with the interviews. One of the applicants was Brendan Rooney, who was working in Lipton's bacon department in nearby Drogheda. Brendan went on to be a very close friend and a key figure in the success of Superquinn as a director.

We interviewed him in Drogheda in the White Horse Hotel and decided that we would put him in charge of our brand-spanking-new bacon department. We wrote to let him know and as soon as he received our letter, he went in to tell the manager in Lipton's to stuff his job because he was going to work in a supermarket, if you don't mind! We were the first non-Dublin supermarket in the country, so it really was a big deal to get a job there.

A few days later, he mentioned his new job to one of the supplier reps who came into the store. The man asked him 'Where's that place in Dundalk you're talking about … Clanbrassil Street? Oh, I don't think you are right. There's no sign of a supermarket going up there!' Poor Brendan got very worried that he might have jumped too soon! So on his half day he got the train and came up to Dundalk. The look of relief on his face was something else when he walked in and discovered that the building work was going on, and the shop was indeed being fitted out!

I loved the buzz of opening a new store. There was a real sense of excitement at starting a new business in a town that I didn't know very well at all. What's more, I was excited about introducing a completely new way of doing business to a trade that had been tied to the old ways for far too long.

* * *

There was one small problem with our new store. On the first day we opened our doors, nobody, with the exception of Brendan Rooney, had any real experience of retailing. I was one of the older ones, at the age of twenty-three! But we soon turned the fact that we were so young and energetic to our advantage. It meant that from day one, our store was all about personality.

The store had 'wooden' gondolas to hold the goods on sale. You walked through the door to be greeted by the back of three checkouts and on the left-hand side was our bacon counter. We didn't sell meat, other than bacon and sausages.

When you came in to the shop you were handed a basket. Again, this was all very new to 1960s Dundalk – you were expected to do your own shopping! *Quelle horreur!*

My father used to tell a story about coming down to visit on our first day. He parked his car and met two women coming along, each with a self-service basket in her hand, bold as brass. He stopped them and said 'Oh, I see there's a new supermarket.' 'Oh, yes – Quinn's.' And he said 'I'm Feargal's father. By the way, you are not supposed to take those home with you.' 'Oh, are you not?'

As they were coming in the door I was saying 'Take a basket.' They would reply 'Ah no, it's OK' and I said 'I insist!', so they thought they got them to keep. We bought a hundred to start but we must have had only sixty left by the end of that first day!

A few years later, we were closing up in the evening. One of our good customers was Miss Martin. She and her sister were spinsters, and had been school teachers. They were retired and I remembered where they lived. I said to Miss Martin 'I'll give you a lift home.'

She had her groceries in a box, and I carried them into the house for her. There on the piano was a Quinn's self-service basket, turned upside down with dried flowers in it. And she said 'That's the one, do you remember you insisted on my having that the first day you opened?'

A big change had occurred in Irish society just before we opened. Until 1959, we had a different economy, one that was based on protectionism, dating back to the 1930s where there was a 'packet tax' on imported goods. It was imposed in order to encourage the sale of only goods manufactured in Ireland.

This meant that I grew up in a time when you couldn't afford to import anything. We couldn't get a Mars bar because they weren't made in Ireland and they were too expensive to import. The only cigarettes that were available were the ones made in Ireland by the likes of PJ Carroll, John Player and Wills. The only matches were Irish. Cars couldn't be imported in one piece; they had to be imported in pieces and assembled in Ireland. Basically everything had to be made in Ireland. This was seen as a way of creating jobs for workers.

Then something quite revolutionary happened. The esteemed civil servant Dr T.K. Whitaker, who is a good friend, published the Programme for Economic Expansion in 1958, and it was implemented under the Government of Seán Lemass from 1959 onwards.

Lemass had taken over as Taoiseach from Éamon de Valera, and resolved to do away with the 'protectionist' attitude of the past. It was an extremely forward-thinking move, which caused havoc. It meant that the car-assembly business disappeared almost overnight; all of the jobs that had been created, based on that policy, were going to go. It was a very brave thing for any Government to do.

But it was also a major factor in allowing us to open our doors successfully, as it meant the retailing climate in which we operated was suddenly vastly different.

In general, we were buying from companies that were not the big, established brands. We were able to get those brands a lot cheaper. For example, our flour supplier was Dock Milling, whereas Odlums was the more expensive, bigger brand.

By that stage, several companies were also beginning to provide pre-packaged goods. For example, we were selling sugar but it was now coming in 1 lb or 2 lb bags, rather than us having to measure it out for customers. Therefore the whole process of self-service was far easier to introduce.

However, goods like rice still came in large sacks, and had to be measured out. Flour was beginning to come in smaller sizes, but we still sold huge amounts of flour in sacks: people were still baking a lot and would buy entire sacks.

My idea of circumventing the bigger suppliers was a major factor in allowing us to be more price-competitive from day one at Quinn's supermarket. For example, Chivers' and Bird's jelly were big sellers back in those days. I don't think anybody really buys jelly now, but at that time no house would have been without jelly once a week.

Selling less well known brands meant we could undercut our competitors. So whereas others might charge sixpence for Chivers' or Bird's-branded jelly, ours would retail at maybe fourpence ha'penny.

This is not unlike what we would have done at a later stage when we introduced our own 'Thrift' range of goods at Superquinn, the idea being that you offer the same product but from a cheaper brand. The likes of Aldi and Lidl have refined this concept further in recent years by introducing their own 'brand name' value goods.

We also stocked some big brands, like Jacob's biscuits and later Boland's biscuits, as we knew our customers would expect to see them in our store. When we opened first we didn't stock Lyons Tea. Instead we stocked Hughes' Tea as it was much cheaper and we were able to sell it at a lower price.

Lyons eventually agreed to supply us, as they could see they were missing out on our trade. I was hugely excited at the idea of dealing with these 'big boys' so directly.

From day one, I would do anything to get publicity: just to get our name in the paper. Our store opened with big signs outlining all of our special offers. We gave out balloons, and took photos of our customers. Later we played games of hide and seek, as well as a form of in-store bingo.

My enthusiasm for publicity was partly a result of my time in Red Island, with its emphasis on entertainment and fun. But it was also a reflection of the competition we faced: there were twenty shops competing with us in Dundalk alone. Put simply, we had to find a way to be different.

We decided we would do this by making as much 'noise' as possible around our store. We wanted people who bumped into each other at the other side of town saying 'Do you know what's going on down there? Do you know what they are doing down there this week?'

I wanted to turn what was a pretty mundane experience – doing the weekly household shop – into something far more interesting for our customers. By comparison, most of our competitors were continuing to do the same things they had always done.

Our other main advertising method was our 'newspaper', the *Quinn Supermarket Herald*. It contained details of all our special offers and news from the store. We distributed it around the neighbourhood by getting young fellows to drop it into letterboxes.

Again, in a lot of ways this is similar to what the German discounters do nowadays with their newspaper booklet 'inserts' featuring special offers.

It is fair to say that I was obsessed with trying to come up with fresh publicity ideas; I had my colleagues driven mad with my mantra that we had to do something new each week. We wanted to be talked about in people's kitchens, and around the town, each week.

My late friend Declan Gibson was a musician and photographer. At one stage I got him to photograph the members of staff, all eight of us together. We ordered big photographs and put them in the window, to show how proud we were of our staff members. And obviously, their parents, cousins, uncles and everybody else were delighted to see the photos, and would talk about them.

Getting the newspapers to pick up on our stories was another part of our early 'PR' mission, although we had never heard of 'PR'!

I remember writing a letter to the *Evening Herald* and being absolutely thrilled when they carried it. It had the name and address, 4 Clanbrassil Street, of our store on it. So anybody who bought the *Evening Herald* would see it was 'that fellow Quinn who has that new shop'.

I knew the papers wouldn't generally carry stories about us that looked like an advertisement. So a little while later we came up with a masterplan to create a bit of mischief. We gave our customers a free goldfish with every two bags of Silver Label tea. And then? Well, I got somebody to complain about it. It was a great way of generating controversy around the new store.

I was also keenly aware of the benefit of selling established staples at below cost. Again, this was simply a great way to get publicity for our new store, and to separate us from our competitors. We sold discounted Zip firelighters, which would normally sell at one shilling and threepence. They cost one shilling to buy and I put them on sale at ten pence ha'penny. It meant we lost a penny ha'penny on every box we sold.

Because we were selling twenty-four packs in a case, potentially there was a large cost to us in doing this. I was losing three shillings with every case sold. But the move more than paid for itself, as our opposition were howling about this below-cost selling! I didn't care, as it meant that word was spreading like wildfire that we were the cheapest in town!

And then we cut the cost of cornflakes. Our rivals, the McCourts, cut their price to keep up. So we cut further. And they matched us. This continued until our rival was selling them at one shilling and three pence. I knew it couldn't keep going like that, so instead we put up a sign in our windows:

'We will buy your cornflakes from you for 1 shilling and 5 pence!'

Well, to say it caused a kerfuffle would be an understatement. No-one could understand how we could make money by offering to buy cornflakes from our customers rather than selling cornflakes to them! Of course, I saw it as a great way to generate publicity and to make sure people chose our store for the rest of their weekly shop.

One of the locals came to me with twenty-four packets of cornflakes, tied to the back of his bike. He had rightly figured out that he would make two pence profit on each pack simply by selling to me the cornflakes he had bought from McCourt's!

Now Mr McCourt was no fool. He had stamped the cornflakes with the McCourt logo, so that if we tried to sell the cornflakes people would know where they had come from originally. What he didn't know was that I was secretly swapping the cornflakes with the batches that were bought at Red Island. And they got through an awful lot of cornflakes in Red Island!

At one stage, the rivalry between our shops became so intense that the local Parish Priest – an archdeacon, no less – got in touch to ask if he could help to broker peace. He told me quite solemnly that he 'hated to see the town at war like this'.

He changed his tune a little when I explained that there were more people coming to Dundalk to shop than ever before. They were coming from places like Drogheda and Ardee just to avail of the special offers. So the 'price war' was good for the town.

Then one day, I was in the shop and I spied another member of the local opposition furtively bringing six cases of Zip firelighters to the checkout. I realised he was paying one shilling or more for them from the supplier, while we were selling them below cost for tenpence ha'penny.

I couldn't let him away with that. I had a camera with a flash, so I took a photo of him in flagrante, so to speak. In fact, I got a few customers and some staff to get around him and I said 'Hello' just as I clicked the camera.

'What the hell are you doing?' he said. I said 'Ah, no, we just like to show photographs of our regular customers in our shop.' 'You can't do that! You can't do that!', he said to me. I told him I would let him have the Polaroid photo if he decided not to buy the firelighters. A form of blackmail, if you will!

All of this was great fun, I have to say. There was a real buzz in trying to compete for business, at a time when the economy was emerging from the old ways of doing things.

I went to Dublin's Liffey Street to buy a tannoy system for the store. We had dealt with the company that supplied the tannoy in Red Island, so I knew the boss, Col. Watchorn, who was ex-British army.

I told him I wanted a tannoy system with microphones, music and loud-speakers. He looked puzzled at the very idea. 'For a shop? What sort of a shop is it?' I said 'A grocery shop.' He said 'You are putting music and a microphone into a grocery shop, into a supermarket?'

He was perhaps the biggest sound system supplier in the country, delivering to theatres, ballrooms and churches. And it had never dawned on him that there might be a future in supplying music to shops!

But there most certainly was. I got on the microphone in-store regularly. It was a great way of allowing me to make announcements and to entertain as well as to play music. Again that was very much a product of my Red Island days. I would announce the special offers or new products that people hadn't tried. That was all new: there was nobody else in town with music, nobody on a microphone telling of the special offers or the new products.

From day one of opening in Dundalk, I had a feeling that we were going to do well. I remember that evening saying to Brendan Rooney, 'Do you know how much we took in?' If I remember correctly it was £437, and he was surprised that the owner of the shop was telling him. It was a lot of money in those days.

He said they would never have done that in Lipton's. The manager of the shop would have been told that you don't disclose that sort of thing. It suggested that the tone in Quinn's Supermarket was quite different to anything that had been tried before.

I was thrilled with our success on that first day. What's more, I was utterly convinced that we were onto something.

* * *

Over time, the new shop began to really 'bed in' around Dundalk town. We won regular customers, and got to know many of them by their first names.

The big shopping days were Fridays and Saturdays. Monday, Tuesday and Wednesday weren't busy so we spent those days filling the shelves. We ordered the goods on Monday, they were delivered on Tuesday and we spent the rest of Tuesday and Wednesday getting our merchandise onto the shelves. Thursday was a half day as the whole town closed at that time.

All the other stores in town began to feel very threatened by what we were achieving, even in those early days. Compared to us, there was no life in them. We were bringing a little 'showbiz' into the business too.

Underneath all of this, our price competitiveness was key, alongside our nimbleness in introducing new products that you couldn't necessarily find elsewhere.

One example was a 'Collarstick'. It was a little tube that you rubbed on your dirty collar so you didn't have to wash the shirt. I remember the rep for the product came in and said 'You wouldn't believe this, but we had to take it off the market to change the wording on it. We have had it for sale in Britain for a long time but nobody ever noticed. It said, "To use, push up bottom"! When I brought it to the Irish retailers they said 'You couldn't do that!'

I loved that! We stocked it, as I knew it was just something different to what was on offer elsewhere. So when people came into our store, they said 'That's an interesting product.'

Even in those early days, we had a competitive advantage over established English multiples like Lipton's. We were Irish, and knew our market and our customers very well. A good illustration was in 1960, when the Irish troops went to the Congo on a peacekeeping mission. I remember going with Denise to Baldonnell to see the planes going off. It was such a big national event, and there was a great sense of pride in what they were doing.

Lipton's management in London decided they had better do something to mark the occasion. They put a photograph of the Irish troops in the Congo on all of their sixty store windows around the country. If you could identify a family member then you got a big prize. But the sign they put on it was: 'The Éire troops in the Congo, see if you can identify them.'

I said to Brendan Rooney, 'Brendan, can you believe that somebody is so out of touch? I would have thought the Irish managers would have pointed out that nobody here uses the word "Éire" when it comes to our Defence Forces.'

It was a real reminder of how much more in tune with our customers we were. I mean if London came up with that slogan, the Irish management should have said 'Take the bloody things back and do it right.' But there was a centralised management in Ireland and they let it through.

In those early years, Denise and I had not yet married. She was more than willing to chip in, and would often lend a hand by working on the tills at the weekends. She was very much a part of the team that helped to start that first shop.

My father never actually worked in the store, but he would come down on Saturdays. He was very proud of it, which meant a lot to me. And of course, he was always on hand to give advice.

By this stage he was able to afford to go away on holidays quite regularly, during the winter months. Red Island was only open from May/June to September and he and my mother went to the Canary Islands for about four to six weeks in January and February. He had a notebook and he would write giving me advice. I still have some of the notes he sent.

He was very enthusiastic because he had made a success of his own grocery shops and he still had that retailer's drive in him. He had also invested in a range of other businesses and had diversified with Red Island and Bray Head, which were open throughout the 1960s.

Another of his businesses was Prima Foods, which supplied us with pre-packed rashers and sausages. Again this was an innovation: the idea of supplying pre-packed meat.

Of course there were big similarities between my father's Payantake business and mine. While Payantake was not self-service, it was low priced and therefore you did anything you could to offer cheaper prices. It also had a firm handle on its stock control, which other more 'traditional' stores did not.

One of the principal rules I learned very early on was that if you listen to your colleagues, if you listen to your own people, you learn a great deal. I think most of my education in business has come from just listening to my colleagues, regardless of their 'rank' within the company.

An early, if inadvertent, lesson I learned in this regard was from a young colleague, Richard Donoghue. Usually we went to the market early each morning to buy our fruit and vegetables for the day. As I knew I wouldn't be in until a little later one Saturday morning, I left Richard in charge. I told him: 'You go down early at 8 a.m. tomorrow, see what's available and buy it.'

When I arrived at the store, I was shocked to find that Richard had bought a load of strawberries. Where I had bought three dozen punnets of strawberries each time previously, he bought about thirty dozen. So when I came in at 9.30 or so they were stockpiled in our store. Let's just say I was far from impressed!

He had used his initiative to get a great price on the strawberries, which had been retailing at two shillings. He was able to buy them for 10 pence because of the quantity he was purchasing. There had been a glut of strawberries and he took them all. And he sold them at one shilling a punnet, which was much cheaper than anywhere else.

I asked myself: 'Will I give out to him about it now?' I thought 'No, I'll leave it until later and then I'll tell him what he did wrong.'

You can probably guess what happened: the strawberries were all gone by lunchtime! What was really interesting to me was they were gone at a profit of only two pence, instead of a shilling. But because he sold twenty times as many, we made more money at the lower price than we would have at the higher price.

I learned a really important lesson from Richard that day, which stood to me throughout my career in retailing: if you have the right product, you can make more money at a lower percentage once you increase the volume sold. I know it sounds simple, but in those days it wasn't how things were done.

Even years later, I discovered that (bloody) accountants tended to measure success based on percentage profit on the items you sell, rather than money you are making from selling the products in volume.

In fact I often quote this lesson in the Seanad. I remember citing the example to Minister for Finance Charlie McCreevy when he announced he had reduced the betting tax from 20% to 10%. The members in the Seanad howled about it, accusing him of looking after his horsey pals in Kildare. But he argued it was the right thing to do. And he came in the following year and said 'I made more money at 10% than I did at 20%, so I'm going to reduce it to 5% now!'

And then he came in the following year to say he made more money at 5% than at 10%!

6

ONE BECOMES TWO

Looking back on it now, I think I knew from an early stage that just one shop wouldn't have been viable in the long term. We would have to expand to really thrive. A trip to the USA, a year after we had opened in Dundalk, served to reinforce this conviction.

The trip was organised by the National Cash Register Company, and I was the only Irish person on it. You had to pay to go. If I remember correctly the charge was £425: quite a lot of money in those days.

It was organised by RGDATA, the grocers' association. There was Government sponsorship: they would pay 50% of the trip if you came back and were willing to lecture to grocers around the country about how to introduce modern methods. I was more than happy to oblige.

We were there for about 14 days, and the trip was a real eye-opener for me.

We learned about supermarkets, shopping centres, department stores and self-service. I could see people succeeding with this new way of retailing. I came back to Ireland very excited and resolved to lead the way in revolutionising how the grocery market operated here.

It turned out that I was not alone in being impressed by the American way of doing things. In fact, two retailer cousins – Denis and Jacques Defforey from Annecy in the South of France – had taken part in the same tour a few years before me. They went home and opened a big new store at the crossroads (*carrefour*) in Annecy. That store eventually grew to become the huge multinational chain, Carrefour!

The main thing I learned during this trip to the USA was that the future of retailing wasn't going to be on the main street: the future was going to be out of town. This meant that parking was going to be very important. In 1960 in Dundalk it had not been very important to us at all, but parking was a big problem in America, just as it is now here in Ireland.

It was fairly clear that while New York had big shops on the main street, the food shops were no longer there. The supermarkets were located outside the towns. And in general in towns like Dayton, where National Cash Registers was headquartered, the city centres were devastated because people with cars were driving outside of the cities for shopping. The whole shopping mall culture was just starting to take off.

I came back to Ireland and talked to my father about further expansion, bearing in mind everything I had learned during my trip. This was in November 1961. So we went looking for a suitable site and came up with the idea of locating our second store in Finglas.

We chose Finglas for a very good reason. In those days, Finglas was in an area with rows upon rows of houses. The houses didn't have garages because nobody had cars. They didn't have phones either. There was a bus service, but the planners didn't build proper infrastructure: they built a church and a school, but it was crying out for more shops and services.

At the time, there was a lot in the papers about people moving out to Finglas and having to go back to the city centre to do their shopping.

It would take us three years to get Finglas up and running (it opened in 1965). I did my research and called to the local cinema, the Casino. It had been built ten or fifteen years earlier. I discovered that the man in charge was from the same part of the world as my father. The two of them hit it off. Beside the cinema was a big site, lying empty. We asked if we could put a supermarket there.

I remember getting Mr Tierney, our bank manager, to come out to visit the site. He was the same bank manager who had lent us £14,000 to buy the Dundalk property. I drove him around to show him Finglas, and to 'sell him' on what we were doing. He said 'But of course it wouldn't be as big as Dundalk.' 'No, of course not,' I tut-tutted. 'It will be an awful lot bigger. I think we would probably need £70,000 to do it properly!' He nearly fell off the seat!

By this stage, Dundalk was doing so well that we had already paid off the £14,000 we had borrowed. We weren't short of cash. He hadn't agreed to give us the loan, and I remember him trying to trim me down a bit in terms of my expectations!

Denise and I went on our honeymoon in October 1962. My father met me at the airport on our return, flushed with excitement. He told me he had just received a phone call from his friend in the cinema to say they would be willing to sell the empty site.

We got the money from the bank because, as far as it was concerned, we were very good clients. We had borrowed money and paid it back way before the due date. This was another important factor in our early success – maintaining a good working relationship with our bank.

But then a problem arose. Not long after we bought the site, we realised we didn't have enough space to do what we wanted. We needed more room. We went back to the solicitor for the man who owned the cinema. I was very nervous and said to my father, 'You better come in with me and help me because this man knows that we have taken the site and we need a little bit more. The space is available there but he's going to screw me, knowing that he can charge me what he likes.'

My father came with me and we met the solicitor. My father explained, somewhat casually (while I secretly sweated beside him!), 'Actually we would like a bit more space.' The man replied 'Oh, that's great news.' Trying to mask how nervous I was, I asked 'How much are you going to charge?' and he said 'Ah, whatever we charged you for the other one, the same rate.'

I could not get over this level of 'old school' decency. In theory at least, they could have charged us way over the odds. But instead, this man was a gentleman about it. About five years later, we ended up expanding further and buying the cinema from them too.

They really were different times. When we applied for planning permission for Finglas, we were told we would not get it unless we had a plan for car parking – for the sum total of nine cars!

My father mentioned this to his friend, the TD Paddy Burke. Virtually nobody had cars in those days. Soon after hearing this, Paddy stood up in the Dáil saying that a friend of his was building a supermarket in Finglas and 'he has been told he couldn't go ahead with it until he put in car parking spaces. Did you ever hear such rubbish? Car parking spaces! It isn't car parking spaces they want in Finglas, it's pram spaces they want!'

Even though Finglas was a really big expansion for us, I wasn't nervous about investing in the new venture. I suppose I must have been a bit cocky, although on the day it opened in June 1965 I was fairly nervous as to whether it would do the business it needed to do!

When Finglas got up and running, it was on a totally different scale in terms of ambition. Dundalk was 2000 sq. ft when we opened, but by 1964 we had extended it to 5000 sq. ft. That made it quite a big shop for the area.

But this one, Finglas, was going to be 10,000 sq. ft. I had grown up!

The move from one store to two presented another challenge. With Dundalk I could be *in situ* all the time, meaning I was around to make key decisions as and when they were needed. I realised that opening Finglas would preclude this. It meant I had to learn the importance of delegating, trusting my colleagues to run the show. This was a huge shift in mentality for me.

Luckily, I had Brendan Rooney to manage Dundalk. He would remain my 'right-hand man' for many years subsequently. But it left a vacancy for the new store in Finglas that had to be filled.

I was twenty-eight when we advertised for a manager for the Finglas store in 1965. One of the applications was from Kevin Gilmore in London. Kevin was in his fifties and had opened a shop of his own in Clontarf, but unfortunately it had failed.

He had to go to England to get a job to feed his family. He followed the Irish papers from there, and had spotted the ad. My father was going to England on a regular basis and interviewed him there.

When my father came back he said 'I met this man, he's a real old-fashioned Lipton's-type manager. He would be a lovely mix with you.' So while I was the owner of Finglas, Kevin became the manager. He was a real old-time grocer, with a love for and appreciation of just what it takes to enthuse a customer to return.

To coincide with our big opening in Finglas, we made a deal that Jacob's would produce a tin the size of a packet of cream crackers so you could fit a packet into the tin. They gave us 1000 of them, and the first 1000 customers through our doors got a tin. Twenty or thirty years later people would say 'And we still have the Jacob's Cream Cracker tin.'

People didn't have telephones, so shortly after we opened we ran a competition with the prize of a three-minute phone call to America. To enter you had to buy three specific products. Well, we had hundreds of entries.

On a Saturday morning we drew a name out of the hat with everybody gathered around in the store. Then we went to the house of the winning family to tell them the good news. They wrote to America, saying 'We will phone you at such and such a time on such and such a day.' Then the family came in to our office and made the phone call to their brother in America. It really was a different era!

About two years after Finglas opened a colleague, Marie Delaney, came to tell me that she was engaged to be married. I congratulated her and said 'I'm sorry to lose you.'

Marie said 'That's what I was hoping to talk to you about. Is it possible I could continue to work?' And I thought 'But who will get your husband's dinner?' She said 'We were talking about it and we really need the money.'

In those days, I didn't know any woman who continued to work after marriage. I said 'If you are happy to do it then yes', and so she continued to work until their first baby came. I thought her very progressive for doing so. Again, how times have changed!

During our time in Finglas we were determined to innovate with development of the self-service model. In particular my father was worried that people would steal the goods as they were not behind a counter.

I remember him writing from his holidays to say he was concerned about the back door in Finglas: there was too much freedom for people to come and go and perhaps take goods out, as we didn't have security there. When he came back, he parked in the car park and went to come in the back door himself.

To his surprise, a security man was on duty and said 'Sorry, you can't come in this way.' My father asked 'What are you doing?' and was told 'I'm here to make sure that nobody except suppliers comes through this back door.' My father said 'You have a job because of me: I'm Feargal's father.' 'Oh, I'm delighted to meet you, Mr Quinn.'

My father said 'I've always been concerned about the back door and I'm delighted he listened to me. Best of luck now, young man; I hope everything works out well for you.' He went to walk in the back way and was told 'You can't come in! I was told nobody was to come in.'

So he had to walk around to the front door. He was thrilled!

7

DARING TO BE
DIFFERENT

The years from 1960 to 1965 were among the busiest of my life. I opened my first store in 1960, and two years later married the love of my life, Denise. As I have mentioned, we got engaged on 9 May 1962 and were married on 6 October. I opened my second store in Finglas in 1965. And in between all of that, in 1963, we were blessed with the birth of our first child, Eamonn.

We would go on to have four more children: Gilliane, Stephen, Zoe and Donal. Denise's role in the family was very much that of a home-maker. There was really no question of her working outside the home: it just wasn't the 'done thing' in those days. But she would often lend a hand, coming down to help on the checkouts on odd weekends, even when she was pregnant. We were very much a team.

Although business was booming by 1965, I still worked in Red Island every summer. I would go there every Saturday night and often, coming back from Dundalk, I would go home via Red Island during the week. I never really stopped going to Red Island; it would never have dawned on me to stop.

I suppose in a way I was like a farmer's son. If you swap farming the land for helping to entertain guests at Red Island, you get the picture. It was just something I automatically did.

It is fair to say that the political climate in 1960s Ireland brought more than a few challenges for a young retailer like myself.

For example, it was simply unheard of for shops to stay open late in the evening. Now I had been to America and had seen it working there. It seemed to suit a lot of people who were working from 9 to 6. I said to my father 'I think there's an opening for late-night shopping in Ireland.' The only time people who worked regular office hours could shop was on a Saturday, as stores were closed on Sunday.

I knew I would face a battle. First we had to deal with a long-established practice of half-day closing, whereby it was enshrined in legislation that all shops had to close for a half day once a week (it didn't matter which day). Dundalk always closed on a Thursday; Finglas closed on a Wednesday.

As I wondered about this I looked up the law and discovered that it didn't apply to tourist shops, such as a souvenir shop. In other words, if you were in a tourist area it might not apply. The law was so vague that I reckoned if you sold postcards to tourists you could then call yourself a tourist shop, even if you also sold groceries.

This was 1965. We sold postcards, so our argument was that we were a tourist shop. Then we announced to our customers that we wouldn't close down for the half day. We also informed them that we would have postcards and souvenirs for sale, as well as our groceries! Luckily we were never brought to court for doing this, and eventually the law changed.

The next battle was to allow us to stay open until 9 p.m. on Thursdays and Fridays. I went to the trade unions and they said 'Well, if you want us to work after hours you will have to pay double time.' I said 'OK, I'll pay you double time after 6 p.m.' So they went to their members, who said 'That's a great chance to earn more money.'

We listened to our customers and said 'We'll try it out and see if it will work.' Delighted, we announced we would be open on Thursday and Friday nights until 9 p.m. from the following week. We were very busy between 6.00 p.m. and 9.00 p.m., as all our competitors were closed.

Then one evening a Sergeant Prendergast from Finglas Garda station paid a little visit: the shop was packed as he approached me.

He said 'I see you are selling meat.' I said 'Yes, we are,' and he replied 'I'm afraid that's against a law that says you can't sell meat after 6 p.m.!' I said 'I never heard such rubbish in all my life. To hell with that, you prosecute me!' He said 'Well, I'm taking a note' and marched out of the store.

He was true to his word! We ended up with thirty-eight breaches of the law, because every Thursday and every Friday he would come in and note that we were selling meat.

The local butchers had complained to the master butchers' association, and it had looked at the law and found a stipulation about the selling of meat in the Dublin area, which dated back to 1938, when trade associations could dictate opening hours for their entire trade: for example, if the hairdressers' association decided that all hairdressers would close at 6.00 p.m., then no hairdresser could remain open past that hour.

It meant that every trader was happy because you couldn't take business away from one another. Of course, the poor customer lost out.

The Statutory Order that applied expressly stipulated that all butchers must close at 6 p.m. The third section of the Order said 'Meat is beef, lamb and pork.' It didn't apply to chicken, and it didn't apply to fish or bacon because they were sold by grocers too.

It transpired that when the Minister in 1938 announced this new regulation, he had to give a month's notice. The kosher meat shops – there were two of them in Clanbrassil Street, Dublin – said 'This shouldn't apply to us. We can't open until sundown on the Sabbath.' So the Minister of the day put a section in the legislation to say 'This won't apply to meat sold in kosher shops.'

I saw this Order and was confident that I had found my loophole! Luckily one of the courses I had done in college was Constitutional law. Article 44 of the Constitution said: 'The State shall not ... make any discrimination on the ground of religious profession, belief or status.' So I said 'I'm going to defend this!'

I made an appointment to meet my old college law lecturer, Rory O'Hanlon, in the Law Library. I told him what had happened and he was somewhat reticent at first. But then I showed him the law.

'You told us you couldn't have a law that discriminated on the grounds of religion', I explained. To my delight, he said 'My God, I think you might have something here!' He got excited. So much so that I wanted to stand up in court and defend it myself, but he wouldn't let me!

We went to the District Court and Sergeant Prendergast dutifully gave evidence of thirty-eight instances where we had breached the law. And with much gusto, Mr. O'Hanlon stood up and said 'We want to defend this on the grounds of discrimination in the Constitution'. The judge said 'Oh, that's OK; it will need to be heard in the High Court.'

Our case took a long time to get to the High Court, but it eventually made it. We brought over a Jewish chef from Manchester. We brought housewives in to say they wanted to shop, to the extent that the exasperated judge said 'We know all that now.' It was pure theatre, and great fun. My father got a huge

Above: My father's family. This photo was taken in 1915. My father, Eamonn, is pictured second from the left.

Below: 'Quinn's of the Milestone' in Newry, probably 1918.

Above: My mother, Maureen, was quite a beauty!

Right: My parents on their wedding day in Maghery, Co. Armagh, in 1931.

Above: Denise's parents (third and fourth from left) at their wedding in 1932. Monsignor Casey (far left) would introduce me to Denise in 1958.

Right: Wasn't I a dote? Aged two.

Below: Proud as punch at my First Communion, Clontarf, 1943. (That's me in the back row, first on the left.)

Red Island Holiday Camp in Skerries was a great place for an eleven-year-old in the summer of 1948.

Left: With Eilagh on the chairlift in Bray around 1951.

Right: Tony O'Reilly and me at the Senior Cup in Donnybrook, 1954.

Above: One of the first photos of me with Denise, in Red Island in 1961.

Below: On our wedding day, 6 October 1962. After our marriage in Chapelizod, we made our way to Mount Sackville School to say 'hi' to the nuns who had taught Denise.

Above: My parents, Denise and me with famous entertainer Dickie Rock in Sutton in 1969.

Below: The proud family with baby Donal after his baptism, 1978.

Above: A fun advertisement in 1975.

Below & right: We only found my father's will forty years after he wrote it. (See Appendix 1.)

To be opened only in __ case of the death of _____
Eamonn Eugene Quinn
of "Roscaoin"
Newtownpark Avenue
Blackrock
Dublin.

Page no. 1.   "Roscaoin"
Newtownpark Avenue
Blackrock
June 3rd 1933

My last will and testament.

1 Everything, real, personal or otherwise, of which I die possessed, I bequeath absolutely to my wife Maureen.

2 My desire is that my executors be:—
(a) My wife Maureen.
(b) My father, John Quinn.
(c) My friend, John Lavelle.

3 I place no obligations on my wife, Maureen, as to what use she may make of my property, but it is my wish that she be guided in this respect by the other executors in seeing that the business, which I have helped to build up will be helped as far as possible, while at the same time I believe she will find it a good investment.

4 If my wife, Maureen, desires to remarry she has my whole-hearted approval. She

Right: The late Con Smith, who died in the Staines air disaster in 1972.

Those whom death seems to take from us
do not abandon us.
We are n the shade,
They are in the Light.
They are near to us,
More present to us than ever
n passing on to the True Life,
They have lost nothing of their tenderness of soul
Nor of the affection of their heart
Nor of their intimate love for their own
The Dead are invisible to us,
But they are not absent from us.

(Monsignor Baugand)

CON A. SMITH

A
Dublin 29-X-1928

Ω
Staines (London) 18-VI-1972

Left: I loved riding at the RDS!

Right: Mother (now Saint) Teresa at the Mansion House in 1993. That's Lord Mayor Gay Mitchell, TD, on the left!

kick out of it as well.

And we won our case! We could now let the world know that Quinn's Supermarket was open until 9 p.m. And boy did we milk the publicity from the case.

What did the State do? It appealed to the Supreme Court! I remember saying 'Oh no!' and going to Rory O'Hanlon, who said 'It's going to cost a load of money to go to the Supreme Court.' Of course at this stage the case was getting banner headlines in the newspapers. So we went to the Supreme Court. And again, eventually, we won the case – in 1971. We could not pay for that kind of publicity!

Despite our victory over late-night opening, I was extremely reluctant to challenge another existing practice: the tradition of stores closing on Sundays. There were a number of reasons for this.

First, I wanted us to have the best staff. I felt if they had to work on Sundays we would be unlikely to attract the best people, because naturally they would want to spend Sunday with their family. The added difficulty was that as we had skilled people like bakers and butchers, we couldn't just have part-timers in to work on a Sunday.

But I suppose there was a bit of traditional thinking at play too. I just felt that Sunday was the Sabbath and it's a day of rest. Why should we be like everybody else? Dunnes Stores were the first to open on a Sunday, and they only opened four weeks before Christmas. Others followed suit. I was extremely reluctant to do it.

Once we did start opening on a Sunday, a neighbour of ours, whom I used to see at Mass quite regularly, wrote to me saying it was a disgrace that I had succumbed. I was delighted when I met her in the shop some weeks later. On a Sunday!

Of course, in the 1960s we were still very much a Catholic country. Every new store opening would include a blessing of the building by the local priest. The Angelus would ring at noon and again at 6 p.m.

Most people don't think of that nowadays. You would hear the Angelus ringing from the local church and everybody would stop to say it: the customers, the staff; everyone in the store. It was just an automatic thing that everyone did.

When we started selling paperback books, an eagle-eyed customer from Clontarf found a book that had been banned. It was quite salacious, by all accounts. She was a 'do-gooder' who was just thrilled that she had found something she could kick up a fuss about. She was talking about going to the papers and the Gardaí, which was something I wanted to avoid if possible.

I went to meet with her. I made a fuss of her, apologised and told her I appreciated her efforts. I asked her to keep an eye on us for the future. Thankfully, my strategy worked a treat. Instead of launching a very public (and potentially damaging) tirade against us, she became our eyes and ears on the ground to protect against any grave risk to public decency.

* * *

In 1966, a year after we had opened in Finglas, I thought 'I'm succeeding with this, we are making a profit, we are doing business but how are we going to expand?'

I could see the Findlater's shops that were staid, based on counter service, credit and delivery, a bit like my grandfather's business in the 1920s. I bumped into Alex Findlater one day; he was of the same generation as me.

The following day I picked up the phone to Findlater's in O'Connell Street from Finglas and said 'Alex, could I come and see you sometime?' He said 'I'm free this morning.'

I drove to O'Connell Street and went in to Alex to pitch for his business. I said 'I've got a formula in Finglas and Dundalk that's working very well. I think I could do a marvellous job with your shops. Would you let me have one of your shops: you can leave your name over the door, but I will run it?'

'Feargal, you are too late,' he said. 'We have just decided to go into the supermarket business ourselves and have taken a lease in Stillorgan. We have sat back long enough ...'

It was a pity, but I wished him well. True to his word, Findlater's did open in Stillorgan. But they didn't have anything like our flexibility.

They had trade unions locked in to traditional ways in terms of opening hours and everything else. We had trade unions too, but we were also flexible about breaking the rules.

The big difference was that we were establishing our working practices as we went, whereas they had years of practices built up. It meant that even when they opened a huge shop in Stillorgan, they weren't able to get the same 'buzz' that we had.

Sadly it didn't last, and in December 1968 Alex announced in the Gresham Hotel that Findlater's was closing, with the loss of 150 jobs. One of our biggest competitors, and a company that had been in existence for generations, was no more!

My other major bugbear within the grocery trade was a general belief that went against pretty much every instinct I had: the belief that competition was unfair.

The 1960s were a time of huge emigration and huge unemployment, but rather than trying to generate turnover and increase employment, the

Government persisted with the policy of resale price maintenance that had so limited my father's ambitions in the 1930s.

The policy meant you couldn't sell below the recommended retail price. If you did, the suppliers were within their rights to refuse to sell to you. Sometime during the 1960s, the British Government announced they were going to abolish resale price maintenance.

The opportunity I had been waiting for had arrived, and I was more than happy to propose a similar change here in Ireland. Also, I was conscious at the back of my mind that any such move would help generate publicity for my business.

I wrote to the papers and made statements in favour of abolition. My clear argument was that the customer was right, and why shouldn't the customer have a lower price if they could get it? What right had the supplier – in most cases large companies like Jacob's and Cadbury's – to say 'We won't supply you unless you agree to sell at the full retail price'?

I was at the forefront of the campaign. Dunnes Stores, led by Ben Dunne Sr, wouldn't have anything to do with it politically. It was just not their way to put their head above the parapet. Meanwhile H Williams and Findlater's (who were still going at that stage) would have been quite happy to have left things as they were, because they had their share of the market. So it was left to smaller operators like me to make the case for change.

Again, I saw publicity as an important weapon in our arsenal. I decided we would sell Macardle's Ale, which was costing us one shilling a bottle, for tenpence ha'penny, and took an ad in the paper.

Well, there was a huge outcry. Everybody else was selling it for 1/6 and here was a supermarket in Finglas selling it for tenpence ha'penny!

The following year – around 1967 – a meeting was held by the trade representative group in a hotel in Dublin. About twelve people were invited and the session was along the lines of 'This year, let's make sure we make a profit. So, can we have an agreement between everybody that we will not sell beer at less than 1/4?' It went right around the table and the big boys all agreed.

You might look back at that now and say it was anti-competitive. And it was. But that was the way business was done at the time.

It came to me at the end, and they said 'Are we all agreed?' I said 'If you don't mind, we won't agree to go along with it.' Here was a guy with only one shop in Dublin and the whole trade – Findlater's and H Williams and all the big players in the business – saying they wouldn't sell for less than 1/4.

But I was determined to hold the line. I said 'If you don't mind, could you leave me out? You see, it's all right for you fellows, you have your business. But we don't have enough business, so I might happily do that in a few years' time if I had a few more shops, but not at this stage.'

Every face in the room turned towards me! Their aim was to convince me, this young fellow just out of his twenties, that I was wrong. All the big names in the business were focused on me. And I realised suddenly that I liked this: I really liked being the underdog!

They all agreed their plan, but they were furious with me as the meeting broke up. They said 'But do you not understand? We all lost money last year' and I was trying to say 'Well, *we* didn't lose money last year because we got an awful lot more people to come in to Finglas.'

My argument was that even if they didn't buy much beer, our customers thought our place was very cheap compared to everyone else. So they would buy their turkey and their ham and everything else from us too.

That meeting was a very big moment for me. What surprised me most was that I would always have been timid and shy in such a situation. But here I was, standing up to the big guys – and loving every minute of it!

As you may have guessed by now, I would do anything to get the name of my store in the paper. And business was really booming for us: so much so that in 1968 we were able to open our third store, in Sutton, north Dublin.

We built the new supermarket from scratch on the site of the Grand Cinema, and opened it with a baby elephant which the kind people in Fossett's Circus were good enough to lend us for the day! Unfortunately, the elephant was not house trained! But to say it generated interest in the locality, and the media, would be an understatement. People just could not understand what on earth such an exotic animal was doing at the opening of a supermarket: which, of course, was the point!

A year after we opened in Sutton, a general election was called in Ireland. Our manager in Sutton, John Gunnigle from Sligo, was about my height. One day the prominent journalist, politician and author Dr Conor Cruise O'Brien came into the shop handing out election leaflets. John said 'What are you doing in my shop, without my permission? You can't be using this as a place for electioneering.' So he threw him out!

Conor, who was a big, burly fellow, said he had 'never been thrown out of a place like that' – one hand on the lapel and the other hand on the trousers – and 'by a little fellow: he was only about up to my shoulder!'

He couldn't get over it. I have to say I was secretly impressed by John's commitment to our store! But Conor made the point that 'We have a democracy: we should be allowed meet our clients and our customers.' Of course I saw the potential in this.

So I said 'OK' and announced we were going to have a public meeting of all the candidates in the area. We got the loan of a big flat truck from our fruit and veg supplier and we put it in the car park.

From 5 p.m. that day all the candidates were invited to put their names in the hat. Charlie Haughey was one of the candidates and he was reluctant to come, as he assumed this was a stunt by one of the Fine Gael candidates. But Conor Cruise O'Brien and the other candidates attended. We got a big crowd to come along to hear them speak.

Until then the only way to meet prospective voters was at Mass on a Sunday. As there were a number of masses and a number of churches, it was difficult for the candidates to get around to each one.

What pleased me most was that the 'hustings' in our Sutton car park was on a Friday evening and the Saturday morning's *Irish Independent* carried it with a photograph and a story on the front page.

From my point of view it was brilliant 'free advertising'. I remember going down to Red Island the following day to my father, and he was thrilled to see that Quinn's Supermarket was all over the news. Again!

You might be beginning to see a theme emerge here!

* * *

In 1970, business was going so well that we decided to open our fourth store, in the newly built Northside Shopping Centre in Coolock. Unlike our other stores, we didn't own Northside. Instead we rented space in part of a shopping centre.

The shopping centre owners decided they would have a grand opening to attract attention. The tenants got together and were putting money towards it. It was suggested that we would bring Frank Sinatra over. I was a huge Frank Sinatra fan and thought this was just fabulous. We had a budget of something like £20,000. You can imagine my chagrin when we realised that Frank Sinatra would cost £2 million or more! It turned out there was never any way we could do it. But at least we thought big!

Instead, we got another 'big star' – Simon Dee, whom I have to confess I had never heard of – to do the opening. He was British, and the others thought he was the best we could get for the money we had. This was at the height of the Troubles, and there was real tension up North.

With just three or four days to go, after a killing in the North, Simon Dee announced that he wouldn't come to a country where people were killing each other for religious reasons. Suddenly we had nobody for our big launch!

Denise and I got in the car and drove to the North Circular Road to see John Cowley, an actor who played the role of Tom Riordan in the famous RTÉ soap opera, *The Riordans*. On the television he was married to 'Mary' (Moira Deady), but 'Minnie' – his real wife, Annie D'Alton – was also on the show, playing another character. Annie told a story about how they would book in to a hotel in Ireland and the hotelier wouldn't let them sleep together because they only knew them from the TV!

They very kindly agreed to get the whole *Riordans* team to come to the launch. One very popular character was Benjy (played by Tom Hickey): the son who drove a tractor. Lo and behold, he arrived to Northside on a tractor. It was a far bigger publicity event than even Frank Sinatra would have been. They were bona fide Irish television royalty!

On 1 October 1970, to coincide with the opening of Northside, we changed our name from Quinn's Supermarkets to Superquinn. I sat upstairs in Finglas with Richard Donoghue (of the strawberries fame) as we talked about how to differentiate our company from Quinnsworth, a big rival.

We nearly chose the name Super Q, but decided it might give the wrong message about the length of our queues! We settled upon Superquinn, and it worked.

At that stage, we were not specifically known for our 'quality' innovations like in-store bakeries, Superquinn sausages, playhouses, etc. All of that would follow in due course.

Instead, there were perhaps two key things that served to separate us from the competition in those early years. One was certainly price. Superquinn as it entered the 1970s was most definitely a discount retailer. It cost less to shop in Superquinn in Dundalk, Finglas and Sutton than elsewhere. We would engage in below-cost selling regularly in order to coax customers past our competitors.

The other key difference was how we entertained our customers. There was always a sense of fun in those early days; the idea that you never knew what was going to happen if you went to one of our stores.

A ring was hidden in a cake of cheese, and people would compete to find it. The one who found it got the chance to win their weight in groceries. Needless to say it was quite embarrassing for the heavier ladies!

Without doubt, Superquinn, as it was now known, was thriving as we faced into the 1970s. Business was booming, and I was enjoying every minute of it.

But within two years, disaster would strike our family. Over the course of a few short weeks, my world would be turned upside down.

8

THREE DEATHS IN A ROW

My sister, Eilagh, started dating a young businessman called Jack McCabe when she was only eighteen. Jack ran his own wine and spirit distribution business north of the border in Portadown, and was probably the leading Catholic businessman in the town.

Eilagh was studying hotel management in Cathal Brugha Street when they met. Not long after, she got a job in Cruise's Hotel in Limerick. One of the staff there got in touch with my parents to say 'Do you know that your daughter is being courted? There's a guy from Northern Ireland who comes down all the way to take her out. He's a lot older than her. Is that OK?' I think he had his eye on her as well!

Now my parents knew all about Jack, and approved of him. But when he proposed to Eilagh a little while after, she was just nineteen years of age. As far as they were concerned she was very young to be getting wed, particularly as Jack was a full ten years older: my mother in particular was quite resolute about this.

I was still in school at the time, and I remember thinking it would be just great if they got married because I would get some time off school to go to their wedding!

Just that week, I had learned at school about how Our Lady, the Blessed Virgin, was only fifteen when Our Lord was born. I quoted this to my mother when she said that she felt Eilagh was too young to be getting married. I remember Eilagh phoning Jack from a coin box to tell him what I had said.

Eventually my parents relented, and agreed they could marry. A short while after, the biggest hamper I had ever seen – in fact the biggest tea chest I had ever seen – arrived in Newbridge College, packed with goodies like apples, nuts and chocolates. It had a note on it from Jack saying 'Thank you for knowing Our Lady's age!'

The pair of them got married in April 1954; Eilagh wasn't twenty until July of that year.

Throughout the previous years, tensions remained within my father's family over the court case involving Payantake. Eilagh tells a lovely story about how her wedding to Jack managed to heal some of those divisions.

She was unsure, when doing the invitations, whether to invite Grandfather Quinn and all of my father's brothers and sisters. My father felt they would probably not come along, but she decided to send the invitations out anyway.

Lo and behold, not long afterwards a beautiful solid silver tea-set arrived for herself and Jack, with no name attached. Eilagh was sure it had come from Grandfather Quinn.

It had indeed come from him. In fact, every one of the family who had been invited attended their wedding, which meant an awful lot to my father. Such was the thawing of relations that when Eilagh had her first child, Gráinne, the following year, Grandfather Quinn came to the christening and held her in his arms. She recalls him saying how happy he was to do this. He quoted from the Bible: 'May you see your children to the fourth generation.'

He died not long afterwards, in May 1955, at the age of eighty-nine.

When Grandfather Quinn died, I decided to take this new spirit of detente a little further. My first cousin Ruairi Quinn, who would go on to lead the Labour Party, and I both grew up in Dublin. But in part because of the bad blood which the whole Payantake disagreement had generated within our family, we did not really get to know each other well when I was growing up.

After our grandfather's funeral in Newry, I took Ruairí and a couple of other cousins for a drive in my father's car. I was eighteen years old at the time, and Ruairi was only nine, so still very much a child. As Ruairi recalled in a television interview many years later, when we got into the car I said, 'Our fathers had a falling out some ten years ago. Now let's make sure it does not continue into our generation.'

And so we all resolved there and then that the problems of the past would remain where they belonged – in the past. Put simply, we would bear no grudges. Despite this, Ruairi and I would still not have seen very much of each other during his early teenage years.

Some years later, I was driving near Skerries when I stopped to pick up a hitchhiker. The young man who got into my car seemed a little familiar, but I could not quite place where I knew him from. He wanted a lift to Skerries, and we got talking. He told me that he was sixteen and had family in Newry. I asked his name and was flabbergasted when he said 'It's Ruairi ... Ruairi Quinn!'

Well, I certainly did not let the fact that I had failed to recognise my own first cousin – who was now nearly a man – get in the way. We went down to Skerries harbour, where I bought fresh mackerel, and Denise cooked a lovely meal while we took the chance to catch up properly. It was a wonderful day, and I am proud to say that our Quinn family links have continued to prosper down through the years.

Almost forty years later I found myself quite regularly having to convince Ruairi, who was by then a senior Government Minister, of a point I was making on the floor of the Seanad. So my early efforts at detente certainly proved worthwhile in that arena too, although I'm not sure Ruairi would entirely agree!

Alongside my father, Jack was one of my most influential business confidants throughout the early years of Superquinn. He owned a number of businesses north of the border, and being older than me he was someone I could turn to whenever I needed advice. I came to rely on him so much that I made him a director of Superquinn a little while later.

There were others I turned to for advice. Back in the very early days, I would regularly pick up the phone to Con Smith. Con had been very helpful to me in business, acting as a sounding board for my ideas.

His father, Con Sr, was a good friend of my father's, and Con was a very successful businessman in his own right, owning a number of companies. These included car dealerships and an agricultural machinery business. He was also a shareholder in Red Island.

I remember Con saying on one occasion that the Red Island board was a bit too old. His suggestion: 'What you should do is leave the guys who are already there on the board, but people like yourself and myself should join the board. They will automatically respect us because we are a generation younger, with fresh ideas. They will listen to us. We can do great things!'

We were making plans to do exactly that when fate intervened.

Eilagh and Jack had come down to Dublin for my parents' forty-first wedding anniversary. It was 17 June 1972, a Saturday. We went out for a meal to a new hotel that had just opened in Kilternan. Nowadays it is the Dublin Sport Hotel, but it was Oppermann's Hotel back then.

The Oppermanns, well-known restaurateurs and hotel managers, had just built the hotel. It was by far the 'snazziest' of its kind in the area. We had a lovely meal. As Denise and I drove home, I remember thinking how lucky my parents were to have had such a long married life together.

The next day, we were shocked to hear on the Sunday evening news that there had been a plane crash near London, in Staines. The plane had just left London for Brussels. Ireland voted in 1972 to join the European Economic Community, a precursor to the European Union. A group of eleven leading businessman decided to go to Brussels to help negotiate the terms of entry. Apparently, the plane had been in the air only a minute or two when it crashed. All 118 of those on board were killed.

They included, to our utter dismay, Con Smith. He was only forty-three years of age.

All of us, including Eilagh and Jack, were absolutely devastated to hear the news. My father was terribly upset when he learned of Con's passing.

Con's funeral was the following Thursday, in Ballybrack, south Dublin. I attended with my father and he let me drive his car. It was a huge funeral, with cars parked right up to the entrance of the church.

As we parked, my father said 'Would you ever get a bit closer to the church?' So I drove a little closer, thinking little of it and not realising that my father was suffering from angina. Even though it was just a short walk from the car, suddenly he collapsed at the steps of the church.

We called an ambulance immediately, and a doctor attending the funeral did his best to help. I remember feeling panicked as we could actually hear the siren of the ambulance about 200–300 metres away, but it couldn't get to us quickly enough. Some of the cars parked for the funeral had blocked the way.

Eventually the ambulance got through to us, and brought him to St Vincent's Hospital. But by that time it was too late.

The man whom I looked up to most in the world, the single biggest influence on my life, was dead. He was only seventy years of age, and he died on the church steps at Con Smith's funeral.

Looking back on it now, my father had been ill with chest pains for some time. Not ill enough to stay in bed: not that he was ever the kind who would take to the bed easily. But he would stop sometimes and take a rest. I remember on one occasion he dropped in to Denise and he just wasn't feeling great. Denise would say he didn't get nearly enough exercise. He had a set of golf clubs but seldom played. Apart from that, we had no warning signs, no inkling at all about what was going to happen.

He had only bought the car that I drove to the funeral a few days before he died. Typically for him, the only reason he had bought it was that he had been wowed by the power steering on Jack's car. He couldn't get over that it had power steering. But he never got the chance to drive the car much himself.

We had opened our fifth store, in Walkinstown, in March 1972, shortly before he died. I remember seeing my father there at the opening, full of pride and excitement. He had a tremendous lust for life, right up until the end.

Eilagh remembers travelling in the car with me to his funeral a few days later with Denise, Jack and Eilagh trying to comfort me. I was utterly distraught, and inconsolable.

I was thirty-five when my father died, and it hit me very hard. He was such an important figure in my life that I could not believe he was no longer around. Even years later, every now and then, I would go to call him, to tell him about something that had happened in one of the stores that day. Denise would have to remind me, gently: 'Feargal ... he's gone.'

It was a horrific time for me on a personal level. Unfortunately, our trauma was not yet over.

Two weeks after my father's funeral, in July 1972, a young Protestant called Paul Beattie was coming home one night with his father in Portadown, north of the Border. This was in the middle of the 'murder triangle'. The two of them were stopped and told to face the wall. Young Beattie was shot dead with a bullet through his head in a vicious sectarian murder.

The following night was 12 July. Fearing the worst, Jack sent Eilagh and their seven children down South to be away from the Troubles, as it was the height of the 'marching season'. She was staying with our mother, as much to keep her company as anything else; we had three of her children staying over with us in our home in Sutton. I will never forget the phone call I received from my cousin Leo Power that night.

I was told that Jack had walked into one of his bars at about 11 p.m. and there was a man sitting there who said 'Hands up everybody' and took out a gun. One of the customers, William Cochrane – an older man and in fact a Protestant – decided to finish his drink first. The man shot him dead.

Jack said 'Look, take what you like from the till; you can have anything you like.' 'That's not what I want' he responded. And he shot poor Jack through the head.

'That's for Beattie', he is reported to have said.

In absolute shock, Denise and I asked our friends, Frank and Patsy Fagan, to come down and mind the children. We got in the car and went to Black-rock, where my mother and Eilagh were staying.

Then we had to break the awful news that Jack, Eilagh's husband, the father of her seven children, had just been shot dead. She was numb with shock. I remember her saying 'Ronan will never know his Dad.' Her son, Ronan, was only two years old.

I headed north, to see what I could do to help. Denise had to take the children north on the train, but was asked not to break the news to them straight away. When she got on the train she met Eilagh's friend Aylne O'Sullivan, who was company for that awful journey. Eilagh travelled North by car. When they got home, Denise had to help Eilagh to tell the children, which must have been a very difficult thing for both of them to do.

That month is one of the defining periods of my entire life. I didn't get over the sense of loss with any ease. I kept busy, partly as a way of coping.

Denise, of course, was by my side throughout. I would go over to my mother every Saturday, after I left whatever shop I was visiting. I would drop in and have lunch with her, to spend time with her. Eilagh was now a widow, with seven young children up North. I was very aware that she needed all of my help to keep Jack's businesses running.

Jack was a wine and spirit wholesaler, but happened to have two or three pubs as well, including the one in Portadown where he was killed. He also had the agency for Bell's whisky in Northern Ireland.

Before his death, planning for the future, he had just opened a huge warehouse. It was a modern bonded warehouse, the first of its kind in Northern Ireland. He had gone into very heavy debt for it, as an investment for the long term. His death meant that, among other problems, Eilagh suddenly had this big financial burden to deal with too. She asked for my help, and I was determined to do whatever I could.

It was a very tough year, but somehow we got through it. I remember New Year's Eve, 1972, we were in Nuala's house, Denise's sister's. When midnight came Denise gave me a hug and said 'OK, let's put that year behind us, it's gone.'

Looking back on that time, more than forty years later, in many ways I think being so busy helped me to just keep going. I had five shops of my own to run, my sister Eilagh needed my help looking after Jack's businesses, and my mother, who was obviously in a lot of pain, needed my help as well.

When I went into one of my shops, I automatically thought 'I mustn't pass this sadness on to anyone who works with me or to any customers.' Now everybody would have known what I was going through, but I did not want them to feel they had to tiptoe around me as a result.

It is a real tribute to Eilagh that she managed to get through such a horrible, gut-wrenching loss. And happily, some years later when she was in her forties, she managed to find love again. One Sunday morning she rang and she said 'May I come and see you?'

She came out the following day. I well remember having a cup of tea with her in our office in Sutton. She said 'I just want to tell you that I've met somebody I like, he's Jim Hyland and we are talking about getting married.' I was absolutely delighted for her.

'There's only one thing … you see, Jim was married before. His wife died two years ago and left him with nine children', she added. So Eilagh, with seven children, married Jim, with nine! It was one noisy house, I can tell you! But it was a fabulous marriage, and they were deeply in love. He passed away on 28 January 2009, and is sadly missed by all.

We also had to tie up my father's business affairs, which was very difficult to do. We had closed Red Island in 1972, due in no small part to the effect that the Troubles in Northern Ireland were having on tourism south of the border.

On 30 January of that year, the Bloody Sunday massacre had happened in Derry, leading to the burning down of the British Embassy on Merrion Square in Dublin. Pretty much overnight, all the bookings for Red Island stopped. My father decided there was no way he could open Red Island that summer; the business simply was not there.

After my father died in June, I was approached to see if we would sell the

Red Island site. A ballroom promoter and estate agent, Shane Redmond, who is still in business, rang to say he thought he had somebody who could be interested in buying the resort.

While there were other shareholders in Irish Holidays Ltd, the company that ran Red Island, clearly they were not going to get a dividend that year as it was closed down. So they were quite happy when I said 'We have got a bid in.' It was twelve acres of prime land, and we sold it to Shane Redmond and his business associates, who were in the building trade.

They got permission to build apartment blocks on the land. I felt that this was a pity, as it was a glorious site. But they owned it now and it was theirs to do with as they saw fit.

Thankfully, when they were getting ready to build, out of the blue Dublin County Council came to them and said 'Actually, we would like to make a park out of that. Would you be interested in getting double the space in Blanchardstown in return for the space here?'

So, they got around twenty-four acres in a land swap for the Red Island site. The builders were delighted and the Council showed remarkable foresight. Instead of a block of apartments, there's now a lovely park and playground where Red Island stood. Dublin County Council demolished the hotel building and everything else associated with the resort, except the Martello Tower, to make way for the new park.

I go back there every now and again. I leave my car in the Red Island car park and walk along the path by the sea front.

As I watch the children and their parents in the playground, I remember my own wonderful childhood in that place, in a very different era. And I pay my own silent tribute to the vision and foresight of my dear father. Gone, but not forgotten.

9

FAMILY MATTERS

As our family sought to come to terms with the terrible events of 1972, I found myself travelling the country more and more, helping Eilagh to run Jack's businesses up North and also operating our own stores.

I knew Eilagh needed my help, and as her only sibling I wanted to do everything I could to help her through her trauma. While it was a busy time, in truth I welcomed the distraction, such was the extent of my own private grief.

Family has always, always, come first with me. As far as I am concerned, it is the foundation stone for everything in life, the reason I get up in the morning. No matter where I was in the country, I could hardly wait to get home in the evenings to see Denise and the children. In fact, I have always hated being away from home, even for a night.

For the same reason, Sundays are sacrosanct in our home. Sunday was, and remains, the one day of the week that is absolutely ring-fenced for family.

People often ask why we didn't expand Superquinn into Northern Ireland and further afield. The truth is that we could have; we seriously considered such a move on a few occasions.

But fundamentally, I realised I was happy with Superquinn's rate of expansion, even if it meant we stayed small in comparison to some of our competitors.

This was a key learning point for me, and something I will explore in a little more detail later.

Also, I didn't want to be away from home more than necessary. The same was true for many of our managers in Superquinn. So while we continued to expand, we made a 'quality of life' decision not to develop outside the Republic of Ireland. For me, despite what others in the market were doing, family life was quite simply more important.

I was very much a 'doting' Dad when it came to my five children – and still am! Denise would say I was a lousy disciplinarian with our children, and there is probably some truth in that!

Clearly there were occasions when we had to present a united front if the children were being deliberately 'bold'. But overall I would have left a lot of the disciplinary stuff to her; it was very much her role in the family to ensure the children 'toed the line'. And that was the real hard work!

By contrast, like my own father I was very much a 'tickler' who loved to play with the children and tell them stories. I would come in from work and they would come running up, asking 'Dad, Dad, what happened today?' They were expecting an adventure. So I would tell them all about my day.

Denise and I travelled extensively, for both business and pleasure, over the years. But we have never missed one of our children's birthdays.

I remember meeting Brendan O'Carroll, of *Mrs Brown's Boys* fame, at an event. Brendan said 'You know, I always enjoyed your house.' I said 'What do you mean?' I did not remember ever inviting him to our house!

'Well,' he said, 'I was in your house many times when I was trying to break into show business. I worked as a waiter with Aer Lingus Catering and used to go to your house on a regular basis.'

The penny dropped. We always used Aer Lingus Catering when holding a function in the house. If there was a children's party and we wanted to lay on a spread, we would get Aer Lingus to help us do it. And apparently Brendan O'Carroll was in our house about twenty times over the years!

He said 'I have often talked about you. You never missed your children's birthdays. I can remember going to other parties where we used to cater for other people but the father wouldn't be there.'

Now my time-keeping was not always what it should have been. I remember Gilliane, our eldest daughter, saying when she was about six or seven years of age, 'Daddy, do you think Dads should be at their children's party?' and I said 'Yes, and that's why I'm always there.'

'But do you think they should be there at the very beginning, like when their friends are coming?' Apparently the party was set for 3 p.m. and I didn't come until 3.30 p.m. As far as Gilliane was concerned, that was a disappointment. So I was never late for a party again after that. If it was important to her that I was there on time, it was important to me.

Denise was absolutely central in creating a sense of calm at home from the 'busy-ness' of business life. She always made me feel welcome when I came in the door, no matter what time of the day it was. If there was a stressful time at work, she would always make sure that this didn't apply at home. In that way, and others, we complemented one another brilliantly.

I remember reading an article about Jackie Kennedy. When speaking about her husband, the late President John F. Kennedy, she said: 'I don't meet him at the door when he comes in and say "How are things in Vietnam today?"'

In other words, she felt he came into the house – into the home – to get a break.

Denise adopted a similar approach. She wasn't going to grill me on the latest problem or issue that had to be overcome at work, unless I asked for her advice. If I came home talking too much about 'Vietnam' she would say 'Enough of that now. Let me tell you what happened with the children today.'

She has always been fantastic at helping me get a sense of perspective. With Denise as my anchor, home life provided an oasis from everyday business life. I think it is terribly important for anyone running their own business to have some place where they can switch off from the stress of a busy working life.

As I have mentioned, Denise very much pulled the strings in the home while I went out to work. This is similar to the kind of relationship my own parents would have enjoyed. I am aware that it is a traditional view of family life. Nowadays, in many families both parents work outside the home. I am just grateful that we were able to find, and maintain, a structure that worked so well for us.

As a couple we were always early risers. We were surprised whenever we learned of others lying in bed, especially if they were related to us! I probably don't need a whole lot of sleep, although I welcome it when I get it. Denise is exactly the same. She would say her early rising came particularly from her father Ned, who was an army officer and had great discipline.

I think the fact that I start the day at 6 a.m. or so set an example for everybody else in the company. If I was up and in work early, invariably they were too!

Of course it helps if you enjoy what you do for a living, and I most certainly did. I think I inherited my energy from my father. He had mental energy as well – a real zest for life.

I would look for that enthusiasm for life in our staff. Rightly or wrongly, I would assume that if someone is not good at getting up, then they are probably slow at doing everything else, including thinking!

Denise and I are similar to my parents in other ways, too. Like them, we discuss and debate everything. Denise has been central to every major decision I have taken, every plan I have hatched.

I would always consult her first. Of course there were occasions where we would disagree. But if it was to do with business, I think she would probably have said 'Well, I think you are wrong but you better go ahead and do what you think is the right thing to do.' And that would usually have just as big an influence on my decision as us arguing the toss!

Also I learned a very useful technique from my father many years ago, which helped me to manage stress at work. Whenever I was very annoyed about something, I got it off my chest by writing a particularly angry letter to the person who had annoyed me. In it, I was brutally honest about just how annoyed I was feeling and why I thought this person had let me down.

But instead of posting the letter straight away, my father's advice was to put it in a drawer and leave it for a week. A week later, of course, once I had cooled down I would invariably decide not to post it, but I had certainly got my frustration off my chest!

One instance where I employed the technique occurred back in the 1970s, when a guest from Britain who had been invited to speak at a charitable function in Dublin wrote to say he had no intention of coming to a country where people were killing one another. I was furious, to say the least, and (kind of) gave him a piece of my mind!

Even before my father passed away, I found other ways to 'switch off' from the pressures of building and running Superquinn. One of these was horse-riding, which became a real passion of mine. Eamonn, our eldest son, started riding when he was seven with Gerry O'Brien in Howth, who rented out horses.

We lived in Offington, an estate in Sutton, at the time and I resolved to learn to ride too. I figured if Eamonn could do it at the age of seven, so could I! I went out and bought a pair of jodhpurs and a pair of boots, got a few lessons, and took it from there.

The legendary hotelier P.V. Doyle once said to me that if you are seen early in the morning you can take the rest of the day off, because people assume you are there. It was a lesson I put into good practice at Superquinn.

During one of my first appearances on *The Late Late Show*, the host Gay Byrne said to me: 'Do you get any time for relaxing? You seem to be always on the shop floor.'

I said 'Yes, I love to go riding', and he said 'Where do you find time for it?'

'I cheat,' I replied. 'I do my best to do it in the middle of the day if Gilliane or Eamonn are free on their school holidays. I can have a longish lunch break and nobody misses me.'

Then I said 'Do you know the name of my horse, Gay?' and he said 'No.' I said 'I'll tell you if you promise not to tell anyone! Well, it's actually called "Business" – It means that if someone comes looking for me, Anne Ó Broin, my personal assistant will say "I'm sorry, he's not here: he's actually out on Business"!'

Now, that was back in the 1970s and I still get people coming up to me asking 'How's Business?' It just caught the imagination. The *Daily Telegraph* asked me about it during an interview one time. The journalist said, rather incredulously: 'Is it true you have a horse named Business?' and I said 'Well, actually, I got the idea from a parish priest in West Cork that I had read about who had a horse named Parish Affairs!'

Two days later somebody wrote in to the *Telegraph* to say he had thought of a wonderful name for his horse. He was a solicitor and he had a horse called 'Bail'! A few days later, another came along with a name for a horse for a judge or a barrister: 'How about "Remand"?' So we got a week's coverage as a result of that one story!

I just loved any opportunity to get out on the horse, and took part in many events over the years.

I would go to work early in the morning, come home, get the horse into the horse box, drive out and go riding. Later I would change and get back to work, and nobody would know that I had been out from 11 a.m. to 3 pm!

I never had much style or finesse on my horse, often coming back with mud on me, and have been known to have to run after the horse to try and catch him!

'I see you have acquired some North Dublin land' was the ribbing my fellow riders gave me. And I would say 'No', thinking they thought I had bought some land for a supermarket. Of course they were really talking about the soil I had on my jacket from falling off my horse. Or being thrown off by the horse, as I prefer to describe it!

Another way I managed to 'switch off' was by playing golf. I joined Portmarnock Golf Club in 1986. Although I was not a highly proficient golfer, I loved the experience of getting out on the fairways. It is something Denise and I can do together, as she is an avid golfer.

I was even fortunate enough to win the gold medal at Portmarnock in 1996, which is a knock-out competition played over the course of several months. My youngest son Donal had won the medal the year previously, so it was quite an occasion. To the best of my knowledge it was the first time since 1920 that a father won the competition after his son. What's more, on the same day, Denise and Donal won the All-Ireland 'Mother and Son' competition in Malahide Golf Club! As you can imagine, there were huge celebrations in the Quinn household that day.

A few years later one of the people I played against en route to the medal told a pal of mine how he had said to me that he didn't like to chat while he played, as it interrupted his concentration. To which I replied, 'Oh, great, isn't that wonderful?' And, being the chatterbox that I am, I promptly kept on talking!

* * *

One day in May 1974, just two years after we lost Con, my father and Jack in quick succession, I was in more of a rush than usual to get home to see my family.

I had left our Walkinstown shop at about 6.30 p.m. and I remember thinking 'Gosh, I'd love to go home but I wonder should I go to Finglas instead, on the way?'

I noticed there were quite a few people at bus stops on this particular day. Back then, it was quite usual to stop and offer people a lift. I saw a man standing at a bus stop and I pulled over. 'There hasn't been a bus here for half an hour,' he explained. 'Somebody told me there was a bomb in Dublin.'

Now this was long before we had the Internet for breaking news, or mobile phones. I had not been near a radio or TV so I had not heard anything about it.

I knew Denise was going in to the city that day, and it got me thinking. But I told myself not to be worrying unnecessarily; sure we had never had a bomb in Dublin during the Troubles before.

I asked the man where he was going, and he said 'Well, I live in Glasnevin.' I said 'I can leave you there because I'm dropping in to Finglas.'

We talked along the way, and I must have mentioned something to him about Denise being in town, as when we got to his house he said 'Do you want to come in and phone to check with your wife?' I was very glad I took him up on his offer. When Denise came to the phone she was in a panic.

She had been in Marlborough Street, in a car park, when a bomb went off on nearby Parnell Street and Talbot Street. The blast from the bomb knocked her off her feet. God forbid what might have happened had she had been much closer. She had a little car of her own, a Triumph Spitfire, at the time and she couldn't wait to get in it and drive away. She was in floods of tears all the way home.

It transpired that thirty-three people, as well as an unborn child, had been killed in a coordinated series of bombings in Dublin and Monaghan.

After Denise told me what had happened, I put down the phone and raced home. When she met me at the door, I gave her the biggest hug possible. Once again, the horrific situation in Northern Ireland had been brought home to me in a very real and personal way that day.

* * *

The loss of my father had a real impact on Superquinn. On a practical level, I had lost not only my hero, but the man I would turn to most often for advice and support. Coupled with the deaths of Jack and Con in such quick succession, this left me in a very difficult position. I knew they could never be replaced.

Colleagues working alongside me in Superquinn – people like Kevin Kernan, Terry Young, Joe McDonnell and Tony Gilroy – were a huge source of support and advice to me when it came to the day-to-day running of the business, but I felt I needed to find someone else whom I could trust, who could act as a 'sounding board' for me.

Over time, I began to lean increasingly on Vincent O'Doherty, who eventually became our Executive Chairman. Shortly after my father's passing, Vincent joined the board of Superquinn as a non-executive director.

Vincent is about two years older than me, and grew up across the road from us in Newtownpark Avenue in Blackrock. So my parents knew his parents. After we moved to Clontarf, they lost contact somewhat.

Then, when on holiday in the late 1960s in Spain, my parents bumped into Vincent. They came back and said 'You wouldn't believe, Vincent O'Doherty introduced himself to us. He's a management consultant now.'

Vincent had a degree in engineering and a qualification in accountancy, and was an executive director in a private building materials and construction group.

I have mentioned that Superquinn Walkinstown opened in March 1972, not long before my father died. When we were putting together our proposal for the bank, I wasn't quite sure how to proceed. It was at that stage that I got talking again to Vincent, who had real expertise in this area, and he helped me to compile the proposal. It was a huge success and we got the money we needed.

He did such a good job that we invited him onto the board as a non-executive director. And in time, after my father died, I began to rely on his advice more and more, even though he was already working full-time elsewhere.

In fact, just after my father died, around halfway through the year, we got some financial results and we were losing money. I was very worried, and asked Vincent for his advice.

'Well, you are too cheap,' he said. 'You have got to put a penny on everything.' I was concerned that in a very competitive market, such a move might lose us customers. In the end, we agreed to put a ha'penny on prices across the board. To my huge surprise, nobody noticed what we had done!

His simple suggestion got us out of the red at a very difficult time. This meant we made enough money in the second half of the year to make up for what we lost in the first half.

While Vincent and I got on very well together, we could sometimes disagree as to the priorities for the company. In many ways, we were like chalk and cheese.

Vincent would approach business with his accountancy 'hat' on, given his background in management accounting, whereas on occasion I would have to correct someone at management meetings when they would use the phrase 'to maximise profit': I would say 'That isn't the objective. The objective is to make a strong company, even if we don't maximise profit.'

But we've never had a serious falling out. And I always saw these occasional disagreements as a sign of strength rather than weakness. They showed that even though I could be tempted to play the 'IOTFC' card from time to time (we're doing this because I Own The .... Company!), if he felt strongly about something he would challenge me.

That dynamic of having someone with an alternative view is very important, particularly in a company where the founder takes an active role. No matter what, everyone knew that Vincent and I shared the same aim: to make Superquinn as successful as possible.

After he took up his full-time role as Executive Chairman in 1981, Vincent went on to take responsibility for the key strategic financial management of the group, and for all property acquisition and development.

This was absolutely central to the company's successful development and freed me up to focus on being its public face, while at the same time instilling our company's culture among our colleagues as it began to grow even further.

In many ways, Vincent acted as a business partner and coach to me in the absence of my father. When he retired from Superquinn in 2000, I described him as the brother I never had. Given the huge losses that my family experienced over the years, it is an extremely apt description.

GROWTH THROUGH INNOVATION

10

A FORMULA FOR
SUCCESS

B y the mid-1970s Superquinn was trading strongly, with five stores open and more on the way. Unlike some of our competitors such as Dunnes Stores, we concentrated from the outset on food and groceries, rather than including sections such as drapery or hardware.

Our mission was to provide top-quality fresh food alongside a passion for customer service with a very personal flavour.

Over the course of the 1970s and 1980s, Superquinn continued to expand within the Republic, although at a slower rate than many of our competitors.

We took a number of factors into account when it came to the rate at which Superquinn developed, not least my desire to maintain a healthy work/life balance.

At the same time, I recognised quite early that expansion was important if we were to increase our turnover and generate a healthy, thriving business. What's more, it allowed us demonstrate to our managers that there was scope for promotion as new stores opened. Fostering their ambition in this way was a key factor in successfully retaining our best staff.

However, I remained determined that the company would not expand too quickly. Because we were doing very well in sales, we had plenty of spare cash. I resolved to be careful when investing it, by expanding in a sustainable way.

Too often nowadays, there is a logic that takes over in companies. They get a successful model up and running, and then seek to 'scale it up' as soon as possible in order to maximise profits. Sometimes this works; at other times it can lead to over-extending.

My thinking was always that I was not going to bite off more than I could chew. I liked to keep in touch with the shops myself, to know what was going on in them. This meant I was able to really listen to our customers.

I was most anxious not to lose that connection by over-stretching.

So we would open a new shop roughly every two years, in places like Ballinteer, Blanchardstown, Bray and Blackrock, mainly within the Dublin and Leinster region. Much later, we would expand outside of Dublin to towns and cities such as Kilkenny, Carlow, Clonmel, Limerick and Waterford.

But the 1970s and 1980s in particular were about far more than expansion for Superquinn. That period also saw us react to what we perceived as a shift in consumer sentiment. In a nutshell, it became increasingly clear to us that our customers wanted more from Superquinn.

Until that point, we were primarily known for price, for service and for personality. We would take any opportunity we could to preach and reinforce this message to our customers.

We always checked our competitors' prices, to ensure we were not missing a trick. Usually, this involved sending a member of staff to surreptitiously note what they were charging for a range of goods in store. You couldn't send someone to the same store twice, as they would be spotted and asked to leave. There was even one occasion where our 'price sleuth' had the air let out of her tyres in a competitor's car park!

It was an extremely competitive marketplace. If we knew one of our competitors changed their prices on, say, a Monday morning, we would be watching to see what the change was. Then we would adjust our prices immediately to match theirs.

We simply couldn't afford to be beaten on price. Superquinn in Finglas was a case in point. On a typical weekday, mothers would wheel their children in their prams down the street on their way to 9.30 a.m. mass. As they passed, we could see them taking in the newest prices in the windows of H Williams and Quinnsworth, which were nearby on Main Street.

We wouldn't put our prices out until the women were coming back from mass. This was a strategic decision. It meant that we would have checked our competitors too – and matched or beaten them.

I remember standing in the Finglas store, watching people take a right turn into our store rather than choosing to go left to one of our competitors. Of course we welcomed them with open arms!

As a smaller retailer, we gave individual store managers the freedom to decide prices based on what the local competition were doing. So in one store, the price of tomatoes would come down. In another, the price of beans might be reduced. This sense of trusting our staff was another key factor in our success.

Because the likes of H Williams and Quinnsworth were larger and more centrally controlled, they wouldn't have the same flexibility to adjust their prices so quickly. This gave us a real edge.

Another key factor in remaining price-competitive was a price survey that aired each Thursday morning during the 1970s and 1980s on Gay Byrne's hugely influential RTÉ 1 radio show. At around a quarter past ten, Gay would reveal the results of a secret survey of a basket of goods that the show had conducted the day before among the major retailers.

If we had a particularly low price on certain items, we almost immediately saw a jump in business after the show aired. On the other hand, we would have a drop in business if we were regarded as high-priced. Gay's show was really that influential!

It meant that Dunnes Stores, Quinnsworth, H Williams and ourselves were always competing to make sure we had the reputation of being the cheapest in Gay's price survey.

I shouldn't really tell you this, but one day we managed to guess who Gay's 'secret shopper' was! One of our staff had noticed a woman buying only the eight products that turned up on the radio show the following day. I got a phone call from the store manager to say 'It's interesting, as we never see her during the week but she always comes in on a Wednesday!' So of course, we resolved to keep an eye on her. She was a well-known journalist and broadcaster.

The following week she returned on Wednesday and bought another eight products that turned up on the radio show the next day.

Well, this was just great news.

The week after, we asked one of our staff to follow her as she did her shopping in one of our local competitors. As usual, she bought eight different products. They phoned and said 'The eight products she bought were Nescafé, baby food ...'

So we immediately phoned around all of our stores and told them to take a full 10p off the price on each of the eight products! It meant we were selling below cost, but Gay's radio show was so important that we didn't care.

After a few weeks the 'not so mystery' shopper (!) moved on to another area.

But for that one week in particular we were the cheapest of all the competitors in the survey, even if we did have to 'cheat' a little!

* * *

In 1973, we introduced an innovation that was a real 'game-changer' for our company. The idea for in-store bakeries came about during a trip I made to a Carrefour supermarket. Around that time, the French multinational chain had set up in Britain, and I was interested to see how they were doing things.

During my trip, I saw they had installed bakeries in their stores, as had long been the case in the French equivalents. Clearly they felt there was a market for these bakeries in the UK too. I said 'Gosh, it would be great if we could have fresh bread in Superquinn.' So I came home and we talked through how to offer this in-store.

We opened our first in-store bakery in Finglas later that year. Almost immediately we knew we had a hit on our hands. The fact that we could offer freshly baked bread to our customers – who could smell it in our ovens – quickly became a huge selling point.

Soon after, we opened a second and a third bakery; then we introduced a bakery into each of our shops. We had struck upon a winning formula: people were willing to drive past other shops because we had something they couldn't get elsewhere.

We quickly identified this as another string to our bow in terms of the 'boomerang effect': the ability to do whatever it takes to ensure our customers always came back.

I had learned all about the importance of the 'boomerang' during my time in Red Island. From pretty much day one, Quinn's supermarket was about entertainment and putting a smile on people's faces. We were having games; we were having fun; we were having competitions. But others, such as Pat Quinn of Quinnsworth, were doing that as well during the 1960s and 1970s.

Now, for the first time, full in-store bakeries with bread, cakes, buns and scones made from scratch – and many other innovations that flowed from this – allowed us to trade not just on price, but on *quality, freshness and taste as well.*

This idea of creating products and offerings that were not available elsewhere was absolutely key to what Superquinn would become over the next few decades. We would not claim that our bakery was cheaper: you could sometimes get sliced pans cheaper elsewhere. Later, we would not claim that our sausages were cheaper, or that our meat was cheaper, although we would do special offers on both.

Instead, we could legitimately claim that these products were tastier and fresher in Superquinn than elsewhere.

Food-based innovations like the bakeries, Superquinn sausages, our salad bars and our store-made pizzas allowed us to distinguish ourselves from our competitors in a way we could only have dreamed of before. In addition, you got our famous customer service with a personal touch.

For a company that had placed so much emphasis on price competitiveness up to that point, it was a major break from tradition. What's more, it became a winning formula.

We would still keep a keen eye on our prices: we had to in such a competitive marketplace. But we were now in a position to offer more by way of products that you could only get at Superquinn.

The aim in so doing was to provide another compelling reason for shoppers to drive past our competitors and to come back to our stores over and over again.

Another way in which we differentiated ourselves from our competitors was by constantly refining and improving the service we provided. When we opened in 1960, we were a self-service store. In theory, this meant we were actually offering less service than our more established rivals such as Lipton's and Findlater's.

But our message in those days was that we were offering a *different type* of service to our customers. And they responded to that very well.

Even before we introduced our in-store bakeries, we increased the customer service we provided. One of the most important early innovations focused on meeting the needs of young mothers with children, who made up a large portion of our regular customers.

In the early seventies we had introduced our Superquinn 'customer panels'. These were regular meetings at which customers were encouraged to tell us what they really thought about our stores. And boy did they tell us!

One day a woman said 'Have you ever shopped with three-year-old twin boys? I take a Valium every day, but on Tuesdays when I go shopping I take three Valium! If only somebody could mind my children.'

Her exasperation really got us thinking. What could we do to make her shopping experience less stressful? It was then that one of my most trusted colleagues, Margaret Jones, came up with the brilliant idea of introducing a Superquinn play-bus.

That first play-bus was certainly nothing fancy! Essentially it was a big single-decker bus with the seats taken out. It had no engine so we had to tow it from shop to shop: Finglas on a Monday, Sutton on a Tuesday, Northside on a Wednesday, etc.

We had a trained childminder or two on duty in the bus. Later, we would provide full playhouses in our supermarkets, so parents could leave their children to be entertained while they went about their weekly shop.

The reaction from our customers was immediately positive: by offering a free 'childminding' service as an option, we were again showing we were a company that really listened to our customers.

A little while later, a customer said to me 'You know, I have an awful hassle with the checkout. Would you ever consider having a few checkouts with no sweets at them?' I said 'OK' and we took sweets away from three checkouts. We put a sign over them saying 'No sweets at this checkout'. We got such praise for it that I said 'Let's take sweets away from all the checkouts.'

Of course the accountants said 'Well, we weren't sure what it cost you to have the play-bus: whether it gave you extra business or not. But we can certainly tell you what this will cost you. The money you will lose from not having sweets at the checkout – because you don't sell nearly as much when they are only available at the cigarette counter – will be significant.'

But we did it anyway, because our customers wanted it!

To this day, I am convinced that one of the reasons we did so well as a company was that mothers with children – and in those days mothers didn't really work outside the home – would choose to come shopping with us over our competitors. In the longer term, despite what the bean-counters might have thought, it was the right decision for the business. You (literally) can't buy that kind of goodwill, and it set the tone for how we wanted our company to behave.

More recently the Government agency Safefood approached me to help it with a campaign to encourage the major retailers to reintroduce the concept of 'treat-free' areas, as a measure to tackle our worrying childhood obesity rates. Of course I was only too happy to help.

Initiatives like the Playbus and the sweet-free checkouts served to separate us from our competitors in a very crowded marketplace, by offering 'value added' customer service.

Other innovations were based on giving another type of 'value added' service: food that simply could not be bought elsewhere.

If I were to create an equation for our success as Superquinn developed, it would probably look something like this:

Price + Personality + Entertainment + Service + Taste = Superquinn

Service and taste were hugely important factors in our growth, as they allowed us to stand out from our competitors in the most wonderful way.

11

COMPETITIVE FUN

Throughout the 1970s the Irish supermarket landscape was becoming quite crowded. Dunnes Stores, encouraged by the success of its major development at Cornelscourt, expanded its self-service food operations around the country.

Quinnsworth, Galen Weston's Power Supermarkets and H Williams were all on the scene as well. Meanwhile, former household names like Findlater's and Lipton's had disappeared from the traditional grocery sector.

The late Ben Dunne Sr, founder of Dunnes Stores, had started out in Drogheda before expanding to Cork and then buying Iris Kellett's shop in South Great George's Street, Dublin. That was back in the 1950s. He continued to expand aggressively, opening Cornelscourt in 1966.

Throughout that time, we stayed on friendly terms. In fact, over the years, he had fallen out with practically everybody but me! Dunnes wouldn't join any association, such as RGDATA or the Employers' Association, now known as IBEC. So, if he wanted to know what was going on in the industry – for example, if he opened a new shop and was told that everybody else was paying double time after 6 p.m. – his only way of finding out was to pick up the phone to me!

I was more than happy to help. We had a good relationship on that basis, even though he was a very intense competitor and extremely driven to succeed. I would often make a point of visiting one of his new shops in places like Donaghmede and Ballymun, with a little gift to wish him good luck.

I first encountered one of my other major early competitors way back in 1960, only a few months after we opened our store in Dundalk.

I had heard about a guy called Pat Quinn over in Moate, whose uncle had a shop there. They had changed the name to Quinnsworth, and I was hearing quite a lot about what he was trying to do with the stores.

On Easter Tuesday 1961, Pat came in to the shop in Dundalk with Anne, his new bride. They were on their way to Belfast to emigrate to Canada. He didn't want to go through Dundalk without dropping in to say 'Hello'. He had obviously heard about me too!

Up until this point we hadn't actually met. A few years later in 1966 he came back to Ireland, and arrived in to me in Finglas. The place was very busy and he said 'Any chance of a job?' I said 'Yes, what can you do?' 'Well, I'm big into marketing. I had some great success while I was in Canada.'

Now I wasn't sure what 'marketing' was: the word didn't mean anything to me! I said 'Well, could you work on a bacon counter, or a fruit and veg counter?'

'Ah, no, no, I'm big into marketing and publicity. I could do this ... and I could do that ...' he replied. But back in those days, I couldn't see myself employing somebody just to get publicity. We didn't pay for publicity. So he didn't get a job.

Around that time, the Stillorgan Shopping Centre was being developed in South Dublin. Lipton's and Findlater's both had outlets there. And somehow Pat managed to convince the owners of the Centre to let him have a vacant department store for little or no rent for the first six months or so. He opened around the same time as Dunnes Stores opened in Cornelscourt.

Pat soon proved to be as good as his word when it came to generating publicity for his new department store, particularly in the weeks up to Christmas.

But after Christmas he discovered he was doing little business. So he started selling tins of biscuits and other grocery items. And it was at this point that he realised he could turn over a lot of money that way. Eventually, Quinnsworth became a grocery store.

Pat opened a second and a third shop in quick succession. He came to the northside and opened in Ballymun. He was able to get great deals on his rent because people building shopping centres couldn't get anyone to come in. Often it was rumoured that they would give him the place rent-free for the first couple of years.

The developers would come to us as well, to see if we would consider becoming tenants. But we were only interested in going in if we could own the property. Our thinking was that we had a cash surplus. We wanted to put it to good use, rather than paying 'dead money' in rent. The only exception we made was the Northside Shopping Centre, as outlined earlier.

Pat was getting huge publicity for his new supermarkets from day one. Dunnes would take out lots of ads in the papers and were very aggressive in terms of pushing their low prices. Of course they had textiles too, unlike us.

But Ben Dunne Sr wouldn't give interviews to the press. Dunnes Stores was, and remains, notoriously media-shy. H Williams was around too, and would have been our other main competitor. Although they had seventeen shops, they were seen as a bit dull and boring.

By comparison, Pat would open his new shops in spectacular fashion, with massive publicity. He always wore a different-coloured polo-neck. We weren't used to this because every businessman in Ireland wore a tie.

He made a name for himself by putting his photograph on every ad and even on the jars of jam that he sold. He was a great publicist and it made him different. It is fair to say he would do anything for publicity's sake.

For instance, at one stage he was giving a car away each week. Now a car was a very big thing to give away. In those days, most people simply didn't have cars. And then he announced that the prize one month was going to be a semi-detached house, if you bought a certain amount of particular items over a number of weeks!

It was clear to me that Pat was a very tough competitor because he was selling things at very low prices. He was getting huge publicity, and I have to admit that we had a challenge on our hands to keep up. We changed our name from Quinn's to Superquinn partly in order to distinguish ourselves.

Pat and I were similar in some ways; both of us loved to generate a sense of excitement and publicity around our stores. But our model at Superquinn was based on a far more sustainable rate of expansion.

To be honest, I was always looking for ways to 'get one over' on him, as I am sure he was with me! Around 1970, a real opportunity arose for me to do just that.

At the time, one of the big Government initiatives was the introduction of a new turnover tax on sales; the price of everything had 2.5% put on to it. People were howling about it but we all had to do it, there was no way around it. The only problem with turnover tax was that you could cheat: if you didn't keep good accounts the authorities couldn't find out if you had paid it properly. By comparison, VAT was much more difficult to hide.

I came back from holidays one day to learn that Pat had announced that there would be no turnover tax at Quinnsworth. This was a huge statement of intent, and could have led us to lose serious business to him.

We agreed we simply had to do something to retaliate. But we couldn't afford to follow suit. I racked my brains and eventually came up with a plan: we would suggest that far from not applying turnover tax, Pat was simply 'hiding' it by charging more for many everyday staples.

To reinforce this message, I took an ad out with twelve products that everybody knew the price of – butter, bread, sugar, tea, cornflakes, etc. – and sold them all below cost. At the bottom, I added the 2.5% turnover tax. Below that, again, we wrote 'No hidden turnover tax'.

Now the prices we were advertising these goods at were dramatically lower than they should have been. We were trying to make a point. On the assumption that those coming in would also buy their weekly shop, our calculation was that this would make up for it.

It worked a treat, and we were able to undermine Pat's messaging around his own great publicity idea. Gradually, we began to win back the business we had lost to him as a result of his big plan.

I thoroughly enjoyed the 'tit for tat' of retailing life. But I was always worried about making a sufficient profit to stay in the game. We had to be nimble with everyone, not just Pat Quinn; Dunnes were very aggressive as well. H Williams would have been doing their best also.

By the early 1970s Pat was opening branches in Douglas in Cork, Shannon and Rathfarnham. We were all mystified as to how he could afford to do this. He was a real showman in his personal life as well. He had two Rolls-Royces, and even owned his own racehorses.

Then I got a phone call one Monday morning from somebody who was at a race meeting in Leopardstown to say the whole talk the day before was that Pat Quinn had sold out to the Canadian entrepreneur, Galen Weston.

Now Galen was a serious player. He had come here a few years earlier to learn the business, with support from his wealthy father. He established a chain, Power Supermarkets. But it never really got off the ground; he always felt it was because people saw it as a Canadian company – a foreign company.

So, by buying Quinnsworth and asking Pat to front the new Power – which was to be called Quinnsworth – Galen was confident he could establish an Irish link in customers' minds.

I was due to go on holidays on the day I heard the rumour about the impending sale of Quinnsworth. I rang Vincent O'Doherty: 'Vincent, what do you think I should do?'

Vincent, who would not normally do anything rash, said 'What you should do is get in the car and drive over to Stillorgan. But pick up the phone to the evening papers and tell them you are going over there to try and stop the sale.'

So I called the *Evening Herald*, the *Evening Press* and the *Evening Mail* and headed over.

I phoned Pat to talk to him, but had no luck. It didn't really matter; all I really wanted was to generate publicity for Superquinn: to let the public know we were trying to stop this foreign company from buying Quinnsworth. In reality, I never thought I would be able to outbid Galen Weston.

I was still at Stillorgan waiting to see Pat when I phoned Denise to ask her to pick up the passports. I told her I would meet her at the airport and we would hopefully still make our holiday to Portugal.

'And if it turns out that I do manage to stop Pat Quinn, we'll have to cancel the holiday!' I added.

My 'move' to buy Quinnsworth certainly got banner headlines, to the effect that 'Feargal Quinn tries to stop Galen Weston from buying Pat Quinn's Quinnsworth'.

In fact, there was no way I could have afforded to buy Quinnsworth. They had ten shops and were paying rent on them all. We owned ours and were taking the long-term approach by building one every two years, whereas Pat would rent the shops and open two in the one day.

The sale of Quinnsworth to Galen Weston went through, and Pat got around £50,000, plus all his debts paid off. Suddenly he was very wealthy.

We had a very dangerous new competitor in town. Galen had very deep pockets and Pat, as its frontman, meant Quinnsworth was a real threat. Pat wasted no time in promoting himself as the acceptable face of Quinnsworth. You couldn't help but like the guy. He was brash and was given full licence to trade on his personality.

Luckily for us, it didn't work and the pair had a falling out after about a year or two. The name 'Quinnsworth' remained even after Pat left the company. They took his profile from it, but it was still very much Quinnsworth.

They had to get a new face, and the advertising agent for the company was Maurice Pratt. They asked if he would become the face of Quinnsworth, and he did a very good job.

After Pat's exit, Dunnes, Quinnsworth and H Williams were still our biggest competitors. Dunnes in particular promoted very strongly – 'Dunnes Stores better value beats them all' was its famous tagline.

They were a larger company than us. Ben Dunne Sr was very competitive and would not have been too worried about selling below cost. His stores were known for value but not for service.

He was so successful at getting his message across that sometimes I found it necessary to remind our customers and staff at Superquinn that we could be competitive on price as well!

The opening of our Blackrock store in 1984 was a huge development for us at the time, as it was the single biggest investment we had ever made.

We were also building the shopping centre it was housed in. I did a lot of soul-searching over the selection of the site. I can remember trying to work out how we would do it because the main street of Blackrock was lower than the shopping centre we were building. One night I came home to Howth and even took out one of the children's Lego sets to try to work it out.

I put the Lego on a slope to see what could we do to put two layers there. Of course it was the architect who sorted it eventually, but I found the Lego a handy way of figuring it out in my mind.

Financially, Blackrock was a real stretch for us. Simply, we had to get it right.

This was during the 1980s recession, when there was very little demand for office space. Yet at the same time I had to decide whether we would build offices as part of the development: if not we risked significant disruption and cost should we want to expand in later years.

We went ahead with the full development, and built a lovely shopping centre and store in Blackrock.

Two or three days before we opened, I arrived on site and realised 'I'm not happy.' Something was niggling at me. Eventually I realised what it was.

We had built this lovely new supermarket, which looked and felt very posh. We had a bakery, we had a sausage kitchen, we had a pizza kitchen; it was a lovely upmarket shop.

And that was the problem! My concern was that it would give the impression that it was very expensive to shop there. I talked about this with the team, and explained 'I want it to be upmarket but I want a huge, gaudy price poster on every gondola end and we are going to sell below cost.'

And we did just that. As you walked in the door of our lovely posh supermarket, the first thing you saw was these big gaudy prices.

I was thrilled, although I'm pretty sure I caught our poor architect looking at me as if I needed my head examined.

* * *

Long before we opened our Blackrock store, in 1976 another big threat arrived on the supermarket scene, in the shape of Albert Gubay, a Welshman. Already Albert had a colourful history in the discount supermarket business, having successfully built up and sold a range of such businesses in Wales, New Zealand and the USA.

Obviously he knew what he was doing. He was great at opening a chain, selling at low prices, getting a lot of attention, generating a lot of cash flow and selling off the company to the next guys who would buy it. He had become very wealthy by doing this.

We opened our Superquinn in Bray, Co. Wicklow in April 1976, and were anxious that it would be a success. What annoyed us was that Albert Gubay was getting huge publicity from the moment he arrived in Ireland. Similar to Pat Quinn before him, he really was a great publicist. He announced he was going to call his company here 3 Guys, which had been the name of one of his successful businesses in New Zealand.

He was invited to speak to the Chamber of Commerce; he was invited onto *The Late Late Show*. In fact, it seemed to me he was invited to everything! It finally all got a bit too much for me, and I decided I was not going to do anything to help his cause!

Gay Byrne rang me out of the blue one day. He said 'We are going to have Albert Gubay on *The Late Late Show*; would you come on?' I said 'OK'. Any appearance on *The Late Late Show* was extremely high profile, so I did a rehearsal with Tom Savage of Carr Communications. I knew I had a chance to put Albert down in a 'head to head' debate but I needed some advice on how to do this right.

I went to Carr Communications with Kevin Kernan, Vincent O'Doherty and a number of other colleagues. I rehearsed what I was going to say, and there were three main issues that kept coming up.

I said 'He's not going to pay proper taxes in Ireland', to which Tom replied: 'No – everybody says taxes are too high in Ireland and if that's the reason he's going to be cheaper, well, more power to him. So you can't say that.' Then I said 'OK, well, he's not going to employ trade union labour.' 'Well, everybody says the unions have us ruined! If he's cheaper because he's not using trade unions, more power to him. That will teach the unions a thing or two and his prices will be lower because the rest of you are screwed by the unions. You can't say that either.' The third point was that Irish farmers would suffer. 'Ah, people will say the farmers have us all screwed – you can't say that either!' I was getting a little frustrated: 'You are not letting me say anything!'

Then Tom Savage asked a very pertinent question: 'Why are you going on? What are you trying to achieve?' Clearly my blood was up at this stage 'Well I just want to put him down a bit … to pull the rug from under him.'

'Well, you can't do that,' Tom replied, quite calmly. 'Nothing you can say is going to put him down. Now, is there any other reason to go on?'

I racked my brains a bit. 'Well, I suppose the only other reason is that I would like people to say I'm a nice guy after the interview … that they like our company and want to give us their business!' I said.

'OK, let's make that the target, that you are going to be a nice guy,' Tom replied. 'You want people to say "I trust him." Remember, there's nothing you can say that will damage him, but it could damage you!'

So I went on *The Late Late Show* with Albert Gubay for our heavyweight 'showdown'. The two of us were introduced and he got the chance to say something. Then I was given the chance to respond. With Tom's advice ringing in my ears, I refused to take the bait, even though there was lots I wanted to say!

Instead, I said: 'Albert, the best of luck to you because it's a really competitive market. Competition does nobody any harm. But it's not going to be as easy as you think ... Anyway, it's great to have a bit of competition in the market.' I got great applause for my magnanimity. It clearly didn't work from Gay's point of view as there was no row, but I came out smelling of roses!

I went on holiday and when I came back two weeks later I was told that Pat Quinn had been brought on to talk about Albert Gubay. Pat had obviously said to Gay, 'Gosh, Gay, why did you let Feargal give him such an easy ride? If I had been on, I would have ...' And so Gay brought him on two weeks later. Pat made all the mistakes I would have made if I had not taken Tom's sage advice. He said to me afterwards 'Oh, I made an awful bags of it.' The audience started booing him.

A little while later, Gay asked me to come on his RTÉ radio show to talk about Gubay's plans again. I said: 'You are giving him too much publicity – no, I am not going to go on and talk about him.' Gay said 'Well, I would prefer to have you on because if you don't come along it's John Quinn of H Williams who will do it.' I said 'I don't want to be seen to be knocking him, because as far as the public is concerned this guy is a hero – he's going to bring the prices down.'

So instead I phoned John Quinn secretly. I gave him three relevant questions to ask Albert – 'Is it true that he's not going to employ trade union labour? Is it true that he's going to import everything and therefore damage Irish jobs and Irish farmers? Is it true that he's not going to pay taxes because he lives in the Isle of Man?'

I thought 'That's great, I'll get John Quinn to ask them!'

Now John wasn't going on for a head-to-head with Gubay; he was going on to talk about Albert's plans to enter the market.

I was in the car on my way down to Naas and I remember hearing John come on the radio and say 'I have three questions to ask Albert Gubay. These were given to me by Feargal Quinn'! I nearly crashed my car!

It is fair to say that we were in full Gubay 'pricewatch' mode in advance of his official opening. it was at this stage that we got a helping hand as he prepared to open his first store in Firhouse.

He was getting acres of publicity stating that he was going to be 20% cheaper than all the existing supermarkets, including Superquinn. My colleague Damien Carolan went to Croke Park on the Sunday before Gubay opened, and he phoned me with some news. He said: 'I met a man whose secretary had left him to work for Albert Gubay. But she didn't like it and has gone back to her job.'

It transpired that because they didn't put prices on anything, the staff learned the prices: this girl had spent a week memorising prices.

There was no scanning and no barcodes; the butter was always this price, the sugar X, the marmalade Y. The customer knew the prices because of the sign above the product. Prices didn't change because Albert would buy in bulk and he would buy enough to last for quite a time.

Now we were naturally dying to know what his prices were going to be. We knew he was going to open on the Thursday, and by the Monday before that we knew all his prices. He was on the radio, he was on television and everything was about how cheap he was going to be. His whole thing was price. 'OK, I don't have a palace like Superquinn but I have low prices.'

On the Wednesday I wrote up a news release and sent it to the *Irish Independent*, the *Irish Times* and the *Irish Press*, saying 'You will probably be going out to see what Albert Gubay's prices are like. So here are our prices!'

Of course we were a penny or two pence cheaper on each of the twenty or thirty items I gave!

Albert Gubay was still blowing and blowing about how much cheaper he was. The morning after he opened, the *Irish Independent* carried a survey of Superquinn prices and Gubay's prices. And he was 2p or 3p dearer on each product! I'm pretty sure he hated me for doing that. He couldn't figure out how on earth we did it. We were chuffed, as his opening ended up as a damp squib!

After a few years, Albert Gubay sold out to Tesco. We were delighted with this news, as he had been a real thorn in our sides. Also we felt his selling out represented an acknowledgement of just how competitive we had made life for him.

Later, in 1997, Tesco took over Quinnsworth. I remember hearing about the planned sale the night before it was announced. For the second time, I announced that we were going to compete to buy it.

Now, not unlike Galen Weston, Tesco had very deep pockets, and were paying what seemed a large sum of money at the time. Anne Ó Broin, my Executive Assistant, got a phone call from a businessman telling her he had £100 million sitting in the bank which he would give me to support my bid.

In all honesty, I don't think I really wanted to buy it! Again, I did it mainly for the publicity. I remember going to the *Morning Ireland* radio show on RTÉ to be interviewed.

My plans had generated front-page news. But it didn't happen and, to be fair, I wasn't willing to borrow that much money and expand to the extent that

Tesco did. Quinnsworth by this stage had shops all over the country.

In hindsight it was probably me being more than a little cheeky. And it was all part of the competitive fun. I would have expected nothing less from my rivals.

12

BATTLES WITH
THE SYSTEM

I always operated on the basis that if I felt a Government proposal was wrong, or unfair, I would try to do something about it.

From time to time we even rallied the Superquinn 'troops' to the cause. At one stage in the early 1980s a group called the Irish Association of Distributive Trades (IADT), which was made up of smaller traders such as those in RGDATA (Retail Grocery Dairy & Allied Trades Association), managed to get the Fine Gael Government to agree to put constraints on the 'nasty' supermarkets that were taking business away from the smaller retailers. There was an election coming up, and this was to be part of their campaign.

Under the plans, the five largest chains wouldn't be allowed to open another store. We were the fifth biggest supermarket chain in the country, with seven or eight shops. The proposal would mean we couldn't open a new shop until we became the sixth biggest business – a move that would probably make us one of the five largest again!

The smaller grocers had argued that we were selling below cost in some instances, and doing deals with suppliers. They felt they couldn't compete and their jobs were going; the family businesses were going bust.

While I sympathised with anyone who was facing difficulties in keeping afloat, I felt the proposed solution was just crazy.

So I decided to do something about it. I have to say it was a very exciting time, as it was my first real involvement in a political 'lobbying' campaign.

We decided to hold a series of meetings. We held a meeting in Finglas to which we invited the local Dáil candidates, and all the staff came along with their families.

We told our staff: 'You'll never get promoted if this law gets through. We'll never open a new shop.' We asked them to ask any politician who came knocking on their door if they were in favour of the law, and to say 'It means my son will never be promoted. He works for Superquinn and they will not be able to open a new shop.'

It certainly had an impact!

A candidate at the time told me that when he went canvassing in north Dublin, within half an hour he was tackled in three different homes where people said 'What are you going to do about this law that the supermarkets can't grow?'

He was so concerned that he went to a phone box to ask party HQ, 'What is our policy about this? It seems to be a very big thing!'

Garret FitzGerald came in to Superquinn Sutton in the run-up to the election. There were a lot of reporters with him. He came up to the bacon counter and one of our staff, Declan O'Dowd, tackled him.

Now at the time Garret FitzGerald was a very important man in Irish politics. The reporters couldn't believe that this young fellow said 'Do you support this law?' and Garret didn't know anything about it!

Declan said 'Well, I'll never get promoted: I'm working in the bacon counter and I'll never get to be chargehand if this company isn't allowed to expand, and you are introducing this Fine Gael policy.'

A reporter said to me afterwards, 'God, you must have trained your guys so well that they are quite happy to tackle Garret on it.' But the truth was that our staff could see why this was such an ill-thought-out policy, and they were more than happy to protest against it.

As a result of our campaign, the policy was quietly dropped.

Much later, in 2001, the Government did introduce a restriction on the size of supermarkets, at the behest of the smaller trade groups. As we didn't see ourselves opening any stores bigger than 3000 square metres, the proposal didn't really impact on us, but it was something I opposed on a point of principle.

It meant that the likes of Carrefour and Wal-Mart couldn't easily come in and open huge 'hypermarkets' outside towns. As a keen believer in competition, I always felt this was simply unfair, although I would have hated to see them enter the Irish market.

While we were fierce competitors, on rare occasions the main Irish retailers came together to help one another by acting in unison. As I mentioned, Ben Dunne Sr and I got on very well over the years. Pat Quinn always struck me as someone who wanted to be liked by everyone he met. He was very much a showman.

By comparison, Don Tidey, who had taken over as boss of Quinnsworth, was less flamboyant and was a very clever retailer.

Meanwhile, I knew Ben Dunne Jr – who went on to run Dunnes after his father Ben died in 1983 – as 'Bernard'. This was a way of distinguishing him from his father. He was quite brash and was very well known in Ireland. I liked him but was aware that he was extremely competitive.

I was always keen to make sure my store managers had their offices out on the shop floor. I felt it made the workplace far more informal, and also allowed them to stay close to their customers rather than taking decisions from behind their desk. This was something I did myself, ensuring I was visible in stores by packing bags for customers and dealing with queries on the shop floor.

One time, this lack of formality produced some very concrete results, helping to promote unity of purpose among retailers!

I invited Don Tidey to our house in Howth to discuss an agreement I was trying to put together between the major retailers.

The Government was formulating plans to protect wholesalers, such as Musgraves, by ensuring we had to source our supplies through them, rather than directly from the manufacturers. This had been proposed by the independent small grocers, and would have meant that our scope to cut out the middleman was seriously curtailed. Certainly when dealing directly with the big suppliers we got better deals than the wholesaler could give us.

The move would have resulted in higher prices for customers, and seemed completely illogical to me. However, smaller retailers supported it, as it meant that we would have to source our goods at the same prices as them, via the wholesalers.

Don arrived out to the house for our meeting. It was a glorious summer day and I asked on the off chance, 'Don, would you fancy a swim?' He was very much a keep-fit enthusiast. I had a spare pair of togs, which he borrowed. So the boss of Quinnsworth and I went running down to the beach near my house.

The tide was in. The kids were on the beach making sand castles. Denise had left a lunch at the house for us, and after our swim we went up and changed.

After we had towelled ourselves off, I explained that 'I would like you to agree that we write to all our suppliers saying that unfortunately, because of the new legislation, we will have to close our account with you and only buy from the biggest.'

My idea was that all the tea companies were to be told that we were closing their account and only buying from Lyons from next month. Then we would do similar with the other brands. My thinking was that the suppliers would be so unhappy that they would make representations to the Government about the planned new legislation.

Don was enthusiastic about my plan. 'I see your point,' he said. 'If we just send the letter and give a month's notice it's going to cause havoc. OK, we'll do that too. We'll send the letter out this week.'

I showed him a letter I had prepared and suggested that he did up his own version.

The following day I invited Bernard Dunne out too! I met Bernard in the Marine Hotel in Sutton and we drove up separately. I asked 'Do you fancy a swim?' 'God,' he said, 'I haven't swum in Irish waters for years!' But it was a glorious day and so I got the togs out again and we went down to the beach.

Our son Donal, who was about four at the time, later asked me, 'Daddy, is the man who went swimming with you very holy?' I said, 'I'm sure he is – why?' 'Well,' he said, 'Do you remember when he dived into the water and he came up? All he kept saying was "Jesus Christ!"'

Bernard agreed to take part in our plan too.

The following week all but the main suppliers got a letter from Dunnes Stores, Superquinn and Quinnsworth saying 'We are closing your account.' It was a rare moment of unity between the three biggest competitors in the market – a 'ceasefire' if you like!

Within forty-eight hours the law was stopped. It was a huge victory for me, and was all decided on the basis of a swim in the refreshing waters around Howth.

Not all of my media battles with Government legislation were so successful. In 1987, the Minister for Industry and Commerce, Albert Reynolds, TD, drafted new legislation: the Restrictive Practices (Groceries) Order.

Among its provisions, it forbade retailers from asking suppliers to the grocery trade for donations to guarantee shelf-space for their products. This was known in the trade as 'hello money'.

My problem? I have always been a supporter of the logic behind 'hello money'.

This was because I believed it legitimate that you negotiated as well as you could with your suppliers, so you could offer the best prices to your customers. Quite simply, it made good business sense.

Before the law was introduced, it was by no means unusual if you were buying ice cream that you would expect the ice cream company to supply the fridge.

It was also not unexpected that if somebody came in to sell you a product, you said 'I have no room: I'll have to take some other product off to make room on the shelf.' Suppliers would then have to convince you to stock their goods as opposed to their competitor's.

One of our company directors, Damien Carolan, is recognised as being the creator of the whole 'hello money' concept: something he is quite proud to acknowledge. He would explain his logic to potential suppliers quite simply: 'The fact is, we don't have elastic shelves.'

But that was regarded as bullying tactics by some suppliers. And Albert Reynolds, whose family business was C & D Foods (pet food), was supportive of their case.

My concern was that we would find it difficult to compete with large mul-tinational players like Tesco, which was a very big buyer in the UK too, if this new legislation was introduced.

My logic was that if the Government introduced legislation to say 'Oh, you can't do that in Ireland', Tesco could do it in Britain anyway as the law didn't apply there. And any savings they achieved there could be used to lower their prices in the Irish market too. In the absence of an EU-wide law banning the practice, I just could not see how such a law was enforceable.

If you had your headquarters in Dusseldorf, Frankfurt or London, the Irish Government couldn't do anything to control you, whereas if you were a solely Irish company – as we were – you were being singled out. In my view this was hugely unfair.

I came out very strongly against Albert Reynolds' proposed Groceries Order at the time. But he was adamant, and the legislation took effect.

While the 1987 order stopped 'hello money' and the selling of certain goods below cost, it didn't stop the multiples from demanding a discount from their suppliers, based on the volume of business done in their stores. If, for example, a large multinational had 100 stores, it could demand a bigger discount from suppliers than a chain with just ten stores. As a result, Reynolds' legislation, to my mind, was very much an incomplete law.

More than a decade later, Superquinn came under intense media scrutiny over the whole issue of 'hello money'. Even worse, there was a particular focus on me. In truth, I felt I let myself down badly during an interview with RTÉ's news reporter, Charlie Bird, in 1999.

Charlie rang me to say he would like to come out and talk to me about 'hello money'. I remembered he had just published a book. I had a copy of it with me and got him to sign it. Then we did the interview out in the car park in Sutton, and he hit me with what I felt were very aggressive questions.

I would be the first to admit that I didn't handle myself very well in the interview. I lost my temper somewhat as I was very taken aback by the line of questioning, and it showed.

He had found a supplier who had come in wanting to get on the shelves of our new store in Dundalk. Damien Carolan told him that we needed a better discount, or 'support money' up front.

In effect, the idea was that the supplier would 'support' the establishment of the new supermarket though a payment. In return, they would gain access to our shelves and increase their own sales. Clearly unhappy, the supplier in question did an anonymous interview on television where he recounted what had happened.

The suggestion was that we were asking for 'hello money', albeit under a different guise. Everything we did was within the law. But in my interviews at the time I fully acknowledged that we had sought to find ways to get around it.

I admit it was a very strange time for me. It was the first time I had been openly criticised in the media and it got headlines all over the place, to the extent that the papers continued with it day after day.

In a way, I learned what my obituary would be like, because one of the papers carried a big article with my photograph and my history as a retailer. It was obviously prepared for an obituary – 'this is what this guy has done over the years'. Unfortunately, the 'hook' was the 'hello money' controversy!

The papers made out that the big nasty supermarkets, of which we were supposedly one, were bullying our suppliers. My point was that very often the 'poor supplier' was much bigger than the retailers. They would include suppliers like Danone, which is a huge, multibillion company, bigger even than Carrefour – the biggest retailer in Europe.

My argument was also that any smaller brand or supplier needed to create a product that was exceptional. They could get it onto the shelves of smaller stores and build demand among customers from there.

If we had enough customers asking for a product, then we would stock it. We were good listeners: when customers said, 'I shop with you for everything else, but I have to go down the road to your competitors for this', then we reacted.

What's more, in Superquinn we had a really strong track record of supporting small Irish businesses. We were the first to stock products like Ballygowan water and Fiacla toothpaste. Also, we had discovered a huge niche in the market for local produce, and had introduced one of the first major 'buy local' campaigns in our stores. We found suppliers in the vicinity of our stores, and put their photographs up to encourage people to buy their products.

On reflection, I think one of the things I found hardest about the whole 'hello money' controversy was the idea that I would not be 'well liked' as a result of the negative publicity from that time. It made me realise just how important it was to me that I was respected by my peers and customers. I was deeply worried this would no longer be the case, given how strongly the media pursued the story.

I was aware that I probably shouldn't have done the interview with Charlie Bird myself, but I have always believed that in times of crisis the boss has to stand up.

The Groceries Order was eventually lifted in 2006, in part due to a concerted campaign against it by consumer advocates such as Eddie Hobbs, who used his *Rip-Off Republic* RTÉ TV show to show that the order was keeping grocery prices artificially high.

I can't stress enough that I felt 'hello money' was simply normal business practice, the cut and thrust of retailing to try to secure the best possible deal. I didn't have a problem with it, but others did. In time, the whole controversy passed.

But it was a real low point. On reflection, the most frustrating thing for me was that for once I didn't do a competent job in explaining myself to the public.

13

THREATENING TIMES

In 1981 the prospect of violence once again being perpetrated against my family reared its ugly head. My national profile was quite high at the time, as a result of the success of Superquinn, so I would have featured on shows like *The Late Late Show* and would have been in the newspapers quite regularly.

One day, out of the blue, I got a phone call from a senior Garda to ask if he could meet me. I was going to the Berkeley Court Hotel in Ballsbridge for an event, and we agreed to meet there.

He told me they had intercepted information – in fact I think they had tapped a phone – and there was a plot to kidnap me or one of my family. As a husband and a father, the idea that they would target Denise or one of my children was very worrying.

The Garda pointed out that I would be an attractive target for ransom, as I had large amounts of cash under my control. What's more, it was easily accessible.

There was a spate of kidnappings of supermarket bosses and others in the early 1980s, including Ben Dunne Jr, who was kidnapped and ransomed in 1981.

In 1983, Quinnsworth boss Don Tidey was kidnapped, only to be rescued after a bloody gun battle with his captors in which a Garda and a member of the Defence Forces were killed. There was a similar effort to kidnap Quinnsworth's owner Galen Weston from his Co. Wicklow home in 1983.

So I was neither the first nor the last supermarket boss to be targeted in this way.

'We have reason to believe that you, or one of your family, are next in line', was how the Garda put it. Obviously the authorities had reason to take these threats very seriously. They put a Detective Sergeant in the Special Branch, Pat Byrne – who would go on to become Garda Commissioner – in charge of my security and that of my family.

I always understood that the people behind the plot had links with the republican movement, although it was never made explicitly clear to me if they were the IRA, the INLA or a splinter group.

After our meeting, I went home and told Denise. My attitude would have been 'Thank God they discovered this.' I learned later that it had come up for discussion at a Cabinet subcommittee meeting on crime. I was told that Charlie Haughey – Taoiseach at the time – had said 'Make sure nothing happens to that man.'

In truth, the fact that the Gardaí were already on top of the plot to kidnap me was a big source of relief. It meant I was not in shock at the news, and was able to handle it. The next day Pat Byrne came out to the house and introduced himself to the family. He asked us all to keep our eyes peeled for anything unusual.

Not long afterwards, Eamonn and Stephen, who were about eighteen and eleven respectively, were coming back to the house on horses when the phone rang. Pat was enquiring if we had noticed anything unusual.

Eamonn said 'No, but there was a car parked out on our road earlier.' Normally we wouldn't see a car parked like that in our cul-de-sac at that time of the year.

Pat asked, 'I suppose you didn't notice the number?' Eamonn said, 'Stephen, did you notice the number of that car?' Stephen said, 'Oh, it was ...', and he listed the registration details. Obviously he had taken Pat's advice to heart!

Pat fed the number into the Garda system and said, 'Oh gosh, that's the car belonging to the guys we know are planning to kidnap you.' Immediately he ordered it to be checked out, but the car wasn't there any more. It was spotted a short while later in the Marine Hotel car park in Sutton; the kidnappers were evidently staking out our offices across the road at Superquinn too.

Soon Denise and I found ourselves playing host to about twelve Gardaí who came to live with us in our home, working on a rotation basis. They were there every night and every day, and stayed overnight. There were three or four of them in the house at any time, armed with Uzi submachine guns.

Donal was three or four at the time, and they would keep the guns away from him in case he would crawl over them or try to press them!

Denise got into the habit of giving our visitors a big breakfast every morning. Now we are not big breakfast people – we wouldn't normally have a fry – but of course Denise ended up cooking one for them every day.

She found she couldn't go to town and couldn't go shopping without an armed Garda with her. I assumed it was me that would be kidnapped, because Ben Dunne had been targeted previously.

While it was a worrying time, it was not without its lighter moments. A cousin of mine, Sean McCusker, dropped by the house unexpectedly one evening, as he does on occasion. He was more than a little taken aback to find himself surrounded by armed Gardaí wanting to know who he was and why he was there!

Denise handled the whole situation very well, to the extent that when we went out to play golf Pat Byrne started to join us. If we went walking, Denise would say 'I think we are fitter than those Gardaí.'

We had a set walking route near our house, a forty-five- or fifty-minute walk, and we would put on a pace because there was always a Garda or two behind us. We would walk faster and the guys were breathless trying to keep up with us!

Eventually things came to a head. The Gardaí got information that the kidnap attempt was going to happen on a particular night.

Pat suggested that we move out of the house and the Gardaí would put two decoys in place, pretending to be Denise and me. The plan was that our house would be surrounded should the kidnappers make their move.

At that stage Pat said, 'There's access from the sea – we hadn't noticed that – so we better make sure we cover that as well … Could you make sure the gate down below is locked because somebody could come in by boat?'

I said, 'Gosh, I really would prefer to be here. It is our home, after all.' Denise felt similarly.

Pat told us, 'We've a much better chance if you are here and they arrive because then we can charge them with attempted kidnapping, whereas if you are not here it is attempted robbery.' So instead of the decoys, we stayed in our house that night, waiting for the kidnappers to make their move.

There were about twelve Gardaí with Uzis in the bushes all around the house. It was coming up to Christmas 1981.

Actually, we slept well that night, as we knew we were very well protected.

The children were all in the house too, asleep upstairs. When we came down the following morning, nothing had happened. To be honest, we were both a bit disappointed, as we wanted the kidnappers to make their move and let us get on with our lives!

It didn't happen the next night either, and it ended up that the gang were made aware in no uncertain terms that any attempt on our family would not go undetected.

All in all, the episode must have lasted around three months. Throughout the time, the threats against myself and my family were very real, and very much part of our day-to-day life.

The three eldest children, Eamonn, Gilliane and Stephen, were fully aware of what was going on. Of course we were concerned not to worry them unnecessarily, but at the same time they needed to be vigilant, and the younger ones needed to know why these strange men were in their home. Pat Byrne certainly gave us a lot of confidence that the Gardaí were on top of it.

By this stage Gilliane was studying in Trinity College. She had the use of a car because the Gardaí said that if she walked to college she could be at risk. So we got permission for her to park in the grounds of Trinity.

Because I spent my Thursdays, Fridays and Saturdays visiting all of our stores, I was advised by the Gardaí to have someone with me at all times, lest an attempt be made to kidnap me while I was alone.

There was another reason why 1981 will be etched in my memory forever. I remember well waking up on 15 February, a Saturday morning. It was shaping up to be another typical busy weekend shopping day.

The previous day had been Valentine's Day, and some of our staff in our Northside store had gone to the Stardust nightclub in Artane that night to celebrate. Four of them – David Morton, Liam Dunne, George O'Connor and Martina Keegan (whose sister also lost her life) – never came home after a fire broke out in the former jam factory, just as a disco-dancing competition came to an end.

Later it would emerge that some of the emergency exit doors had been locked and impeded on the night of the fire, trapping those who were trying to escape.

Our four Superquinn colleagues were among forty-eight people who died as a result of the fire. Other staff members were badly burned.

I headed to our Northside store that Saturday morning to see what we could do. It was devastating.

As the northside communities of Coolock, Artane and Donnycarney struggled to come to terms with their overwhelming grief, Fergus O'Brien, Lord Mayor of Dublin, set up an official Stardust Committee to fundraise on behalf of the bereaved families. He asked me to serve on the committee, and I was only too happy to oblige.

I served alongside the famous socialist Noel Browne. We would be on opposite ends of the spectrum politically, but got on well. We did our best to ensure that any money raised went directly to the families affected by this most awful, avoidable tragedy.

The Keegan girls are buried in Balgriffin, as are my parents, and when I am out there I visit their grave too. Another young man who was very seriously injured was working in our bacon department at the time. We were delighted to welcome him back to work in Superquinn afterwards.

It was a very upsetting time, which sent shockwaves throughout the whole city and the wider Superquinn family.

I came face to face with death in a very different way some years later. I received a message around May 1996 asking me to phone the crime reporter

Veronica Guerin. She was a very well-known journalist at the *Sunday Independent*, with a reputation for doggedly charting the activities of Ireland's crime bosses.

I phoned Veronica and she said, 'I was talking to my editor and I said I'm just so busy that I can't fit everything into my life. His reply was, "Well, find somebody who is even busier than you, but who seems to be able to fit everything into their life. Why not be their shadow for a week?"' She asked 'Could I shadow you for a while?', to which I replied, 'Veronica, I would love to have you along.'

Now, I didn't know Veronica, so she came to the office to talk through her idea. She explained that she wanted to write a feature piece about her time with me for the paper.

We talked about it and I said, 'Actually, to be honest there's an awful lot of what I do that's dull and boring. So to have you follow me every day for a week or so is not going to make for a very good piece! What you should do is dip in and out of my life for three weeks.' And she said 'That would be a better solution.'

I had described to her what a typical week would be like running Superquinn, and in my various other engagements as a Senator. So for three weeks, I had Veronica look at my diary and 'cherry pick' the best bits to shadow me!

On the very first day she came along, we were holding a Superquinn dinner that we held every year in the Berkeley Court Hotel, where those who were 10 years in the company were invited with their spouse to a formal meal and night of dancing to celebrate.

Veronica joined us and watched as Denise and I welcomed each couple and had our photograph taken with them. At the end of the night, the photographer came back with the photo duly developed and framed. Veronica was great company that night – and throughout the weeks I spent with her.

She also came to Finglas, where I went through the figures with the staff one Thursday morning, and she attended a customer panel in Swords (she lived nearby in Baskin).

We had great chats over the course of our time together. During that time, my respect for the passion and enthusiasm with which she went about her work soared.

On the final day together, I was particularly busy. I had to attend a board meeting of the Irish Grocers Benevolent Fund; also I was judging the food of the year awards alongside chef Darina Allen for An Bord Bia, and I had another engagement: three different things in three different parts of the city.

When we were finished for the day, Veronica hitched a lift with me to Jury's Hotel in Ballsbridge, where her car was parked.

We said our goodbyes and we both got in our cars. We drove through the East Link toll bridge at the same time, and she passed me at speed. I phoned her and said 'Veronica, were you in an awful hurry to get away?' and she said 'Oh, I'm always driving too fast. In fact I have to go down to Naas court soon because I was charged with speeding.' And I remember saying to her, 'Would you not be able to do something about that?' because every Garda in the country knew her. Quite typically, she said 'Oh no, I wouldn't dare use influence to get off.'

On 23 June the *Sunday Independent* carried her story of what it was like to 'shadow' me. The original intention was that I was also to shadow her, for a week. But instead we agreed that I would do an article, to appear on the same day as hers, in which I talked about what it was like to have her as my 'shadow' for three weeks (see Appendix 2).

On 26 June 1996, Veronica went to Naas for the court appointment she had mentioned. On her way back she phoned a Garda friend. She was on the phone to him at Newland's Cross when he heard the gun shots.

Pat Byrne rang me to tell me the awful news. I was in the car, coming through Sutton at the time. I just couldn't believe it.

Denise and I went to her funeral at Our Lady Queen of Heaven Church beside Dublin Airport. One of Veronica's family insisted on putting us sitting up near the altar, not far from President Mary Robinson and Taoiseach John Bruton. It was a desperately sad funeral, with her young son Cathal and husband Graham struggling to control their grief.

Little did I know it at the time, but the last few weeks of Veronica's life were, to a very large extent, spent with me. After her untimely death, I spoke in the Seanad as we discussed the horrors of her work and those with whom she came into touch, and said 'I realised I could not do her work.'

I meant every word.

14

CREATING A CULTURE OF INNOVATION

When people speak with me about Superquinn today, they often talk about the emphasis we placed on personal customer service, or the innovations we introduced such as our bakeries and our sausages.

As I mentioned already, some of those innovations took time to refine, with others requiring a pretty major shift in our thinking before they really made an impact.

More recently, I have watched with interest as another well-known Irish entrepreneur, with a penchant for publicity similar to my own, has sought to change his company. Over the past few years, he has decided to reorient the tone of his business towards a more 'friendly' model of customer interaction.

His enterprise was previously known for pretty 'rough and ready' customer service, and for providing a low-cost offering without 'frills'. On the surface, it is the polar opposite of what Superquinn was renowned for: putting the customer first.

But dig a little deeper, and there are many similarities between Michael O'Leary of Ryanair and me.

This might surprise a lot of people, but bear with me. I believe the comparison is a most useful way of illustrating exactly what made both of our companies a success.

From his early days at Ryanair, Michael O'Leary identified a different type of customer service than was the 'norm' at the time. Having travelled to the USA to study the methods employed by the low-cost Southwest Airlines, he came back full of ideas as to how best to apply its 'no frills' approach to the Irish (and European) market. His version of customer service was based on offering consumers the ability to travel abroad at a very low price. I used Ryanair quite a lot to come back from Brussels, because it left a couple of hours earlier than other available flights. It was an awful nuisance to have to queue and stand for my flight.

But the service Michael O'Leary provided was excellent, when measured against the goals he set for his company: Ryanair was cheap, and offered more flight options. It 'did what it said on the tin'. For this reason I often chose to fly with Ryanair, despite finding the experience less relaxing than with Aer Lingus or other 'full service' carriers.

O'Leary's approach was in fact a classic example of the 'boomerang' principle in action. He said 'I'm going to give you a low price, and arrive on time. You are going to have to put up with queuing, you are going to have to put up with noise, you are going to have to put up with paying for bags, you are going to have to put up with people selling you stuff, and you are not going to have allocated seats.'

Before Ryanair it cost a couple of hundred euros to travel to London; suddenly we could do it for as little as €10 with Ryanair. Crucially, O'Leary delivered on his promise to his customers. And that's what I call real customer service.

You could say the same thing about a grocery discounter. If you compare an Aldi or Lidl store to the upmarket Donnybrook Fair stores in Dublin, there is a huge difference in the way they look and feel. This is because they are different businesses, offering a very different service.

Customers who go to a discounter know their store may not have the same 'ambience' as their more upmarket competitors, but they know the 'service' they will receive is value and price.

As a retailer, I was always looking for a gap in the market. When we started out in Dundalk in 1960, that gap was price competitiveness alongside a different type of service: self-service. My objective when we opened was to get every customer to shop with us. Doing that meant offering lower prices than anywhere else.

Every other shop at the time was giving far more service to its customers. They were giving credit, they were providing delivery, they were doing the shopping for you; you stood at the counter and gave a list in, which was filled by an employee.

By comparison, when we opened we said 'No, you have to go pick up the basket yourself, you have to go to the checkout, you have to pay cash and no, we are not going to deliver it for you.'

The reason we did so much business from our first day in Dundalk was that we took the sight out of people's eyes with our low prices, alongside our different version of service. And in many ways, that's the same as the Ryanair concept.

In time our model changed to include 'value added' taste offerings, and Superquinn became known as more than a simple discount supermarket. But many people forget that we essentially started out as a 'Ryanair' type discount retailer, so I have more than a little in common with Michael O'Leary.

In fact, the success of the German discounters Lidl and Aldi prompted us to seriously consider emulating them at one stage. We went as far as identifying a site in Rathmines, and crunching the numbers.

In 1999, we sent one of our senior managers, Cormac Tobin, to England to work with Aldi. Cormac's aunt Eithne lived in Birmingham and he applied for a job there, without telling them he was still employed by Superquinn!

He telephoned each week with an update on how they did things. Then he returned to Superquinn and we sent him off around the world to examine the low-cost model.

As part of his intensive research efforts, he spent time working with the Albert Heijn chain in the Netherlands, Pick n Pay in South Africa, Big Fresh in New Zealand and companies like Wegmans and Publix in the USA. He compiled a 'top secret' report for us, weighing up the pros and the cons of such a move.

We did this because Lidl and Aldi had clearly spotted a gap in the market. Put simply, we felt we needed to be there. But we also agreed that we should do it under a different name. Such was the secrecy that we even had a code-name for his final report: 'Fred'!

Eventually we decided that it was not for us. There were a few reasons for this, not least the fact that we would need real 'scale' to be able to offer Lidl- or Aldi-style goods cheaply. We would need to open a lot of shops, and we were not sure that it was the right course for the company.

However, far from looking at what Lidl and Aldi were doing and saying 'Ah, well, that's grand for them, but it is not for our customers at Superquinn', we were keen to experiment with the idea of competing with them directly.

There was clearly a demand for what they were offering and we were prepared to emulate them by providing a very different type of 'service' to our customers than they received in Superquinn.

I like to think that that was typical of my approach to business: if there is a gap in the market, can I fill it, and how will I do it? That is really the primary question that needs to be answered by any entrepreneur.

When I opened my first store in 1960, I realised this gap was about low-cost pricing coupled with a new type of customer service. In time, we refined our model based on the needs of the market. For Michael O'Leary, that gap was low-cost air fares and very little else, but now he has realised that the market wants more and is reacting as all good businesses should do, by making his company far more customer-friendly.

Too many businesses get stuck in the old, comfortable way of doing business. Instead of reacting to a changed marketplace, as we always sought to do in Superquinn, it can be tempting to bury your head in the sand and hope the new challenges you face will simply go away. And therein lies a recipe for disaster.

They won't go away. For any business to succeed, it has to have a culture of innovation at its core at all times.

* * *

I mentioned earlier that I was always 'on the lookout' for anything that would help grab the attention of our customers. From our first day in 1960 to the day we sold the company in 2005, I would constantly say to people like Brendan Rooney and later Damien Carolan: 'What can we do next week? We've nothing to do next week.'

Frankly, I was obsessed with the concept of having something new each week so that people meeting a kilometre or more away from Superquinn would say 'Did you hear what they are doing in Superquinn this week?'

Sometimes we simply copied or adapted ideas that we had heard elsewhere. Carrefour with their in-store bakeries is a good example. Another was when I saw my good friend, the late US retailer Fred Meijer, give away a 'free ice-cream cone' card to his customers. I emulated this by giving out a free donut card to Superquinn customers.

Some of our initiatives were far more ambitious. As the company grew, I was travelling quite a lot to the States and elsewhere. I had a British Airways air-miles card and I thought, 'That tells you an awful lot about your customers. Not only that, you can reward your customers for their loyalty.'

Then I discovered that Ukrop's in Richmond, Virginia, had introduced similar loyalty cards for their customers. I asked if we could pay them a visit to look at what they were doing, and they agreed.

So our finance director, Frank Murphy, who attended the US-based Food Marketing Institute Conference, went on to Ukrop's stores in Richmond. He worked with Scott Ukrop on their loyalty project before coming home to introduce our very own card. Initially I was of the opinion that we should only give it to good customers so that customers would be crying out for them. The other view within our company was 'Let's give it to everybody who comes in and wants it.' In the end (thankfully) we decided to go with the latter idea.

So in 1993 Superquinn became the first retailer in Europe to launch a customer loyalty card, called Superclub. It was an enormous success, and all because of the achievements BA had with its air-miles reward scheme. The benefits to us were huge because it not only encouraged customers to remain loyal but also provided us with a lot of information about their shopping habits.

A few years later, some of the bigger players in the UK, including Sainsbury's and Tesco, came to us to see what we were doing.

Truth was, I was always aware of just how important it was to know what other retailers were doing in the marketplace. And I knew that if I helped them, they would be willing to return the favour down the line.

In order to keep on top of any developments in the trade, we also took out a subscription for every English language food/grocery magazine. But we didn't have them sent to our Support Office. Instead, we would have them sent to employees in our various shops.

It was their responsibility to read the each magazine and tell us what was new in it that we might consider replicating. For example, William Brereton, who worked at the dairy counter in Finglas, was the only one in Ireland to get a dairy magazine from Canada. He knew he was the only one and so he would devour it.

One of our senior managers, Damien Kiernan, was the only one getting a Californian fruit and veg magazine. One day he read about how salad bars were catching on in restaurants in California. So he opened a salad bar in our Naas store.

When I went to Naas he showed me what he was doing. I said 'Gosh, that's a great idea', and we rolled out similar salad bars across our stores.

Similarly, Carrefour had launched its 'Produit Libre' low-price brand in 1981. It was an all-white packet, and hit the headlines in the trade and elsewhere. It prompted a huge outcry from the established suppliers, with some predicting that these unbranded goods were going to bring about the end of brands!

I thought it was just great, so I said 'We should do the same thing.' My good friend Noel Jones, whose wife Margaret had been the driving force behind many of our innovations, came up with the brand name 'Thrift'. Then we announced we were going to introduce plain packaging, without saying what name we were giving to the new 'brand'.

We kept our plans very 'hush hush' as we went about booking our ad campaign. We announced that a press conference was going to be held on a Wednesday at 11 p.m.

Galen Weston owned Quinnsworth at this stage and it was being run by Don Tidey. They panicked when they heard what we were doing, because they had introduced a 'yellow pack' low-price range very successfully in Galen's Canadian stores and they wanted to import the same goods and brand here.

They said 'Could Feargal introduce a yellow pack? If he introduces it, it will be too late because he will have branded it and we're lost.'

So they rushed to bring in their yellow pack by flying the product from Canada. We beat them by a day, but they need not have worried. Our Thrift range was in a black and white pack, not a yellow one!

Another big decision was whether to put the Thrift jam beside the branded jam and the Thrift detergent beside the branded detergent. In the end we decided that we would have a dedicated Thrift aisle, so if you really wanted to get good value you went down there.

In fact, some of the items being sold in our Thrift range were actually supplied by the established brands, so they were the same product but cheaper, and without the branding!

For this reason, I remember being perplexed when Aldi opened near us in Carlow years later. In those days we had switched from Thrift to Euroshopper because we had joined a European group of retailers so we could buy stock jointly, giving even greater savings to our customers.

One day in Carlow a customer came to me as I was working in the store.

'You are very dear', she said, to which I replied 'What do you mean?'

'Well, your Hellmann's mayonnaise: it's €1 but Aldi have mayonnaise for 89 cent.' I said 'But we have our Euroshopper mayonnaise for 89 cent', and she said 'Yes, but that's your cheap brand. Theirs is a big brand from Germany!'

Now, she had never heard of their brand, but where Aldi and Lidl were very clever was in giving 'snazzy' names to their own brands, so people thought they were big brands in Germany. But in essence theirs is the exact same principle of offering a 'Thrift' alternative.

Sometimes we had initiatives that allowed our customers to become involved in the fun themselves. We introduced a 'Goof' scheme whereby we asked customers to keep an eye out for any 'goofs' they might come upon in the shops: for example if food was on display past its sell-by date, or the checkout queue was too long. In return they would accumulate 'Goof points' that could be credited against their shopping. One particular woman became known as the 'Goof lady' because she spent her time going from store to store looking for 'Goofs'.

We placed a big emphasis on creating a sense of pride and camaraderie in the people who worked with us. Shelley O'Shea, a colleague, said to me once, 'We used to feel so proud walking down Finglas in our uniforms.' I loved that: the sense that to get to a job in Superquinn was a real privilege.

In order to foster that sense of pride, we needed to have a culture within the company of really listening to our staff as well as to our customers.

With this in mind, we tried to spread the gospel of innovation among our staff. The tone we set in Superquinn was very much that anyone, however senior or junior in the company, could come up with an idea and potentially see it implemented. In fact, it was expected of them.

One way in which we encouraged innovation was by remaining nimble.

Because we were small we could do things others simply could not.

Our experience with orange juice is a good example of this. Our area manager, Liam Royal, was visiting our Kilkenny store when he noticed that instead of simply putting a 'best before' date on our freshly squeezed orange juice, the store put the name of the day there too.

This happened because a customer had said 'When I open the fridge I don't know what date it is, but I do know what day it is.' So they put Friday 5th or similar on the labels from that point on.

Liam came to our regular Monday morning management meeting and said 'It's a very small thing but I thought it quite innovative.' We said 'Gosh, that's a great idea; let's do that.'

By Tuesday it was up and running in all our shops. I remember telling Sir Peter Davis, head of Sainsbury's, this story and he was amazed: 'Oh that would take us at least six months, if not a year, to do!' By comparison, Liam was able to see the new label in one of our stores on Friday, talk about it at our management meeting on Monday, and the following day it was rolled out in all of our stores.

Our approach wasn't simply to maximise the profit at all costs. Again this is something I have already spoken about, but it is worth repeating. Most businesses, certainly if they are run by accountants or subject to the demands of shareholders, would think the objective is always to maximise profit.

Instead, I continually set the tone at Superquinn by reminding our staff that 'No, it's not about maximising profit: the objective is to maximise customer satisfaction. Yes, make sure you make a profit, make sure you run a healthy business and make sufficient profit so the company remains viable. But it is not the only objective. Customer satisfaction is the most important part of building a sustainable business.'

Similarly we were determined to have the freshest goods. Our attitude was that to remain competitive we had to have the best, we had to have the healthiest, we had to have whatever it was that would satisfy our customers. So our expectations of our staff were very high.

In return we made a point of incentivising our staff by rewarding and recognising their hard work and innovation.

One way we did this was through the introduction of a 'twinning' competition, whereby two shops would be 'twinned' with one another. For example, every baker in a particular store had to spend time working at the bakery of its 'twin' store.

The competition was judged by customers, who would be asked to give marks for improvement. It went on for around six weeks. During that time, staff went between the two stores, exchanging ideas on how best to innovate within their own departments.

The thinking was that the colleagues would come back to their own stores and say 'Do you know what they are doing in Lucan?' 'Do you know what they are doing in Swords?' 'That's a great idea, let's do the same thing here.'

So each person came back to their store having learned something new. The process allowed them to work closely together, learn from one another, and then apply this to help them 'win' our competition.

We had many such competitions but on this occasion, the two winning 'twinned' shops were Lucan and Swords. So we picked 100 names out of a hat, fifty from each shop: twenty-five men and twenty-five women.

There was going to be at least one butcher, one baker, one checkout operator and ten chosen at random. And we flew them to different stores in the USA, to experience life there. There was one woman in her sixties who had never been out of Ireland and never in an aeroplane.

Again, there was a strong business case for doing this, which the accountants would not always see. But I felt that if we were to promote excellence and innovation in Superquinn, this had to be recognised through investment in our staff.

* * *

There were other ways in which we promoted a sense of teamwork and camaraderie within the company. A great example is our participation in the annual St Patrick's Festival.

Superquinn was involved with the Dublin St Patrick's Day Parade for years, long before it became a three-day festival. As many as 400 of our staff were involved each year and there was always huge excitement as the big day approached.

They practised every Sunday morning in the underground car park in Blackrock for about four weeks before 17 March. On the day itself, we sang and danced along the streets and enjoyed every minute of it. I loved handing out Superquinn sausages to the crowds that had gathered.

Then we held a party in the Gresham Hotel for everyone who had taken part. It really was great fun and a great way of getting the Superquinn team together.

Eventually it was decided to turn the St Patrick's celebration into a festival that would take place over the course of several days. Michael Colgan of Dublin's Gate Theatre took over the chairmanship and it moved in a different direction, away from commercial floats sponsored by companies such as ours.

Then I was asked to take over, building on the work that Michael had done. The major change I made was to put more fun in to it, rather than just theatre.

The big question I asked was 'Can we get people involved, so we make sure they enjoy it?'

With this in mind, we organised a huge sponsored fireworks display for the public to enjoy. I had great fun going to the festival and I always insisted on dressing in green!

Another example of the team spirit at Superquinn came when our store in Sutton burned down on 26 September 1986. Denise and I were away at an FMI (Food Marketing Institute) conference in Italy. Bizarrely, the session that morning was all about crisis management!

I was at a lecture when there was a knock on the door. I was called out and Denise said she had just got a call saying that Sutton was on fire.

This was at about 9 a.m. I got on the phone immediately to Vincent O'Doherty, to be told the fire was discovered at 3 or 4 a.m. and unfortunately the whole building was ablaze. Thankfully there was nobody in the building and nobody was hurt, but the Support Office above it was on fire as well.

I knew the fire had the potential to seriously impact our business. Denise and I left the hotel immediately and went to the airport, having asked the hotel to see if they could get us to London. We flew from there into Dublin, arriving later that afternoon.

I need not have worried about getting back so quickly. Before we even got home, our team, led by Vincent and Alan McDonnell, our marketing manager, had sprung into action. They arranged with Irish Rail that customers could get the DART free if they shopped in Blackrock, and to pay the toll bridge for anyone travelling to Blackrock by car to shop.

We also put a caravan at the Marine Hotel in Sutton. We would do our customers' shopping in Northside, and they could go there to collect it.

I was incredibly proud at the way our team pulled together so quickly in order to minimise the impact of the fire on our business. Luckily, the computer files had been taken off site over the weekend, as a precaution, so at least we knew how much we owed and to whom we owed it. It meant we were able to pay our suppliers on that Monday, promptly.

We didn't know how the fire started, but something similar happened in our Blanchardstown store. Luckily, that fire started in the middle of the day as opposed to 3 a.m., so it was extinguished quickly. In the end, we figured that the same type of faulty fridges had been behind both fires.

The rebuild of Sutton was a huge challenge, but was overseen magnificently by Vincent O'Doherty. The shop was out of action for about three months as we built it and then the office. We moved the Support Office to Blackrock temporarily, so we commuted there and back for a while.

Crises such as the burning down of Sutton reinforced the importance of having a strong management team around me. I always thought it important for business people to be able to both seek and listen to advice. A quote I have always loved is 'God gave us two ears and one mouth so we would listen twice as much as we would talk.'

About 1980 we started to hold an Annual Strategy Meeting. This was followed a few days later by the Annual Management Meeting. The meetings were held in different places and at them we would decide our plans for the year. I would do a lot of preparation for them.

My problem was I wanted fun and excitement at these meetings, whereas Vincent would be more serious. His role was very much about making sure we made a profit, whereas I would say 'You need to make sure that the customer comes back again and, oh, you should also make a profit!'

I knew how crucial it was that our management would feel they had scope to develop their careers with us. In fact, during my time at Superquinn we lost very few managers to our competitors. Those whom we did lose went to open their own shops.

We didn't find it too difficult to expand as we moved into the 1990s. Much of this was due to Vincent's negotiation skills!

He was so successful that in 1994 we opened three shops in one year, which was unprecedented for us. They were in Kilkenny, Carlow and Clonmel, with a couple of months between each opening. It was a big investment in terms of money, time and resources.

Our junior managers could see that this was a company that was expanding. They could see scope to become a manager of one of the new stores. If we announced that we were going to stay small, we wouldn't have been able to hold on to our more ambitious younger managers. So it was a very deliberate decision by us at the time.

People often ask why we did not expand Superquinn internationally. The truth is, we seriously considered it a number of times, as I have mentioned in Chapter 9. At one stage we looked at a shop in Yorkshire that was up for sale.

In the 1990s we looked seriously at opening in Northern Ireland: I had come to know Sir Peter Davis, the boss of Sainsbury's, quite well, and was aware that they might be willing to sell their outlets there.

After giving it a lot of consideration, I said 'Well, I'm not going to spend my time travelling up North every week.' Now, it was still troubled times in the North and I wasn't going to drive up there in a southern car. We had tricolours over all our shops here, and would have had to put a Union flag over those up north.

We sent two of our senior managers, Cormac Tobin and James Burke, to have a look, and it was clear there was no enthusiasm from them for the move either.

By this stage we had seen Dunnes Stores open in England and in the North. Musgrave's had opened in Spain. Others were expanding, and people were asking 'Would you not consider it?'

But I had absolutely no interest in having to be away from home, keeping an eye on the business. And my managers had little interest in spending much time travelling around either.

I loved travelling with Denise and visiting other countries and other supermarkets to see what they were doing and to learn from them. But, put simply, I wouldn't have liked to have to run a version of Superquinn outside Ireland.

15

FAMILY TIES

My son Eamonn claims he started working at Superquinn when he was all of eleven years of age, wheeling trolleys in the car park. Alongside his four siblings, he would have worked every summer in the supermarket.

When he finished college we had already established a policy that any family member coming into the business would have to bring something of value. So Eamonn worked in fund management. It was great, as it gave him the experience of working in different companies, examining them and seeing how they did things.

When he was nineteen he went to the States for the summer to work with Ralphs, a chain of supermarkets in Los Angeles. I felt very lonely when he went on the plane on his own. Neighbours of ours were in Los Angeles and they met him at the airport. Everything was fine, but I remember phoning to see if he arrived safely.

He worked as a butcher and learned the techniques of butchery for that summer. He would go on to be the first of the family to join Superquinn in a formal role. Even so, he started working on the shop floor.

I handed him over to the manager of the shop in question and said 'Here's Eamonn, teach him all you can.' So he put him into the fruit and veg and moved him on to different areas. Eventually he ended up in charge of a department.

Then he worked his way up to assistant manager, store manager and Director of Marketing. Although he had been a fund manager in his previous career, I don't think he had any problem getting his hands dirty, hauling around sacks of potatoes and learning from the ground up.

The other children worked in Superquinn over the summer holidays in various roles – making pizzas or behind the meat counter, for example. They didn't have any problems doing it. Just as I had grown up in Red Island doing almost everything, it was automatically assumed they were going to work in the stores, to get to know the business.

I know members of the Dunne family do similarly.

When Stephen, our second son, finished in college he decided we weren't as good as we could be in terms of taste. So he went to Ballymaloe and did a three-month course to learn about taste and cooking.

Then he went around the world working in Michelin-star restaurants. His ambition was to come into the company, but he knew the rule was he had to bring something with him. So he came in critical of the tenderness of our steaks, critical of the taste of our grapes or our oranges.

It was a valuable skill to bring to the company. He went on to join the business on a full-time basis, too. But both Eamonn and he had to earn their recognition. I always felt it was important that the people who worked with them could see 'He probably would have got that job even if he wasn't family.'

Over the years, I had started putting my thoughts on the culture of Superquinn into internal training notes for the staff. I would use these as references for when I gave speeches to our teams.

Also I would use them whenever I was giving a speech at an event, on topics such as food safety, marketing or ethics in business. I always enjoyed making speeches to people from all walks of life, be they librarians, politicians, local jobs clubs or chambers of commerce.

Basically I had a core speech that could be adapted to different occasions. The adaptations broadened out the speech and it went from there.

Then one day, Anne Ó Broin demonstrated once more just why she has played such an important role in my career. She read my training notes and had a real 'light bulb' moment, thinking 'That would make a great book.'

Anne helped me put the book together with anecdotes and stories. All of it was aimed at being useful to somebody in business.

The concept was, 'Could we manage to encourage our team to look after our customers as a guest would have been looked after in Red Island?' The boomerang principle came from Red Island, and was coined in the book for the first time.

We came up with the title *Crowning the Customer*, a gender-neutral way of saying 'the customer is king' or 'the customer is queen'. There were stories of Red Island in it which I had been telling for years and still tell.

Some of them may even have made their way into this memoir!

When the book was completed, I went on holiday in August 1990. Before I set off, I sent the manuscript to all Irish publishers, stipulating that I wanted it published on my birthday, 27 November. Michael O'Brien of The O'Brien Press rang full of excitement within three days and spoke to Anne. He was adamant that he wanted to publish the book, and was the only one willing to do it in the stipulated time frame.

It was in my mind that we often opened shops on my birthday. I was aware that the President of Coca-Cola, Don Keough, was going to be in Ireland that day. He had asked if he could come and see Superquinn and we brought him out to Blanchardstown. He was quite a character and full of life.

He agreed that he would do the launch, and we booked a room on Stephen's Green to hold the event. At the last minute Don told me that Taoiseach Charlie Haughey had invited him to Kinsealy and so he wasn't going to be able to stay long at the launch. He came in, said a few words, and left to meet An Taoiseach.

The launch went extremely well. I was on the shop floor in Ballinteer the following day and the Gay Byrne programme was on radio.

Gay rang me about the book and I took the call without explaining the situation to him. A customer interrupted me and said 'Excuse me, but where's …?'

I had to excuse myself to Gay live on air as I got the item for her. When I came back Gay said 'Where are you?' and I said 'On the shop floor in Ballinteer.' He couldn't get over the fact that I was still looking after customers as I talked to him on the national airwaves!

I was delighted with the success of the book, both in Ireland and internationally. I began to get invitations to speak about its themes all over the world.

It has ended up being translated into fourteen languages. I am amazed at the number of people who still come up to me and say 'That book has been of immense help to me in my business.'

A few years after I sold Superquinn, I got another chance to put my theories on how to run a successful business into practice when I was approached to take part in an RTÉ TV series called *Feargal Quinn's Retail Therapy*. This saw me advising struggling businesses around the country on how to turn things around, and was a real ratings success.

But this was not my first stint anchoring my own show. In fact I was a bit of an old pro by that stage (!).

In 1986, RTÉ asked me to guest-present the first of the Saturday night chat show series *Saturday Live*, which would take the place of Gay Byrne's *Late Late Show* when it switched from Saturday to Friday.

The idea was to get a different non-TV personality to present the programme each week. I was always up for a challenge and readily agreed.

I was invited onto the first *Late Late Show* of the season, in September, to plug the new programme. Gay asked, 'And tell me, Feargal, are you opening any new supermarkets?' I said 'Yes, we are: we will be opening one in Swords on my birthday, 27 November.'

Now I knew that Sisk's, the builders, had told us that, because of changes we had made to the plans, the date of opening would not be my birthday but a week later. We would still get it open in time for Christmas, but I knew that was no good to us: we needed a full four weeks' run-in before Christmas.

George Sisk was at home, enjoying his brandy and watching the *Late Late*. I said to Gay, 'I know we will open on time because Sisk's are doing it and they wouldn't let us down.' George told me that he nearly choked! But they did get it open on time!

I anchored the first Saturday of the new TV series in October 1986. They asked each of the presenters to do a party piece. I remember talking with Denise about it and I said, 'I know what I could do: I could cook mussels.' So I went back to the producer and said 'I'm not going to sing; Denise won't let me sing and I am certainly not going to dance or do a recitation. But I can cook mussels!' 'Gee,' he said, 'that would be great; that's a great idea.'

Now, just to be sure, I visited Aidan McManus in the King Sitric restaurant in Howth the night before and got a lesson to ensure I was doing everything correctly. I announced in the middle of the show that I had been asked to do a party piece and that really my party piece was cooking mussels.

They wheeled in the oven and I started cooking. There were two lines I used:

Above: Zoe and Donal see their first computer in Trinity College, circa 1984.

Right: My sister Eilagh with her husband Jack McCabe and their family in Portadown. Tragically, Jack was shot dead on 12 July 1972.

Above: What a great cake, made by our prize-winning bakers!

Left: As Chairman of An Post, I was happy to do even the simplest job once a month.

Top: We gave 20,000 hot Superquinn sausages away each St Patrick's Day. I loved the occasion!

Above: Vincent O'Doherty, as chairman of Superquinn, enjoyed visiting the shop floor.

Trading . . .

W

Leading investigative journalist swaps places with supermarket chief. Great idea, if it had worked! **Veronica Guerin** and **Feargal Quinn** report on what happened when they tried to trade places.

FEARGAL QUINN

. . . places

I was handed
Feargal's diary and
told, 'Just tell me
where you want to
go.' I was astonished
at the openness

Above: Veronica Guerin and I shared time – and a spread in the *Sunday Independent* – in the weeks before she died in 1996. (See Appendix 2.)

Below: Clouseau was the eighth member of our family.

Above: Can you identify the people selected for a non-political cabinet in a public opinion poll?

Below: The President of Coca-Cola, Don Keough (right), launched my book *Crowning the Customer* in 1990.

Left: I enjoyed my twenty-three years in Leinster House.

Below: My grandchildren Emilie, Charlie and Lucy and I were made welcome at Charles Haughey's home, Abbeville.

Left: Simon Burke took over my role in Superquinn in 2005.

Above: What a wonderful Superquinn team at Malahide Castle on our 40th birthday in 2000.

Below: With Taoiseach Bertie Ahern, TD, at the Ability Awards.

Above: We got a warm reception in Drogheda while filming RTÉ's *Local Heroes*.

Right: With Iggy Ó Muircheartaigh and Aidan Daly at the NUIG conferring of my honorary doctorate.

Left: HRH appears pleased to meet Denise!

'Cooking mussels is so easy that nothing can go wrong' and 'Even a man can do it!'

I showed how to do the mussels and I called on Phil Coulter, one of our guests, to play some music as I prepared them. As Phil played I was waiting for my mussels to cook. To my horror, I discovered live on air that all I could get was the smell of burning rubber!

The RTÉ oven had never been used before and had not been tested! It wasn't working, and there were these flat, dull, raw mussels! Naturally, I got into a little bit of a panic. At one stage I started to call them oysters!

I knew the show must go on. So I handed them to each of my guests – cold and miserable. Luckily the camera focused on me so I ate mine, saying how lovely they were! Well, they say in showbiz that you have to fake it till you make it!

Although I was nervous presenting the show, I loved it, but I don't think a presenter's life would have been for me. I've great admiration for presenters, and often find myself marvelling at their ability to keep things fresh and interesting on screen, but I'm not sure it's something I could have done.

As well as *Feargal Quinn's Retail Therapy*, I did another show for RTÉ TV in 2012: *Local Heroes*, in Drogheda. The thinking behind it was to help an entire community come together to reinvigorate their local businesses and town. Again, I just loved the chance to meet some fascinating people, and to input directly into their lives.

This inspired me to write a second book, *Mind Your Own Business*. It was published in 2013 and leaned heavily on the stories that featured in *Feargal Quinn's Retail Therapy*.

Once again, the aim was to show how many of the techniques I had applied to my own retailing career could help struggling businesses to survive and thrive during one of the worst recessions the world has ever seen.

Some of the approaches it outlines were influenced by my experience of public life too.

SECTION 4

ENTERING PUBLIC LIFE

16

AN UNUSUAL CHRISTMAS

Christmas Day in our family was always a little bit different from most. Denise, like my mother before her, had to put up with having no husband around until well into the afternoon. Later, some or all of her sons would go suspiciously missing too.

The reason? We were at the Mansion House in Dublin, working on the Knights of St Columbanus' Christmas Dinner for the poor. It was a tradition my father started many years earlier through his membership of the Knights, and one I was anxious to continue after his sudden passing in 1972.

I was the third generation of my family to join the Catholic charitable organisation. I distinctly remember, when about seventeen, overhearing my father telling somebody rather proudly on the phone one evening that he had put my name down to join. Later I learned that my grandfather proposed me and my father seconded me for membership.

The Knights were initiated in 1915. If you wanted a job in Ireland in those days, it was seen as most advantageous to be a member of the Protestant-only Freemasons organisation. Due to its wide network of connections in business, being a Freemason meant you stood a good chance of getting a job in certain banks, as well as in companies such as Player's cigarette factory, Guinness and Jacob's Biscuits.

But if you were a Catholic your chances were slim because you didn't have the same contacts.

Although the Knights of St Columbanus organisation was founded by Fr James K. O'Neill for religious reasons, it functioned as a network to help promote opportunities for Catholic workers. Throughout the 1950s in particular, the meetings – where some members would dress up in what to outsiders appeared like mysterious white robes – were very well attended. So there was clearly a need for such an organisation at the time.

I am still a member of the Knights to this day, although I would be the first to acknowledge that I am not as good at attending meetings as I once was. In truth, my biggest association with the Knights was my involvement over 50 years with the Christmas Day Dinner. I was thrilled to be awarded a Papal Knighthood by Pope John Paul II in 1994 as recognition for my work on the dinner over the years.

My father first got involved in organising the dinner due to his role as a hotelier and caterer with Red Island. He was very critical of the catering company running the dinner at the time, and said 'I think we could do a better job.'

Until he got involved they used paper cups and plates at the dinner. Because of Red Island he could provide proper cutlery and delph, which made it more like a 'traditional' Christmas dinner. Soon he took over as Chairman of the overall event.

Each year in the week before Christmas we would go down to Red Island, which was closed for the winter, and turn on the electricity and the heating. A few hundred people would come for the parish's 'Whist Drive', an annual fundraiser based around a popular card game competition. At the same time, we cooked a huge batch of Christmas puddings for the event.

The dinner was held in the Mansion House. As children it was what Christmas Day was all about for us. We woke up very early after Santa Claus had visited and left his gifts. From the age of about ten I was away by 9 a.m. to the Mansion House. It was only men; women didn't go until much later. I would get home at about 2 p.m. and the family dinner was at 3 p.m.

In later years, I would bring my own boys with me to the dinner, with a view to continuing the tradition into the next generation. Denise used to say somewhat ruefully, 'I never see you on Christmas Day until 3 p.m.!' But I always thought it a wonderful way to spend Christmas Day, even if our family celebrations were a little bit different.

Anyone could avail of the free meal in the Mansion House, no questions asked. I took over as Chairman after my father died and I discovered that a number of our guests were saying 'I want to take some food home because I have someone at home who isn't well enough to come in.' So we provided take-away bags. Eventually we were feeding about 700 people and sending out about 300 dinners to people's homes too.

At the beginning of December each year, I would write to various food companies and suppliers to request all of the food, cigarettes (a staple in the early days) and drink that we needed.

They would deliver it to my office, free of charge. We would employ Tommy McCrudden, the Red Island chef, who charged a nominal amount for his time. The turkey, potatoes, vegetables, dessert, Christmas cake and pudding and all the trimmings would be delivered to the Mansion House two days before Christmas Day. Then lots of volunteers would turn up very early in the morning to put the tables out in the Round Room, set the tables and help in the kitchen. It was quite a well-oiled operation.

I had the job of welcoming our guests, Red Island style. One of my main functions was to ensure that people were not too shy or hesitant to come in. I was always conscious that for some people, publicly acknowledging that they were spending Christmas Day alone was a difficult thing to do. I was determined to do what I could to make them feel at ease.

I remember on one occasion noticing two men arrive carrying lovely cameras around their necks. I welcomed them inside and asked them where they were from. In broken English, they explained that they were Japanese tourists.

They were staying in a bed and breakfast but there was nowhere in Dublin to get Christmas dinner. They had been told they could get it in the Mansion House, so in they came and had their Christmas dinner too!

One day in 1993, the Lord Mayor of Dublin, Gay Mitchell, rang. The Corporation had decided that the best way to honour Mother Teresa of Calcutta, who was due to receive the Freedom of Dublin City, was to have a breakfast with various charitable organisations.

Apparently Mother Teresa said she wanted to be with the poor, rather than spending her time being treated as a typical visiting dignitary. The Lord Mayor wondered if I would organise it.

Superquinn staff were a huge help on the day, volunteering to prepare the breakfast in the Mansion House.

There was great security surrounding Mother Teresa's visit and our security officer in Superquinn, John McCallion, made sure that all the preparations were perfect. This was no surprise to me, as John had a track record of handling the security challenges for our family with great sensitivity down through the years.

I remember Mother Teresa as a very humble woman. Although she spoke

English, she seemed rather quiet and very unassuming. She went to each of the tables, meeting everyone present and stopping to say a few words.

Looking back now, events such as the Christmas dinner were an early way of involving myself in Irish civil society. They allowed me to become engaged in public life while I continued to expand Superquinn. After my father's death, I took over his role on the Board of Hume Street Hospital in Dublin, where I remained for over thirty years.

Michael Dargan, the boss of Aer Lingus, got in touch one day in 1973. I knew him as a very prominent businessman, and I was delighted to hear from him. He wondered if I would go on the board of the Irish Management Institute.

The IMI was intended to facilitate a greater exchange of ideas between business and the state. It had a large board with an executive. You had people like the chief executives of the main banks, such as Ian Morrison of the Bank of Ireland, mixing with the heads of semi-State companies such as CIÉ and Aer Lingus.

I was still in my thirties, and I was very honoured to be asked. It meant I was starting to get to know people of influence in the Irish business community, as a younger up-and-coming entrepreneur.

Over the years I learned a huge amount from the various conferences and events that the IMI organised. Taking part in the IMI also represented an early form of networking, allowing me to be on a 'first name' basis with some of the most well-known business people in Ireland.

Even more importantly, learning about their experiences in all types of businesses began to pique my interest in contributing more to Irish public life.

17

RED-LETTER DAYS
AT AN POST

I n July 1979, I received one of the most intriguing phone calls of my life. On the other end of the line was the personal assistant to the Secretary of the Department of Posts and Telegraphs. I was in the office in Sutton at the time, and the call was to make an appointment for the Secretary to phone me.

Now nobody ever made an appointment to phone me, so I knew it must be something important! I said 'Of course, I can take a call right away.' The Secretary came on the phone: 'The Minister would like to see you. When would suit you?' I said 'Well, today will suit fine.' The Minister in question was Pádraig Faulkner.

I went to Leinster House that afternoon and met both the Minister and the Secretary. They handed me a report put together by the Posts & Telegraphs Review Group chaired by Dr Michael Dargan, whom I knew from my involvement with the IMI. The 'Dargan Report', as it became known, recommended that they take Posts and Telegraphs out of the Department and turn them into two separate semi-State bodies.

Essentially, the Government of the day under Taoiseach Jack Lynch knew that the rollout of the telephone system simply wasn't working. It took a year or more to get a telephone installed. Also there had been a lengthy strike in the post office in 1979 that had caused a lot of disruption to services and loss of money.

Another of Dargan's key recommendations was that the Government appoint outside Chairpersons to the new companies, alongside boards that were independent of political interference. They asked me to chair An Bord Phoist, the Interim Postal Board, as it was then known.

While I was intrigued by their offer, I have always believed that if you agree to something, you give it your all.

On one hand, I was extremely busy building up the business. By that stage, Superquinn had opened supermarkets in Ballinteer, Bray and Blanchardstown, bringing the total to eight. We were formulating plans to open another three in Knocklyon (1980), Sundrive (1981) and Naas (1982) over the next few years.

Also, we were in the throes of intense competition with Dunnes, Quinnsworth and Albert Gubay, among others, to grow our market share.

On the other hand, I absolutely relished the challenge of leading such a major reform effort of a key national service. Timing is everything in business, and I was lucky to have a brilliant team in An Post: Michael Sheridan, John O'Callaghan, Ross Hinds, John Dwyer, Terry Reynolds, John Fitzpatrick and Jim Treacy.

I was confident that the Superquinn management would thrive even if I was not around quite as much as I used to be.

I knew that the prestige of being Chairman would reflect well on Super-quinn too. As it happened, my mother, a former post office employee, had died a month earlier. At the back of my mind I would have thought how proud she would have been to see me leading the national postal service.

Denise and I talked it over, and consulted with Vincent and others. I decided to go for it. However, the announcement that I would be chairing An Bord Phoist was not made until Hallowe'en night, 31 October 1979. About a fortnight previously, I heard that the Chairman of An Bord Telecom was going to be Michael Smurfit, the hugely successful paper and packaging entrepreneur. Our appointments were announced on the same day, and boy, did they hit the headlines.

The next day's front pages carried photos of us both, announcing that we were the 'two tycoons' who were being brought in to help shake up the industry.

Soon afterwards, I was asked where I would like my office. I was taken to Merrion Square, where they had a very fancy office in a lovely old Georgian building. I said 'No, I don't want a separate building. I want to infiltrate and influence. I want one room in the GPO [the headquarters, on O'Connell Street]. I want to be close to the action.'

We had about 9000 employees, and there were sub-post offices with a further 1000 staff run by independent postmasters and postmistresses.

Michael Smurfit took a different approach. He wanted to make a total break from the old ways, and took an office on Merrion Road, Dublin 4, away from the existing telecom headquarters, as a way of signifying his intentions.

I was asked whom I wanted on the Board, and I was able to influence who joined. One of the people I recommended was Des Ryan, the chief executive of P.J. Carroll & Co., the cigarette manufacturer, as I wanted an experienced business brain. There were very few women on boards at that stage but we appointed two: Claire Browne and Mary Ridgway. I felt that this was an important signal that we were moving with the times.

The trade unions got one-third of the appointments to the Board. The postmasters' union wanted one appointment as well. So six members out of fifteen were from the existing company. This was a much larger Board than I would have liked.

The other key appointment early on was a new Chief Executive for An Bord Phoist. We advertised and one of the applicants was Tom Garvey. Tom had been head of Córas Tráchtála Teo, the Irish Export Board, up to 1977, and was then the EU Delegate to the Federal Republic of Nigeria. I rang him one Saturday at his home in Blackrock and asked 'Could we meet to talk about your application? I'm in Ballinteer this afternoon, if that's OK.' And he said 'Oh, that's grand, I'll come to meet you there.'

But I had no office in Ballinteer, so I ended up interviewing him for the job in a little cubbyhole, surrounded by boxes of oranges! I could see Tom, who was an erudite and sophisticated man, thinking 'What sort of situation have I got myself into?' But he got the job.

I suppose it was a bit of a culture clash, as that's the way I did things in Superquinn. It wouldn't have dawned on me to do it any other way. Despite the less than glamorous start to our relationship, Tom turned out to be a very good appointment as our Chief Executive. I took up the role of non-executive Chairman.

My initial priority in those early negotiations was to make sure we were able to run the new entity on our own, without undue outside interference. I had been asked on accepting the role what conditions I would be laying down.

I had only one, which was duly agreed to: I didn't want to report to anyone but the Minister of the day. If I needed help, I wanted a direct line to the Minister, without going through civil servants.

In return, I pledged to do all I could to ensure that the postal service began to function more effectively. While there was a fee attached to the role of Chairman of the Board, I donated mine to charity.

On the day it was announced that Michael Smurfit and I were to chair the new companies – 31 October 1979 – the Minister was Pádraig Faulkner and the Taoiseach was Jack Lynch, as I have mentioned. But it was a very strange time politically.

Jack Lynch resigned a month or so later, and in December 1979 there was a new Taoiseach, Charlie Haughey. The new Minister was Albert Reynolds, about whom the few people I talked to seemed to know little. In time, he too became Taoiseach.

I heard about his appointment on the radio at about midnight, and the following morning I went to my office in the GPO. At about 8.30 a.m. I picked up the phone to the Department, asked for the new Minister and got to speak to him. I said 'Minister, I would love to meet you' and he said 'Yours is the first invitation I've got.' I said 'Would you come to lunch?' and he accepted. So I went across to the Gresham Hotel and booked a room.

I picked a red and a white wine for lunch so as to get to know the Minister, get him on my side in order to have him understand the problems of An Bord Phoist. I was delighted to get in there before Michael Smurfit or indeed any of the other influencers got to him. Of course I didn't discover he was a teetotaller until he arrived!

I discovered very quickly that we had a big problem with our name. Put simply, people didn't know how to spell it! Oifig an Phoist (post office) had a 'h' in it, so around the country there were signs saying 'Oifig an Phoist' everywhere. But people were spelling 'Phoist' with or without an 'h' or even with a 'u'. I remember wondering how to change that.

I sought advice, and one of my most trusted advisers from my Superquinn days, Noel Jones, was part of that process. As ever, he suggested a range of possible ideas. Eventually he came up with 'An Post'.

'You don't need an Irish version: "An Post" is Irish,' he explained, outlining its merits. 'And it's also English, so the tourists coming down the street in Caherciveen or wherever will recognise what it is.' And I thought 'That is brilliant.' I took his suggestion to the Board and we decided that it would be the new name of our national postal service.

There were interesting technological challenges in the ether at that time. I remember Tom Garvey said to me one day: 'I would like you to come to Tallaght, to a company that has a new piece of equipment to show you.' It was a strange device called a 'fax machine'! When we went there they asked me to write a note to put through their fancy machine.

So I wrote 'How are you? This is my first time to use this machine. Feargal Quinn.' The paper went in and a few minutes later, to my surprise, my own message came back with 'Thanks very much Feargal. This is Joe and I'm in New York.' I said 'Wha….!?!'

I simply couldn't believe it: this was space-age stuff as far as I was concerned! This was long before email, remember.

'That's going to threaten our whole future,' I said to Tom. 'Why would anybody use An Post to send a letter when they can fax it in a matter of minutes?'

He then suggested a way to combat the perceived threat.

'What we have in mind is to put a fax machine in each post office so people can use it and we will charge them for it', he explained.

In the end, his big plan didn't really work out, because it still meant you had to go to your local post office to collect the fax. And we couldn't be sure that every post office internationally would even have a fax machine!

We were to spend a number of years getting our new An Post service up and running. A few weeks before 1 January 1984, when we were due to formally rebrand as An Post, Tom Garvey came to me.

He was apologetic, but told me he was leaving to become a director in the EU's Directorate in Brussels. Subsequently we appointed Gerry Harvey as Tom's replacement, but for around six months as we launched our new company, I was both Chairman and acting Chief Executive of An Post, while also running Superquinn.

I loved rolling my sleeves up from day one at An Post. As we worked behind the scenes to set up the new company, I resolved to change the way things were traditionally done within the postal service.

One of the first things I asked after I started in 1979 was 'How are we going to influence?' I decided 'I'm going to try to visit every post office in the country.'

Now in my enthusiasm I didn't quite realise that there were 2000 sub-post offices! What I really meant was that I would visit all of the fifty-one larger company-owned offices, whether in Dundalk, Drogheda or Limerick. My idea was to bring some local member of the Board, whoever was there, along with me. This would let the staff get to know us.

And then I invited potential customers of the postal service to join us for lunch. In particular, I was hoping to woo more business customers. We certainly put in the leg work, travelling all around the country to meet customers, instilling our message: we were going to get things done.

It was very much a listening exercise, hearing what they, as customers, needed from their postal service. Many of them had never been asked what they wanted before, which of course was anathema to me given our culture of listening to our customers at Superquinn.

One of the things I discovered very early was that we were sending comparatively small amounts of post per head of population when compared with

Britain, and especially the USA.

I worked out very quickly that we had to get a lot more mail into the system, because the postman was going to be paid whether he was delivering one, two or six letters. The fixed cost to An Post of paying his wages was the same no matter how many letters he delivered.

It seemed to me that if we could get more letters in circulation, even if at a lower price per stamp, we were winning. Of course, this was me applying my experience in the grocery trade to the postal service. Increase your turnover but keep your costs as constant as possible.

I made my case to the Board and they concurred that we simply had to get people into the habit of using the postal service more.

However, we still had a real job of work on our hands to get the investment we needed to do this. I wanted to bring the price of stamps down: not for somebody writing a personal letter, but to introduce a special rate for the business market. As I tried to make my case for this innovation, I found myself going 'around the houses' between the different Government Ministers.

Adding to the confusion, there were three changes of Government within eighteen months between 1979 and 1981, so we had very little consistency (we dealt with five Ministers in total before the launch of An Post!).

Then somebody on the Board said, 'Does anybody know the Taoiseach so that we could get going on this investment issue?' By this stage Charles Haughey was back in power. I said, 'Well, I think I know a way of getting to him.'

I happened to know that Maureen, his wife, shopped in our Sutton store quite regularly. Not long after I spied her there and I pounced! I went to chat to her, and while doing so casually mentioned that 'I would love to meet the Taoiseach sometime.'

An hour or two later I got a phone call from the Taoiseach's office to say 'I understand you want to see the Taoiseach: would you like to drop out to Kinsealy? How about tomorrow morning?' I said 'Perfect.'

I drove to Abbeville at about 8 o'clock the next morning. I remember travelling up the immense driveway and the Squire of Kinsealy (as Haughey was later known by some) came to greet me at the door. He brought me to a room that had its own bar.

I wanted to make sure we would get sufficient capital to be able to start the business properly. The Taoiseach said, 'Look, aren't you wasting your time? Sure there's no future in the post office, that's out of date; it's all telecommunications now. We don't need to spend money we don't have on this.'

'No, you are wrong,' I said, marshalling my argument. 'Picture the postman coming up to your door with one letter. If we can get more people, particularly the commercial mail user, to post more letters, then that same postman has three or four letters: it will make a huge difference.

'In Britain they have three times the volume of mail per head of population compared to Ireland and in the USA they have up to six times that of Ireland.

'It is very expensive to operate with such a low volume, but if we could manage to encourage more commercial use of the mail, then we could make the post office pay within a very short period of time. What I'm going to do is introduce a special rate for commerce.'

Luckily, I was able to convince the Taoiseach of the merits of our case. He said 'OK, I see your point. I'll talk to the Minister.'

I've heard it said before that if you want to get to a powerful man, you should get to his wife or his family. It was certainly true in this case!

Over the course of a meeting that didn't last more than fifteen minutes, we gained the support of the most powerful politician in the country, after several frustrating months of seemingly getting nowhere. True to his word, he contacted the Minister, and we got a commitment for the investment we needed.

It was not the only time I got to see first-hand just how C.J. Haughey operated. Many years later, we were celebrating the birth of my grandson Charlie in Portmarnock Links Hotel when his namesake came over to say hello at our table. After I told him our good news, he was delighted to hear that we had 'named our grandson after him' (!).

I explained that his grandfather on his mother Lorraine's side was a professional musician, and was keen for him to have a reference to music in his name. For that reason, he was to be called Charlie David Quinn (aka CD!).

Haughey chuckled at this, and returned to his table. A few days later, we got a call to the house to say that a State car was outside. Lo and behold, the driver had brought a present for baby Charlie. It was a thimble, with the inscription 'From CJ to CD' (!).

When young Charlie was a few years older, C.J. invited us up to Abbeville, where he got to chat to 'CD' personally.

* * *

I can't emphasise enough, coming from a business background, just how little experience I had of the Civil Service in the early 1980s. For instance, I thought the Secretary was the one who did the typing, not the person who ran a Government Department! It was definitely a steep learning curve.

In fact, I was to learn that my theory wasn't quite right when I told Taoiseach Haughey that the costs remain pretty much fixed regardless of how much mail was in the system. I thought if you managed to get the postman coming up to your house with six letters instead of one, he had the same distance to walk.

It didn't cost him anything extra, so it shouldn't cost us either. But I hadn't factored in some of the 'interesting' working practices that had been in place for many years.

Although I was a part-time, non-executive Chairman, I thought it worthwhile to spend a day a month actually doing the various jobs that are involved in delivering the mail. I wanted to get out and about to see what it was like to serve the public. After all, they were the customers who actually used the postal service.

So I worked in a different section of An Post each month: I went to Tuam, worked behind the counter and then spent some time in the sorting office to get a handle on how that worked. Much like in Superquinn, I felt that my being 'on the floor' allowed me to get to know the business and become visible to the staff.

Mind you, while I had no difficulty relating to the customers, I was having real difficulty in getting my cash to balance at the end of a session on a post office counter!

One of the old hands told me this was often the way – the chatty people (aka Yours Truly) made mistakes, while the person who kept their head down and hardly looked at the customer was usually the one who never made mistakes with the cash.

Then one evening I took the post office sorting train that left Dublin at 9 o'clock. All the mail for the south of Ireland was delivered to Connolly Station for this post office train. The sorting took place on the train.

Our first sorting was for Portlaoise, followed by Thurles, Limerick Junction and then Cork. When we got to Portlaoise we got rid of the bags of mail for that area, and went on to the next stop, until we got to Cork. We arrived in Cork at 2 o'clock in the morning and the mail was delivered to the sorting office there.

It was a smashing system that worked really well, even if it was a little old-fashioned. It meant that if you posted a letter before 6 p.m. in Dublin, it would be delivered the following morning in Laois, Tipperary, Cork, Kerry or wherever you wanted it to go.

I asked the sorters on the train, 'Do you always get the post sorted on time? It must be quite busy at times?' 'Oh yeah, even when we are very busy we always get it done on time,' was the proud response. 'It's great when we get that much extra to do, because we get overtime.'

I said 'What do you mean, overtime? It's only taking you three hours to get from Dublin to Cork, so how do you get overtime?' 'Oh, we negotiated it. When there's a lot more mail we get extra; we call it overtime, but it's not really overtime. Before we start we look to see if there's more mail than usual. We have to be paid more to work faster.'

I was flabbergasted at this revelation. I could not understand why it should cost the company more to have extra mail sorted on time when there were more than enough staff to get the job done. We would never have allowed this in Superquinn, and I simply could not comprehend this way of thinking. I still can't!

As our launch date – 1 January 1984 – approached, I was keenly aware that we needed to generate as much noise and excitement around the launch of An Post as possible.

Morale among the 28,000 or so people employed in Posts and Telegraphs was quite low at the time. In particular the post office was viewed as being slow, out of date, 'snail mail'. By comparison, Michael Smurfit's new Telecom Éireann (as it would become known) was seen to be far sexier and 'modern'. We heard that Telecom was going to spend a large amount of money advertising, with big billboards saying that the future is in Telecom. Meanwhile we had nothing like its resources to publicise our new company.

So I asked, how will we change that narrative, and take on Telecom Éireann directly?

With this in mind, I invited seven or eight well-known business people with marketing expertise to a meal at the Grey Door restaurant in Dublin. I asked for solutions: 'How do we handle this? We have no money to spend. We want to be seen to be "with it". Telecom are going to take TV ads; they are taking big billboards too ...'

Jerry Liston, former Chief Executive of United Drug, said 'Would you ever think of launching the new An Post by going back to the penny stamp as a once-off promotional tool? People could post letters to anywhere in Ireland for the price of one penny.'

Now the Penny Black was the famous stamp from 1840 when the British post office started. I loved the idea! It had it all: a sense of tradition, a bargain for the customer, and real word-of-mouth appeal.

We printed a load of penny stamps and sent them to every post office in the country. But we couldn't tell anybody what the stamps were really for, for fear that businesses would stockpile them. This led to more than a little confusion among staff and postmasters.

I remember bumping into the local postmaster in Sutton a week before Christmas. 'Feargal, may I just say to you, I think you are making a big mistake,' he said. 'If the first thing you do when you take over is to put the price of postage up by a penny, it's going to have a real negative effect.' That's what he assumed when he saw all the penny stamps arriving. The cost of postage was 22 pence: he thought it would be going up to 23 pence.

Of course, he had it wrong. But although I knew him well, I couldn't tell him the truth! This was because on the weekend before we launched the new

'An Post' with its penny stamps, I went on *The Late Late Show* to make the big announcement.

I said 'For Tuesday, and for that day only, it will only cost 1 penny to send a letter from anywhere in Ireland. But the envelope has to be handwritten.' (Tuesday, 3 January 1984 was our first business day as Monday was a public holiday.)

I didn't want the banks sending out all their statements with the new stamps, or people sending out commercial bills!

My announcement created a huge stir. On the day of our launch the post offices were packed out the door. You went in and bought forty stamps and wrote forty letters to the likes of Aunt Maisie who hadn't heard from you for years!

The company offices and the 2000 post offices were extremely busy, the postmen were busy delivering and the sorting office was on overtime because there were so many letters! It was a huge success and everybody was talking about An Post and the new 'sexy' post office.

And of course the vast majority of people who received a letter wrote back, using a full-price stamp! It was the polite thing to do. So it was a real win–win situation.

It gave us great confidence within An Post, as everybody was talking about our launch initiative. I was delighted, as it allowed us to change the perception of the organisation and raise staff morale.

Also I loved the fact that the very same people who had been branded as unimaginative and dull turned out to be bright, innovative and entrepreneurial. One postmaster who ran short of penny stamps ended up cutting 2p stamps diagonally in half in order to satisfy his customers! And of course those envelopes are worth quite a penny now!

* * *

During my time at An Post I was always eager to inject a sense of urgency into the way we did things. Coming from a retailing background, I knew the key to success was being nimble and fast when it came to implementing ideas. Working in a semi-State came as something of a culture shock when I was faced with the more 'old school' practices that had developed over the years.

A good example was when I had the idea of doing a pre-paid St Patrick's Day card initiative, as a follow-up to the successful penny stamp promotion. The plan was to offer people the chance to send a pre-stamped card anywhere in the world.

Around the middle of January, I said to some of the staff: 'How about this idea for a St Patrick's Day card that's already stamped? Could we do it for 25 pence, going anywhere in the world?' And they said 'Chairman, what a great idea. Yes, certainly, we'll get to work on it straight away and we'll have some samples for you by the end of March.' I said 'But St Patrick's Day is 17 March!' 'But you didn't mean this year?,' they exclaimed.

I most certainly did! And when I set the challenge, the staff responded immediately. It was a marvellous example of the talent in the organisation being able to respond once they were given the opportunity to stretch themselves to see beyond the old way of doing things (slowly).

We got an advertising agency to come up with designs for six different themed cards. And we told them we wanted them back within forty-eight hours! They commissioned individual designers to do each one, so there was a funny one, a scenic one, a religious one and so on. And within forty-eight hours, we had picked the best.

I went on *The Late Late Show* again to promote it. It was huge. We sold a million in the first run and had to print another million, which sold out. We showed that this new semi-State company was able to do things very quickly.

Suddenly everybody was talking about An Post again because of the St Patrick's Day card. The following year, somebody came up with the suggestion of a 'love stamp' for St Valentine's Day, so we did that too.

We were trying to get people back into the habit of using the post office with each of our initiatives. What's more, we were trying to generate enthusiasm among the post office staff around the country, to make them feel proud to be employed by An Post. And it was working.

Another way of generating business for An Post was to encourage the Government to award us the licence to run the first Irish National Lottery.

We had felt for some time that, despite the existence of the Irish Hospital Sweepstakes since the 1930s, the Government was missing a trick by failing to have its own State-run lottery, as some other countries had.

Amid intense competition for the licence, not least from the operators of the Sweepstakes, we argued our case successfully: the new National Lottery was to be called An Post National Lottery.

On the day we launched, in 1987, I remember driving past protestors from the Sweepstakes outside our launch venue, Dublin's Royal Hospital Kilmainham. They feared (quite rightly) that our new service represented a real risk to their jobs.

We invited several hundred people to the launch. Our big idea was to give five Lottery scratch cards to each and ask them all to scratch them at the same time. We had spent a lot of time and effort convincing the Irish public that they would have a great chance to win significant prizes. It's fair to say we had visions of our attendees excitedly jumping up and down as scores of them won huge cash prizes and the like.

But of course Murphy's Law intervened – only a dozen or so people won anything at all!

Throughout my time with An Post, I was always very impressed by the diligence of the post office staff, particularly in many of the more traditional rural post offices, where it seemed to me that the role of postmaster was almost a vocation.

One such visit was to the post office in Athlone. The staff there were insistent about not letting a customer down. They would say 'The other day, we got all the mail cleared; we were all ready to go home when we discovered one more letter that had slipped behind.' They said 'We just couldn't go and leave that letter, even if it would only be a day late. Luckily one of the staff lived quite near the address. We asked him if he would deliver it on his way home – and he did.'

There was pride and a great tradition there, especially among the longer-serving staff, that I wanted to foster.

Another of the practices I tried to introduce to An Post was to get all of the senior executives to work on the shop floor for part of the week to learn from our customers, as I did in Superquinn. 'But Chairman, we did that twenty or thirty years ago' was the immediate response.

'*Éist le fuaim na habhann is gheobhaidh tú iasc*' [Listen to the sound of the river and you will catch fish]. The water in the river today is different from the water yesterday and certainly far different from the water twenty years ago,' I replied.

I was trying to introduce a cultural shift that I felt needed to happen. Can we get you out on to the floor, or to deliver the mail? They agreed, but with no great enthusiasm. I felt it was half-hearted, particularly with certain senior people.

Meanwhile, as Chairman at the Board meetings, I tried to avoid putting issues to a vote. Instead, I focused on reaching consensus. Over the course of my chairmanship we were usually able to get agreement around the table, despite the variety of interests represented.

I was devoting a large amount of my time to An Post in the first couple of years, particularly during the six-month period around the launch in 1984 after Tom Garvey left and before Gerry Harvey, his successor, came in.

Until then I had been running Superquinn, and it was very much a hands-on job. But the demands of the An Post role meant that, even if not attending to it full-time, I was certainly needed at the end of the phone every day.

An Bord Phoist started in October 1979; Superquinn developed quite fast in the early 1980s. We opened Knocklyon in 1980, then Sundrive a year later, followed by Superquinn Naas in 1982 and Blackrock in 1984. Swords opened in late 1986.

I had no choice but to delegate far more within Superquinn. Much to my (sort of!) chagrin, I found that Superquinn started doing better without my full-time attention! I realised that the area manager who was coming back to me every day for decisions now had to make decisions for himself. And that seemed to work very well.

Pat Kelly, who ended as a senior executive in Superquinn, tells the story of his mother criticising him for being late home from work at our shop in Northside when he was still very young. He had started only a few weeks before, and he said 'But I had to put the burglar alarm on and lock up.' And his mother said 'What do you mean, you had to lock up?'

'Well, Feargal gave me the keys.' She couldn't get over the fact that her son was trusted so early in his career with us. Pat always says it is because he was trusted that he accepted the responsibility he had been given.

So there was a real benefit to my being somewhat 'distracted' from Super-quinn due to my commitments with An Post. I would never miss a Monday morning meeting or the Thursday morning figures in different Superquinn bramches.

The business actually thrived, partly because the managers had been loaded with more responsibility. Put simply, they rose to the challenge, allowing me to delegate even more.

I finished in An Post on 16 December 1989, having served ten years. The farewell took place in the GPO Arcade between Prince's Street and Henry Street, and my children were impressed recently to see my name on the plaque there!

While I enjoyed my time with An Post, I think the first few years were the most worthwhile: there was a huge sense of achievement in getting the new organisation up and running successfully.

The time was right for me to go when I did. I believe every Chairman of a State board should not stay in the role for too long. Now you could say the same thing about Superquinn – maybe the Chief Executive should move after a given time – but I always disagreed with that!

Overall, I think my major success at An Post was that we re-instilled a sense of pride among the workers, the postmasters and, I believe, the customers. I like to think we had some success in making An Post relevant to people again.

Throughout my time there, I was worried that we had too many staff and not enough work. My big concern was that we would have to downsize – that there might be job losses. This was something I was anxious to avoid if at all possible. My solution was to do all I could to get people using the post office more, to generate more mail per head of population.

It is more than twenty-five years since I stepped down from my role as

Chairman of An Post. In the intervening years, I have watched as the debate continues to rage about the closure of rural post offices around the country. There is little doubt that these post offices can play an important role in their local communities, as a focal point for the people who live in the area. It is something I witnessed first-hand on many occasions during my time with the company.

But I remain convinced that the original logic we employed at An Post all those years ago still applies. It is imperative to make more work for the post offices so they can remain open. In the age of Internet, mobile phones, text messages, services like WhatsApp, Skype and email, this is a real challenge. Unless it can happen, I fear that many more closures might come.

Just as it doesn't make sense to have a rural Garda sitting in a station on his own with no car, it doesn't make sense to have a post office that does not have enough business to justify remaining open.

Plus ça change ...

18

APPLYING MYSELF TO THE LEAVING CERTIFICATE

I n 1993, a few years after I stepped down from An Post, the Minister for Education, Niamh Bhreathnach, rang. I had spoken about different intelligences at an education conference in Marino a few weeks earlier. She told me the Government wanted to introduce a new Leaving Cert Applied curriculum that would focus on recognising a non-academic Leaving Certificate, very much in line with what I had spoken about. The committee they were putting together was primarily made up of education experts, but they wanted someone outside the sector to chair it.

The traditional Leaving Cert says you study for two years and then you go in to a three-hour examination and write everything you know about that topic, whereas the Leaving Cert Applied concept is 'We want to measure your other intelligences.'

It was an idea that really appealed to me. I loved the principle of recognising people's intelligence in a way that the traditional Leaving Certificate had not achieved.

I mentioned earlier that my father had always emphasised real-life experience and skills over academic achievement. It was something I valued in my staff in Superquinn throughout my career. I saw the Minister's offer as a real opportunity to recognise such skills in a more formal way.

But I was a grocer by trade, and was somewhat apprehensive about taking on the job, as I would be mixing with education experts.

Also, business was thriving at Superquinn. We had opened a new store in Lucan in 1991, bringing our total number of stores to fourteen. What's more, we were knee-deep in planning to open three new stores the following year: an unprecedented rate of expansion for the company. These openings would see us move even further outside of Dublin, to Kilkenny, Carlow and Clonmel.

But even though I was hugely busy with Superquinn, I simply couldn't resist the Minister's call. I felt that a new version of the Leaving Certificate, targeted at identifying non-traditional intelligence, would be extremely important in encouraging people from all walks of life to stay in school, to learn practical skills that they could apply to the workplace and to have them reach their potential.

So I became Chairman of the new body in 1993. The committee was made up of people representing academics, teachers' unions and others from within the education sector. Usually we met in Dublin Castle once a month.

As Chairman, I wasn't trying to make the decisions. I was trying to listen to the best ideas and say 'That sounds great' or 'Hmm ... I don't think that will work' and to steer the deliberations. It wasn't always an easy process.

It took about two years to put the new Leaving Certificate Applied curriculum together, building on work that had already begun behind the scenes. Then we put it into operation and I stayed on for another three years to help oversee its implementation, before stepping down in 1998.

I visited as many schools as I could during my tenure. About fifty schools introduced the Leaving Cert Applied in the first year, and I must have visited about forty of them.

I loved going to the schools. The whole concept was to encourage the students. It was fascinating to see some youngster who, from the age of five, six or seven, was in effect told 'You are dumb, go to the back of the class. Just sit there and don't be interrupting the rest' and by the time they got to fourteen or fifteen they really felt left behind. Then they joined the Leaving Cert Applied curriculum and discovered they were the best in the class at, say, cooking, hairdressing or woodwork.

Also I loved that our measuring the ability to communicate didn't focus just on writing skills. So you could find that you went to a school for the graduation and the class cooked for all the parents. Then those who were good at communicating acted as orators. It was lovely to see somebody who was considered to be below the standard now proudly showing off their innate skills and talents! In many cases it was quite emotional.

Also we taught the Leaving Cert Applied students that 'You have to learn the practical subjects, but you have also to learn how to work together with others.' This is a key life skill.

I remember one class with twenty-one students that was told to break into teams of three. 'You have to build seven garden ponds with year-round gardens in which the water flows all the time.' Now, to do that, they had to learn maths, botany and physics as well as engineering skills.

They had to learn to work together to build a garden pond with year-round colour. Then their family would go to see their work and the students showed what they had done through teamwork.

The other big bonus was that success wasn't measured in a two- or three-hour exam at the end of the year. Instead the students were continuously assessed.

We met with quite a lot of resistance after we proposed this as a method of marking students. A number of the teacher unions didn't want to be involved in measuring their own students. Teachers in other countries actually wanted to be able to mark the skills of their students, but in Ireland the attitude was very much 'No, no, no, we live in this town and if we gave X a poor mark we would be ostracised.'

This was a difficult nut to crack, but eventually we reached agreement so that teachers from another town were allowed to undertake the continuous assessment that we felt was so vital to the success of the programme.

There was a real and unfortunate snobbery around the new curriculum too. On one visit to a school I was told that the Leaving Cert Applied was looked down upon. The academic teachers didn't call it the Leaving Cert, they called it the LCA.

There was one school where the teacher even said 'OK, those doing the Leaving Cert over here and those doing the LCA over there.'

I felt that this was very demeaning to the students, so I arranged for a 'swear box' to be installed in every school that ran the programme. Any teacher who referred to it as the LCA had to put 10 cents in the swear box!

I'd love to tell you the Leaving Cert Applied has been a brilliant success. But in all honestly, it saddens me to think that take-up levels remain low. Unfortunately, it suggests that some of the same snobbery remains.

* * *

In my 'day job' with Superquinn, I was very fortunate to get involved with various international organisations from a very early stage.

Denise and I attended our first international conference in 1976, when we flew to Rio de Janeiro for an event hosted by the Paris-based food business forum CIES. We got to know practically every major player in the supermarket business around the world. As a result we learned all the trends long before anybody in Ireland identified them.

Simply by listening to other retailers from around the world, we identified the trend towards healthy eating and the increased focus on nutrition and interest in the environment very early. Thus we could look at how best to provide organic and non-genetically modified foods in Ireland long before this had entered broad consumer discourse here. Also we got the idea to introduce initiatives like the 'Guaranteed Irish' shamrock sign and later a breakdown of Irish purchases on till receipts.

This gained international attention, to the extent that a customer came to me in our Blackrock store to tell me we had been mentioned in the British House of Commons. Apparently, during a debate on stimulating British business, a member of parliament had proclaimed that 'We should be doing what they are doing in Superquinn!'

I was a member of the board of a number of international organisations such as CIES, the US-based Food Marketing Institute and the Brussels-based Euro-Commerce. I became Chairman of EuroCommerce not long after I sold Superquinn. It represents retailers of all varieties in Europe, and the role required me to travel around Europe a lot, addressing their various national bodies.

Attending these conferences over the years was also a brilliant opportunity to mix with people from all backgrounds with many different business experiences.

They say travel broadens the mind. A few years earlier, in 1969, Jack McCabe, Brendan Rooney and I witnessed first-hand how culturally different even countries like the USA were from Ireland in those days. We were midway through our lunch on a domestic flight from New York to Fort Lauderdale when an announcement was made over the intercom.

'We are now approaching the State of Georgia, which is a dry State on a Sunday. Our staff will be around to your table to collect glasses from anyone drinking alcohol.'

And with that, the air hostesses set about 'confiscating' the glasses of wine and beer that we were thoroughly enjoying alongside our meal! As you can imagine, we were more than a little taken aback by this somewhat puritanical (and nonsensical) approach to the licensing laws.

All the more so when, after about ten minutes, we were told that we could order alcohol again – as we had left Georgia airspace!

Denise was a great 'mixer' on these international business trips. She has a great sense of style. In many cases we were younger than most of those present. We always enjoyed these meetings, and I got huge benefit from attending them.

I knew my role at the various conventions was to entertain and be good company. So when we would arrive, people would want us to sit with them, to join them, to play golf, whatever. And we ended up having a lot of fun.

Later, when I joined the Food Marketing Institute, I got to see barcode scanning in operation for the first time. I found it fascinating to see that you didn't have to put a price label on every single item, every tin, every packet.

One of the biggest problems with the old 'price ticket' was that it was cumbersome. Suppose you were selling something at 1/6 and you had done a big display. Then your competitor down the road had dropped its price to 1/4. In order to match this you had to take your labels off and put on new ones. This was both time-consuming and expensive. So the concept of scanning really excited me.

I wondered how we could get it into our stores. I knew that for it to work, it would need 'buy-in' from all of the main Irish producers and retailers of food. So I worked with the food group within the Confederation of Irish Industry (now known as IBEC) and we hosted an information event with speakers outlining how it would all work.

Then we set up our own association and I became the first President of the Article Numbering Association of Ireland (I know, it's a catchy title!). It took five years before the first shop opened with only barcodes: a shop in Co. Cork. And it was swiftly followed by Superquinn.

Some of the international invitations we received came from major brands such as Coca-Cola, PepsiCo, Georgia-Pacific and Sara Lee, the American cake company. Often these companies invited us to attend and we paid our fare, which was fine.

We met the most interesting people, who, more often than not, would be keynote speakers at the events. We met Henry Kissinger, Jack Welch of General Motors fame, Lee Kuan Yew of Singapore, King Juan Carlos of Spain, President George Bush, Rudolph Giuliani, John Major, Nelson Mandela, etc., all of whom have addressed small private conferences that we attended over the years.

Sometimes we literally got to 'bump into' international figures at events a little closer to home, too!

In 1988 President François Mitterrand of France visited the French-owned Yoplait factory in Inch, Co. Wexford. Along with many others, I was invited to meet him. Mitterrand and his entourage arrived in Inch in three helicopters; the first had his security personnel, the second the press and the third had Mitterrand.

We lined up to greet him, and he shook hands with everyone he met as he went along. People were saying a brief 'hello' and it was all very formal.

He didn't speak much English, and when he came to me I started yapping away to him in French, which was great from his point of view as he had somebody with whom to talk. We were getting on like a house on fire!

Then formalities started. The lights came on and the television cameras turned around as the chairman of Yoplait in Ireland went to a rostrum with lots of microphones to make his welcome speech.

Now I was still chatting away with Monsieur le President when I realised that somebody was trying to come between us. I thought 'This is some local County Councillor looking to be seen with the President', so I stuck my elbow out!

But the guy was persistent, and he tried to get in between Mitterrand and myself again. I held my ground to the extent that when he moved I gave Mitterrand a bit of a dig in the ribs by mistake! The man moved over to the other side of Mitterrand and the speeches started. Who was he? The interpreter!

Luckily my lack of manners does not seem to have gone against me in the eyes of the French Government; in 2011 I was both delighted and honoured to be named a Commandeur de l'ordre national du Mérite by then French President Nicolas Sarkozy.

In 1993, I had a 'run in' with the Iron Lady herself, the former British Prime Minister Margaret Thatcher, at another event.

Sara Lee Cakes invited a group of business people to the Bahamas, and Mrs Thatcher was the keynote speaker. Her topic was 'Where in the world are we going?'.

There were only two non-Americans in that group. Mrs Thatcher was a very strong and a very right-wing speaker, and as far I could see the Americans were wowed by her.

She was very anti-Europe, and when she finished one of the Americans asked her some simple question about Russia.

Then I piped up. 'Mrs Thatcher, may I take you back 200 years? A group were drawing up the American Constitution. Can we go back there and think what would have happened if they had agreed to have thirteen different States, each with its own immigration policy, each with its own currency, each with its own passports. Would we now have such a successful United States?'

'Mr Quinn, the situation is not the same,' she replied, waving her finger at me like a school teacher. 'People who came to the USA came of their own free will, instilled with ambition and drive and entrepreneurship to create a nation, not like the bureaucrats of Europe sitting on their backsides in Brussels with different languages.'

She ended with a resolute 'So there, Mr Quinn', firmly putting me in my place. But I could see that I now had the Americans on my side. I had them thinking and sympathising with me.

There was a lovely sting in the tale. As I sat wilting, up jumped Vernon Jordan, a respected US lawyer and a good friend of President Bill Clinton. Vernon Jordan happens to be black. 'Can I make a point, Lady Thatcher?' he said. 'Not all of us came of our own free will!'

And the room erupted with laughter, as Dame Maggie looked on, perplexed.

19

JUMPING THE FENCE: FROM BUSINESS TO POLITICS

As a businessman interacting with politicians regularly over the years, Irish politics always held a fascination for me. I spoke earlier about how I was interested in politics with a small 'p', even bunking off college on occasion to attend Dáil debates. Also I was keenly aware of my family's Republican past.

However, the party whip system never really appealed to me. Both Fine Gael and Fianna Fáil tried to woo me to run for them at various stages during my career. I remember in particular, when a European election was coming up, getting a call from Taoiseach Garret FitzGerald to ask if I would consider running for Europe.

Now Garret and I went back a long way, as he had been one of my lecturers in UCD. He was a brilliant lecturer in transport economics. He never had any notes and often veered off the subject. This certainly kept his talks very interesting!

Before he became Taoiseach, Garret had taken to ringing me out of the blue when I was in Superquinn to ask if I would help him to identify inflation. As a professor in UCD, his theory was that any inflation in the products we were selling in our grocery shops would be visible with the wholesalers six months or a year earlier.

As a result, he realised he could detect what the retail prices would be in six months' time by comparing them with the older retail prices charged by the wholesalers. He was developing a sort of 'early warning system' if you like. I was very happy to oblige by supplying him with the figures he needed.

I sought advice from Vincent O'Doherty when Garret asked me to run on the Fine Gael ticket as a candidate MEP. At this stage Vincent was on the board of Superquinn. He asked 'Why would you do that? What are you trying to achieve?' As ever, it was a very good question. And I realised that apart perhaps from the prestige of being in Europe, the role held very little attraction to me. I felt I could achieve more in Ireland.

So I never gave Garret's proposal any serious thought; I couldn't possibly run the business and be an MEP based in Brussels, if I were fortunate enough to get elected.

As far back as 1973, not long after my father died, I made an early unsuccessful attempt to 'jump the fence' from business to politics by securing a seat on the University panel in Seanad Éireann, running as an Independent. I was thirty-six at the time and still in the relatively early stages of developing Superquinn.

Although we had just joined the European Economic Community, much of the way the country was run reflected a much earlier era – an inward-looking time, dominated by a cosy protectionism and a lack of interest in the out-side world. In particular, those of us who worked in business did not find the atmosphere very encouraging.

One example of this lack of a business perspective in the Oireachtas was when the Government of the day proposed a Wealth Tax in 1974. This was to be paid by Irish residents who owned a business or company. Since the only source of income from such a resident was his business, it meant the tax had to come out of the business itself.

While I could see why this was a politically popular (and populist) move, I was extremely concerned about the impact it would have on entrepreneurship in Ireland.

Our competitors at the time included Albert Gubay, based in the Isle of Man, and Quinnsworth, which was part of Associated British Food, based in London. Neither of those businesses would have to bear the cost of a wealth tax.

One day while talking to Vincent Gallagher, our architect, I mentioned the unfairness of the situation and he arranged for me to meet Richie Ryan, the Minister for Finance, whom he knew. I remember well climbing the steps of Government Buildings in Merrion Street and being ushered into the hallowed offices of the Minister.

I think I made a strong case. 'Do you understand the unfairness of this tax, Minister?' I argued. 'It is most illogical because it only applies to Irish residents. The future development of the Irish economy depends on Irish entrepreneurs. It has no future if we introduce a tax that only applies to the very people upon whom our future depends.'

I got very little sympathy. The Minister's words were something like, 'I see your point and you argue it well. However, we have decided to introduce this tax so you are going to have to live with it, even if your competitors can avoid it.'

This made no sense to me, and I felt it was extremely short-sighted.

Also I had been struck by the fact that those who were elected to the Seanad by the universities were mainly academics. There were some businessmen in the Seanad at the time – Paddy McGrath of Irish Sweepstakes and Lord Iveagh of Guinness were members. But there were few, if any, Senators who had actually run a business and created a job for anyone. As far as I could make out, they were all very clever bods, good writers and good speakers. But I felt there was room for somebody in business there too.

Under the (strange) Irish Seanad electoral system, only those who have attended certain universities are allowed to vote for some of the candidates, who are placed on a university panel. Other candidates are voted for by members of the Dáil, the Seanad and city and county councils, while some are directly appointed by the Taoiseach of the day.

Fifteen candidates went forward for three seats when I ran in 1973, and I came in ninth, which wasn't bad. But my friend Noel Jones later joked that the number of votes I got was lower than my golf handicap!

I was very innocent as to how it all worked, and perhaps a little naive. I was on the National Universities of Ireland (NUI) panel, so only graduates of NUI colleges could vote for me under the Seanad electoral system. I learned very quickly that I could generate support by getting my hands on the list of eligible voters.

It came to around 100,000 names. I would invite people I knew from the list out to the house and ask them to find their friends and acquaintances on the list.

Next I would ask them to write a letter to their pal seeking a vote on my behalf. As you can imagine, this was a painstaking and time-consuming process, given the sheer volume of names involved.

Patricia Keaveney, my secretary at the time, would drive to the office, type out the letter and the person signing it would handwrite the envelope. We posted the mail the following day.

What we didn't twig, of course, was that most of the people were from the same college and had the same friends. It meant that duplication was a real problem. One guy got nineteen similar letters over the course of a couple of weeks. He was inundated to the point that when he saw a letter arrive he thought, 'Ah, not another bloody letter about Feargal Quinn and the Seanad!' So my grand plan didn't work!

Almost exactly twenty years later, a chance conversation led me to mull over whether or not to run again for the Seanad. In the intervening period, I had served ten years as Chairman of a semi-State company, with my term of office at An Post ending in 1989. This brought me into closer contact with the corridors of power than was customary for a business person at the time, and kept alive my interest in how the country was run.

Also, Superquinn was thriving and I had become increasingly involved in various international bodies. So I felt I could really contribute.

In 1992 I attended a Dublin Chamber of Commerce lunch in the Berkeley Court Hotel to honour the visiting Prime Minister of Canada, Brian Mulroney. I mentioned that I had just returned from South America, where our daughter Gilliane had been volunteering her services in Chile as a management consultant. We had also visited Argentina, which was regarded at the time as a 'Third World' country.

Someone at the table said, 'In 1922, when Ireland became a Free State, Canada and Argentina were practically equal in population, in wealth and in their natural resources. Now one is a Third World country and the other is one of the wealthiest in the world. The only difference is the Governments that were elected to run their countries.'

That lunch was the spark that got me thinking about ways in which I could contribute more to building up our own country. It came out of the blue; I had not really thought about running for the Seanad again until then.

I thought 'Yes, it's doable. I think I could get elected without having to join a party. I am sure the Seanad isn't going to be as intrusive on my time as being a Dáil deputy.'

I knew Noel Mulcahy and T.K. Whitaker; both had been Senators. They shared an office in Kildare House. They had talked to me about what it was like being in there. It wasn't a full-time job, and as far as I could see I could still run Superquinn and make a real contribution.

Shortly afterwards, I went fishing for four days in Laerdal in Norway and had the opportunity to give my plan a little more thought. When you go fishing, even with a group of three or four others as I had done, you are on your own all day. I remember thinking it would be a shame if I looked back at the end and thought 'Gosh, I could have done something to make sure that Ireland was more like Canada than Argentina.'

I remember coming back with my mind made up. Anne Ó Broin asked 'How did you get on?' and I said 'I actually made a decision while I was there.' But I wouldn't tell her what the decision was just yet, even though she was itching to know!

I bided my time a little longer, and after an event where my friend Murray Raphel, the marketing expert, spoke in Dublin, I sat Anne and Noel Jones down for lunch in the Yacht pub in Clontarf to tell them I wanted to run. Not long after, I formally announced my intention to go forward for the Seanad.

Nomination day was 1 December and the counting of ballot papers was on 1 February 1993.

Noel was incredibly enthusiastic, as of course was Anne. But I do remember detecting a certain note of apprehension in her voice. She would later say she sat there wondering if she would be able to do all the work expected of her, behind the scenes!

As an Independent candidate, I had to be innovative second time around when competing against people who often had strong union, church or political backgrounds. My platform was summed up neatly in my slogan: 'Put a doer into the Seanad!'

In that election, there were three seats on offer and a number of other high-profile candidates, including Joe O'Toole, an incumbent Senator and teachers' union leader with huge union support; Brendan Ryan, sitting Senator with the Simon Community and lecturer at Cork RTC; Joe Lee, the esteemed historian and professor from UCC; and Dr Anthony Clare, the renowned psychiatrist and broadcaster.

I was reasonably well known from a business point of view, but when I mentioned to someone that Anthony Clare was going forward they said 'Oh, you haven't a chance against him!' Anthony was a very well known TV personality who had come back to Ireland after a successful career in the UK with the BBC.

I invited everybody I knew and asked them to bring their pals. Then they consulted the voting lists and I asked them to write to the graduates they knew. Whether they were business colleagues, neighbours, pals, pals of our children – everybody and anybody was invited! We established two offices; one in Sutton and one in Blackrock. It was a three-week campaign and on Mondays we went to Limerick, Galway and Cork and replicated the system there.

The aim was to have them in and out in fifteen minutes! We had tea, coffee, sandwiches, scones, biscuits, etc. on offer. When they were leaving they handed back the lists with their letters.

The next day Anne started handwriting the envelopes and slotting the letters into them. But we didn't yet seal the envelopes: we wanted to avoid nineteen letters going to the same person! I learned from my mistake during my 1973 campaign!

We put them in alphabetical order; all duplications went to Anne and she decided which letter was sent.

We had a team working on the campaign, mainly volunteers. Nuala Grennan, my sister-in-law, helped, as did Fiach, Anne's husband. We had family, the Superquinn team, everybody. At the end of the Superquinn day, a number of staff would come in to lend a hand.

There was a lot of *craic* around it, even though it was a lot of work. A day could start at 7 a.m. and finish at 11 p.m., and we would do that six days per week.

Once the ballot papers were posted, we would stop campaigning. Our thinking was to leave people to decide for themselves based on the strength of our message. So we got all of our work done a week before the poll.

The count for that campaign was on 1 February 1993 and the result was announced two days later, in Carysfort College, later known as UCD Michael Smurfit Graduate Business School in Blackrock. I remember a reporter from the *Irish Times* talking to one of the candidates. She asked 'Are you confident?' and he said 'Yes.' She asked 'What about Feargal Quinn?' and he said 'Ah, these names always crop up but never get anywhere; they never transfer.'

I didn't come top of the poll – Joe O'Toole did – but I attracted transfer votes very well, to the extent that I was elected first. There was a bit of prestige in that, as whoever is elected first has to make a little speech. It had been assumed that as Joe had all these teacher votes, he would be first.

So, the hard work really paid off. I was absolutely delighted to be elected to Seanad Éireann in the National University of Ireland constituency. Joe O'Toole and Joe Lee were elected alongside me.

Now I had to prepare myself for an entirely new role as a public represent-ative. I couldn't wait to get started.

20

SEANAD STORIES

My first day in Leinster House was a few weeks before the House was in session. I arrived and was about to say to the ushers at the gate 'My name is …' when they immediately said 'Welcome in Senator, congratulations!' It certainly made me feel a lot more welcome than the last time I had tried to gain entry to its hallowed halls!

On that occasion I had sponsored a charitable function in Howth, which involved putting some expensive seafood up for auction. Hugh Byrne, one of our local TDs, suggested we get publicity for the cause by staging a rather impromptu photo opportunity in Leinster House. I loaded all the fish and a big display of oysters into the back of my car, and duly arrived at the Leinster House gate – only to be refused entry.

Hugh came along, saw what was happening, and asked the ushers to let me through. But they said no, it was Budget Day and parking was restricted solely to members. So Hugh pushed me out of the way and got behind the wheel of my car, saying to the ushers 'It's my car. Let me in!' And they did, of course!

Luckily, this time around, there were no such issues!

The first person I met that day was the late Senator Tom Fitzgerald, from Kerry. Tom very kindly showed me around the House, and brought me into the Seanad Chamber and the offices. As I stared at the portraits of former Taoisigh on the walls, I felt a great sense of pride at being chosen to play a part in Irish political life, however small.

About a week later, the Taoiseach announced his eleven appointees. Among them was Gordon Wilson, from Enniskillen. His daughter Marie was one of eleven killed in the Enniskillen Remembrance Day bombing by the IRA in 1987.

I had met Gordon a few months earlier. When I read that he had accepted the nomination I rang and he said 'Oh, I'm going down to Dublin tomorrow.'

'I'll be there to meet you and show you how everything works!' I replied. I showed Gordon around even though I hardly knew the place myself!

I had a huge amount of regard for him. He always corrected me when I said 'Gordon represents the Unionists.' He would say 'No, I don't. I may come from that background but I don't represent the Unionists.'

He was a valuable and highly respected member of the Seanad until his untimely death in June 1995.

My office in those early days was in the basement of Kildare House, rather than Leinster House. I was sharing with two others – Joe Lee and David Norris. We would go back and forth to Leinster House all the time.

I was amazed to discover that the pedestrian lights outside Leinster House are the best in Dublin! They change almost immediately once you press the button. This is because some TDs and Senators might have to rush over for a vote. You have only eight minutes to get into the Chamber. The notification bell rings for four minutes and you have another four minutes to get there before the doors are shut. So if the pedestrian lights are delayed you could miss the vote!

I soon got into the habit of working in my office with my ear and half an eye cocked to the television screen on my desk that carried the proceedings of the House. Working on papers while listening to a debate is discouraged within the Chamber, but it is quite practical to do so while in your own office. It enables you to get to the Chamber when your turn to speak is approaching.

Meanwhile, the public watching their legislature on television are always scandalised by the sight of all the empty seats. I have often thought that we do a very bad job of communicating to people exactly how the Oireachtas works. It is a little-known fact that for most of the time, Senators and TDs are not in their respective Chambers but in their offices, attending to the mountain of paperwork that comes with the job!

One of the biggest criticisms thrown at the Seanad is that it is simply a 'talking shop', a retirement home for failed politicians or a 'staging post' on the road to the Dáil for up-and-coming party stalwarts. There is no doubt that the way the Seanad works needs to be reformed (more of that anon), but such criticisms serve to seriously underestimate the potential impact that the Seanad can have.

I would not have sought election six times unless I sincerely believed this to be the case. In truth, it would have been a waste of my time and energy.

I never took a wage for working there. In An Post, I opted to donate my wages to charity, so essentially I worked for free. This was a purely personal decision on my part. Obviously not everyone is in a position to do this. But I was convinced that I could make a difference in the Seanad and wanted to give something back.

I wanted to 'gift' my Seanad salary back to the State. To my surprise, when I sought to do so, I was told this was not possible! So I had to receive my salary, and then gift the post-tax amount to charity.

This situation changed only after the collapse of the 'Celtic Tiger', when

I point-blank refused to take my salary. Eventually a mechanism was found whereby the monies in question went back to the State rather than to me.

I had put myself forward to the Seanad electorate as an Independent candidate, free of any association with any political party. I decided I would be genuinely independent: I would support or oppose the Government of the day on the merits of each issue as it arose.

If I felt the Government was doing the right thing, I would support it; if it was going in the wrong direction, I would oppose it. In practice, what I sought was to improve the actions of Government rather than either blindly support them or oppose them on a 'knee-jerk' basis.

Also, I resolved to make it clear that I did not enter the Seanad as a representative of business, but as a person with business experience who could bring that experience to bear on the political issues of the day.

Within the Irish Constitutional framework, the Government is answerable only to the Dáil, not to the Seanad. For instance, this explains why there is no Ministerial question-time in the Seanad, and it is what marks out the Seanad as primarily a consultative body.

Some people regard this as a weakness, but I regard it as a strength: it makes for a more relaxed, less confrontational body; one in which considered arguments can be made.

I am often asked about the differences between my life in politics and in business, but the truth is I have not found all that much of a difference.

I have always believed that management is 'getting things done through other people', and I have never been the kind of manager who throws my weight around and orders people to do my bidding.

Politics, like management, is about trying to change things through influence – not by giving orders. One of the lessons I learned early on in the Seanad is that the achievements any individual Senator can hope for are generally small and incremental, rather than the kind of flashy coups that make head-lines.

Sometimes you will succeed in getting an amendment accepted to an important piece of legislation. But more often, you get things done slowly and undramatically by influencing the way the decision-makers think.

Each time a Minister comes to the Seanad, he or she will be accompanied by a number of civil servants. It took me a little time to realise that, while it is hard to get a Minister to change his or her mind (or even, sometimes, to pay close attention to what you are saying), the civil servants may be very inter-ested in what you have to say and may well take it into account when they formulate recommendations for future policy.

This realisation made me acutely aware of the need to prepare very carefully what I would say on each occasion that I got to my feet in the Seanad Cham-ber. Off-the-cuff remarks are fine at the time, but if you want to influence policy you must present an argument that is well developed. This is not made easy by the Seanad convention that reading a scripted speech (except by a Minister) is not acceptable, though it is permitted to rely on notes.

So I got into the habit of first committing my speeches to paper, and then memorising at least the first page of what I intended to say. Also I learned that you sometimes have to repeat a message again and again before it begins to sink into the official consciousness!

I realised early on that there were a few ways to become an influencer in Seanad Éireann. One was through taking an active part in the Committee system, which involves scrutiny of proposed legislation. Another was by ini-tiating my own Bills on issues that I felt were important enough to warrant this.

I had campaigned on a platform of putting a 'doer' in the Seanad, and was fortunate to get some early victories in terms of scrutinising proposed legislation.

The very first Bill that Mary O'Rourke brought in as Minister was the Unfair Dismissals Bill. Now in 1973, I had visited a hotel during my first election campaign. I knew the manager quite well, and he contacted me a few weeks later. He was putting together a group of people who were going to buy the hotel, and wanted to know if I would be interested. I had some spare money at the time and decided to invest. It was one of the very few times I really invested outside of Superquinn.

At one of the investor meetings a short while later, someone suggested: 'Put a bright, attractive young woman behind the reception desk because the auld one you have there is ... well, you know ... it's not the best image for the hotel to have her there.' The manager said, 'Well, she's very good. She knows all the guests and knows what everybody wants.'

'Yes, but when I walk into a building I don't want to see an auld one like that; I want to see an attractive young one. Get rid of her,' was the reply.

Now when I looked at Mary O'Rourke's Unfair Dismissal Bill 20 years later I remembered this incident, which struck me at the time as grossly unfair. So I suggested an amendment to say it should be illegal to dismiss someone on the grounds of age.

I couldn't believe that age was not specified in the proposed legislation; indeed it seemed absurd to me that it had been overlooked. To my delight, given that I had only been in the Seanad a couple of weeks, the Minister accepted my suggestion.

About a month later I met a union official, Paddy Cardiff, who told me that all of the unions had circulated the proposed Bill to their members two or three months beforehand, and nobody had proposed that age should be included.

He told me: 'What we couldn't get over was that it was a boss who spotted it and introduced it, instead of it being a worker.' But for me, it was about taking each issue on its merits. I have always been a firm supporter of protections for older workers. Managing to have my amendment accepted so early gave me real confidence from the 'get-go'.

Something similar happened during my first term as Senator. Micheál Martin, Minister for Education, reluctantly accepted, against the Attorney General's advice, an amendment I put in to the Mitchell Scholarship Bill. The Bill allowed the Government to cover the cost of scholarships for American students to come to Ireland. However, it was restricted to students enrolling at colleges within the State.

As the students were likely to be studying the peace process, it seemed ridiculous to limit it to the twenty-six counties. I argued the case, and the Minister didn't accept it at Second Stage or Committee Stage. But he accepted it at Report Stage, and the amended Bill went back to the Dáil to be approved. Once again, I was beginning to get a real sense of just how much input individual Senators could have on pieces of legislation.

Overall, my first few terms in Seanad Éireann were focused primarily on scrutinising proposed legislation and making amendments.

Very early on I made the case that we should switch to Central European Time, as should the UK. I have long campaigned for this as it would lead to fewer road deaths, reduce our energy costs and bring us more in line with the European working day. While it would give an extra hour's daylight at the end of every day, it would also require us all to get up an hour earlier. I'm told that children and teenagers around the country hated me for this reason!

But we could never convince farmers in particular to support the move. When they argued it would mean darker mornings for them, I responded by saying we should simply not tell the cows! I'm not sure they saw the funny side!

I sat on various Committees in Leinster House, so I could argue my case before any legislation went to the Dáil for final approval. It wasn't until a little later that I started to introduce my own Bills.

In the meantime, there was certainly plenty of political drama in the Oireachtas. One Monday night in December 1994, I was the only one in the mezzanine of the Dáil when the Fr Brendan Smyth scandal broke. It had emerged that there had been a seven-month delay at the Attorney General's office in handling the extradition warrant for the notorious paedophile priest; this caused huge tensions within the Fianna Fáil/Labour Government.

Tánaiste and Labour leader Dick Spring stood up and made the announcement that he would no longer support Albert Reynolds. Albert walked up to the mezzanine and I shook hands with him.

The next day I was playing golf in Portmarnock at about 9 a.m. I was on the thirteenth tee, and going past on horseback was Charles J. Haughey with the prominent builder and equestrian Standish Collen. They stopped and we chatted. It was clear from Charlie's demeanour that all was right with the world. Albert had just had his comeuppance and Charlie was sure that the northsiders were back in power with Bertie Ahern as Taoiseach!

Instead, within a few days, we had the 'Rainbow coalition' of Fine Gael, Labour and Democratic Left, with John Bruton as Taoiseach. So, for the first time ever, and for two and a half years, the Government wouldn't have a majority in the Seanad: the 'Taoiseach's nominees' had in fact been nominated by his predecessor.

The balance of power rested with the six Independents: Mary Henry, Joe

Lee, David Norris, Joe O'Toole, Shane Ross and me. That was a wonderful time, because nothing could get through without our agreeing to it.

Some of the six Independents voted against the Government most of the time; others, such as myself and Joe Lee, were more willing to support the Government if we felt it was merited. As a result, when a new Bill was being proposed, it was not unusual for us to receive a personal phone call from the Minister in question, asking for our support to get it over the line!

Not that my willingness to support the Government was ever guaranteed, then or later. Despite cross-party support for the 2015 Marriage Equality Referendum, as an Independent I took the somewhat difficult decision to oppose it. I did this primarily because I had concerns about the lack of an 'opt-out' clause for religious reasons. Also I felt that many of the issues around equality had already been addressed through Civil Partnership. Nevertheless, the Irish people voted in favour of the referendum, which of course is their right in a modern democracy.

Over the years, there were some people, Ministers in particular – Michael McDowell was one – who were very good performers when they came to the Seanad. You could see they were listening to every word, and they would even interrupt at times to ask for clarification on what you were saying.

There were also some who quite clearly did not want to be there. Sometimes a Minister would address the Seanad and everybody there would respond, putting forward their views and making their points, and the Minister would be looking down the whole time, or talking to one of their party colleagues in a row in front of them.

You have only five minutes to make your point and you've planned it, and then the Minister starts talking to someone as you are speaking. The first time it happened to me I got quite upset; the next time it happened I just stopped speaking. It doesn't happen too often now because of how I react. I see it as a matter of basic good manners.

One particular former Minister came in one day, and as I was making my point he started talking to the person in the row in front of him. So I stopped, and he kept chatting. Then the Cathaoirleach said 'OK?' and I said 'I'm just waiting for the Minister's attention!' To this day, that former Minister has never spoken to me or acknowledged me; if we meet in the corridor he ignores me!

The other main frustration in the Seanad is the length of time it takes to get something done, particularly when compared to the business world. I have talked about changing the label on the orange juice in Superquinn and getting it done quickly. It would probably take years to get that done in the Oireach-tas! It is most frustrating to put forward a piece of legislation and find that there's no objection to it, and yet it drags on and on.

If there is a determination on the part of the relevant Minister to make something happen, then it can be done quickly. For example, the Government moved fast on the night of the bank guarantee. But unfortunately the political will is not always there.

Very often in Irish politics, practically all of the fifteen Cabinet Ministers were teachers or lawyers before getting elected. You would be lucky to find one of them who was ever in business.

I remember talking with Tony O'Reilly many years ago, not long after somebody new was appointed Minister for Finance.

'I think he's a good guy,' I said to Tony.

'He might be, but has he ever had to worry about paying the wages at the end of the week?' he asked. 'I don't have confidence in somebody unless they have had to worry about something like that. Feargal, you've had to do it; I've had to do it. I would prefer to see somebody in that role who has had to do it. But these guys are mainly teachers and lawyers.'

I always held a similar opinion in that regard, even before I became a Senator. I remember bringing it up in Dundalk way back in 1962, at a public meeting when the Government of the day was going to introduce a new profits tax.

It was a great term, because nobody liked people making profit. I stood up at the meeting and said my piece but got no sympathy whatsoever. I was a grocer running a business, saying 'If we are not able to make a profit how can we survive? How can we create jobs?' But everyone in the room believed that profits should be taxed, full stop, with no real explanation as to why.

I would say the vast majority of politicians, representing their constituents, argue on behalf of taking money, without arguing as to where the money comes from. And therein, all too often, lies the problem. Obviously there needs to be a mixture of skills within the Cabinet. But that mix should always, in my book, include some people from a business background.

* * *

Time was running out. I could see my fellow Senator nonchalantly 'loitering' outside before the doors shut for the vote. The stakes were high: if he timed his entrance perfectly, we would defeat the Government on a Bill that I had been working on for some time.

The purpose of my Upward Only Rent (Clauses and Review) Bill was to stop a practice that allowed landlords to charge businesses unfair 'upward only' rents.

The idea of the practice was to get big investors and pension funds to invest in things like shopping centres. The carrot was rent leases that would guarantee that the return on investment could only go up: a 'safe bet'.

Under the system, you might sign a lease in 2005 saying you were willing to pay the agreed rent. Built into the lease was a review of the rent after a set number of years, but the review would be upward only! If you said you didn't want that clause in the lease, then you quite simply did not progress the signing, and the landlord got somebody else to rent the shop who would agree to these terms.

During the 1990s and early 2000s rents were going up all the time, in line with the booming economy. Then in 2008/09, turnover collapsed, so shops couldn't afford these 'boomtime' rents, which were automatically being increased by the landlords due to the upward only rent legislation.

It was grossly unfair. I thought the market should be based on a fair rent – nothing more and nothing less.

Both Fine Gael and Labour had it in their manifestos to stop these leases, and proposals to change the law made it into the Programme for Government. But they changed their minds, only removing upward only clauses from leases signed from 2012 onwards.

The Government were worried about the constitutionality of removing the clause from earlier contracts, and decided that was the limit to what they could do. So I decided to force the issue with my own Bill.

With the support of Fianna Fáil, Sinn Féin and the Independents, we believed there was a real possibility that we could win this vote. It was the Final Stage of the Bill, so if we were successful it would still have to get through the Dáil. To achieve a 'win' in a Government-controlled Seanad would augur well in terms of giving the Government food for thought on this issue.

In February 2014 my Private Members' Bill went to an electronic vote. It was a dead heat until the Cathaoirleach of the Seanad, Paddy Burke, used his casting vote to reject the Bill.

Immediately I called for a 'walk through' vote. I knew there were some members around the House who had promised to be there but weren't. A 'walk through' meant those not in the Chamber would have a further opportunity to come in and vote by walking through on the Yes or No side.

But Senator Paul Bradford, one of my Independent colleagues who had recently helped to establish the Renua political party, was missing. His vote was vital if we were going to win. I phoned him and he ran up to the back door of the Chamber. He didn't come into the room straight away. Instead he loitered outside, trying to give the appearance of 'nothing to see here'!

With just five seconds to go he stepped inside and we won the vote by the narrow margin of twenty-three to twenty-two!

Later he told me that the reason he didn't come in earlier was to ensure that the Government wouldn't realise he was there. If they had seen him they would have known they were going to lose, and would have sought to get another 'body' into the Chamber on the Government side!

There were others coming up on the other side for the vote, but the doors were closed. Once the Cathaoirleach says to close the doors, the ushers do so immediately. They are very strict and there is no admittance.

So we won, with support from some of the Taoiseach's nominees (the so-called Enda-pendents!), other Independents, Fianna Fáil and Sinn Féin. We were also helped by the absence of a number Government Senators.

It was a great victory, if more than a little dramatic given that it was based essentially on a 'numbers game'. The fact that we could defeat the Government on an issue like this indicates that the Seanad could offer a very real form of checks and balances to the Government of the day, if only it were given more scope to do so.

The beauty of being an Independent in Seanad Éireann is that I can pick and choose the issues I want to campaign on, rather than being subject to the whims of the party whip.

I am not stepping on somebody's toes when it comes to choosing the issues I am concerned about. If somebody came to me with a good suggestion, or if I read something in the paper, I would say, 'Somebody should do something about that.' I would then invariably say, 'Well, I suppose I could be the one to do it!'

Also, I am not afraid to vote with the Government of the day where I feel they merit my support. I always think it is much harder to govern than to sit on the Opposition benches. Because of this, I feel it is only right to support them in their work from time to time.

Unsurprisingly, I have always had an inclination towards supporting issues of relevance to business, such as the upward only rent issue.

Another example was my efforts to reform problems with contract law in the area of construction. Now I knew very little about construction contracts when I entered the Seanad, but I knew that cash flow was very important to sub-contractors, many of whom were left high and dry in the recession after the main contractors they had worked with refused to pay them.

So I put together a Private Members' Bill which aimed to tackle the problem.

It sought to introduce guarantees about how much and when a contractor will be paid. It gave them the right to stop work if they were not paid, and if there was a row, rather than go to court which can take years and a lot of money, there would be an independent adjudication system.

Until then, if a sub-contractor stopped work in protest when the bigger contractor didn't pay on time, the sub-contractor could be sued because they had agreed to do the job. The fact that they had not been paid made no difference!

I was delighted when my original Bill was eventually passed into law in 2013, after it was adopted by the Fine Gael/Labour Government. Private Members' Bills are very rarely enacted, so it was quite a coup.

It is by no means unusual for the Government to take a Private Members' Bill and incorporate its key elements into a 'brand new', Government-sponsored Bill.

While the ultimate outcome is the same, and the issues relevant to the Bill are addressed, the Seanad member in question (and indeed the role of the Seanad in leading to the new law) is rarely sufficiently acknowledged.

More often than not, the Government of the day does this because it doesn't want to give the credit to someone who isn't in Government. It is a method I have seen employed over and over again during my time in Seanad Éireann, to great (and rather frustrating) effect.

I had a very personal reason for pushing one particular issue.

David Ryan was nineteen when he learned that a problem in his heart could only be solved with a heart transplant. David, a son of Margaret Ryan, a colleague in Superquinn Sutton, waited, and waited, and waited for a donor heart. As he waited David got weaker. After eighteen months he and his family learned that a suitable match was available.

Margaret contacted the media to highlight the need for a better organ donation scheme. She ran a campaign with our colleagues and our customers to promote the donor card scheme.

David was twenty years old when the operation took place on Good Friday 2000. Margaret told me of the joy when he came back to consciousness. He was unable to speak but wrote '21 soon' to his mother to remind her of his upcoming birthday.

Within two days he was on his feet, chatting and well on the mend, taking an interest in his new life. On Easter Monday he watched the races from Fairyhouse on the hospital TV and appeared well on the road to recovery. His mother and his immediate family were overjoyed.

Unfortunately, two days later, on the Wednesday after Easter, the transplanted heart was rejected. David died the following Friday. The medical opinion was that the eighteen-month delay for the transplant probably contributed to his death.

Margaret, having had time to discuss it with him, was aware that David was happy to have his organs donated to help others. She told me that she felt somewhat comforted in the knowledge that two people have a better life because of his donation.

I'm told that his eyes went to two different people: a twenty-five-year-old and a seventy-five-year-old man.

At the same time as this happened with David, in the same Superquinn supermarket, two other members of staff were waiting for kidneys. I saw their health deteriorate in front of my eyes.

Since then I have taken a keen interest in the whole question of organ donation. Dr Patrick Condon in Waterford initially drew my attention to the different rates of organ donations in various countries. I learned that the number of donations per head of population is much higher in Spain than in Ireland. This is largely due to the fact they have 'presumed consent' in Spain, meaning that when someone dies it is presumed they have consented to their organs being donated unless they specified otherwise.

With this in mind, in 2008 I put forward my own Human Body Organs and Human Tissue Bill. This provided for a presumption in favour of consent in relation to the removal of human body organs and human tissue for organ donation.

I felt something had to be done to ensure that people like David Ryan and others do not have to wait unnecessarily for the vital organs they need.

Ultimately I withdrew the Bill in the Seanad, as the Fianna Fáil-led Government of the day indicated that it wanted to look at the issues in more detail with a view to reintroducing it at a later stage.

I felt it was a victory for my campaign, and took the Government at its word. Unfortunately, little has been done since then to bring about presumed consent.

Nevertheless, it is an issue that continues to be championed to this day by others such as the prominent GAA commentator and organ donor Joe Brolly, as well as the Oireachtas Health Committee. So, using my role as Senator, and despite the failure to legislate to date, I was able to generate significant media and public discourse on this important issue. Again, this shows what the Seanad can do, given the chance.

On a similar health theme, I sought to introduce legislation requiring owners of premises that have a large number of people coming through them to install defibrillators for public use, in order to save lives. I am hopeful that this Bill will be reconsidered by the next Government.

More recently, I sought to introduce legislation to ensure that spouses who kill their partners will not inherit their estate. We have known the Cawley family for years and often holidayed together. Celine was horrifically killed by her husband, Eamonn Lillis. He has since been released from prison, and has received a significant sum of money as a result of her death. As far as I am concerned, this is a situation that should never have been allowed in the first place.

Other areas that my Bills have covered include an initiative to ban the sale of Irish passports, tougher laws to reduce the abuse of migrants by employers, a Bill to ensure that life-saving carbon monoxide alarms are installed in all buildings offered for sale or rent, and another aimed at ensuring that a legislative framework is established to trace the provenance of food. Even more recently I have made the case for tighter regulation of drones to ensure that the public's right to privacy and public safety is not undermined.

There is a reason I have taken the time to outline all of the above.

In total, as just one Independent Senator, I have produced seventeen Bills over the course of my twenty-three-year career in the Seanad. That is more than one new Bill every two years, from conception to drafting to having it laid before the Oireachtas for debate and discussion.

As I have mentioned, some of these Bills have already become law or are likely to be enacted soon, such as the Construction Contracts Bill and the Defibrillators Bill. Others have been adopted by the Government of the day but not in the exact form I proposed.

Many of my colleagues in the Seanad have had a similar impact on a huge range of issues. Without the Seanad, none of this would have happened.

The problem is, the impact of these Bills is often underestimated. Just because they don't get voted through does not mean that they are a waste of time. The very fact that the issues they raise are put forward for discussion with the relevant Minister can lead to real change, albeit down the line.

And even if it can be frustrating when the Government of the day promises but fails to take action on a particular issue, such as my presumed consent initiative, a strong independent Seanad made up of Senators who really value their participation in the political process can serve as a 'watchdog' to hold the Government to account.

Added to this is the capacity of the Seanad to scrutinise planned legislation.

For these reasons, and many more, I threw myself wholeheartedly into the campaign to save Seanad Éireann when, in 2013, it was fighting for its very survival against a Government and Taoiseach that wanted it gone. I drew on all of my entrepreneurial skills, and an awful lot of help from some of the brightest political strategists, to help ensure it survived.

It was left up to our small band of Independents and supporters to articulate to the Irish public just why the Seanad's life support machine should not be switched off.

21

SAVING THE SEANAD

Whehen Enda Kenny stood up at the Fine Gael annual dinner in October 2009 and told those present that he planned to hold a referendum to abolish the Seanad, I was not the only one in shock.

I well remember watching his speech on TV at home. Sitting beside him was Frances Fitzgerald, a woman I had come to know well during her time as Leader of the Fine Gael party in the Seanad, until she was re-elected to the Dáil. From her reaction it was clear she had no idea that Enda was going to drop his bombshell!

For all intents and purposes it appeared to be a 'solo run' by the soon-to-be Taoiseach. At the time, he was struggling for popularity in the polls. Obviously he was going for the low-hanging fruit, the easy target that would draw attention and catch the imagination. And to my mind, the Seanad had been singled out more than a little unfairly.

I admit I was furious at the announcement. If I didn't believe in the vital role of the Seanad, I could have found better ways of using my time and energy over the years! It felt to me as if the Leader of the Opposition was dismissing the work and achievements of the Seanad. What puzzled me was that he had never shown any real interest in the Seanad prior to that point.

Yet even when the proposal was included in Fine Gael's general election manifesto, I still felt pretty confident it would never come to pass. It certainly didn't receive much attention at election time as a 'burning issue' that the general public were exercised about during a time of financial crisis.

But when it was subsequently included in the Programme for Government, I realised the referendum would definitely happen in the lifetime of the Government. And I knew that those of us who did not want to see the Seanad abolished would need to prepare to fight for its continued existence.

In December 2011, Michael McDowell, the former Tánaiste and Attorney General, made what would turn out to be an important speech on the Seanad in Trinity College Dublin. The *Irish Times* carried the speech the following day.

Michael outlined how he had been critical of the Seanad previously but had now come to the conclusion that it was an important element in our Constitution. Essentially, he had changed his mind about the abolition of the Seanad.

Sensing an opportunity, I picked up the phone to him.

'I'm fascinated by what you said,' I told him. 'Would you be free to come in to Leinster House, and I'll get representatives from each party and the Independents to come along?' Michael agreed immediately.

I invited two people from each of the political parties and groupings in the Seanad to meet with us for coffee the following morning. I was delighted when twenty-eight of the sixty members of the Seanad joined us.

Michael explained the background to his change of heart about the Seanad. It struck me that one of his most interesting points was that the Seanad could be reformed without a referendum if the Government of the day was willing to legislate for this. He had some ideas as to how this could come about.

Senator Katherine Zappone was one of those who attended the meeting. She came up to me afterwards and said 'Feargal, you mustn't let this die. That's a very strong case. Why don't you form a group to argue the case for reform rather than abolition of the Seanad?'

I liked the way she was thinking, but I knew that if we formed a 'reform' group and brought everybody in, we would have 28 members and we would never get anything done! Such a large grouping of disparate voices would be too unwieldy.

So I said 'Katherine, let's work together and we'll get some outside help.'

Obviously, we saw Michael McDowell as a key supporter. In addition, we invited the eminent barrister and columnist Noel Whelan to join us, as we were aware that he also supported our viewpoint. I asked the retired teachers' union leader Joe O'Toole to join us. I was aware that Joe, as a former Senator, knew how to get things done and he had been a member of the sub-committee on Seanad Reform chaired by Mary O'Rourke.

We held our first full meeting in the Dargan Room of the Merrion Hotel on 9 February 2012. Anne Ó Broin, who would go on to play a key coordinating role in the campaign, also attended.

We decided to set about ascertaining where various key bodies and lobby groups, such as IBEC, the Law Society, political parties and the Seanad nominating bodies, stood on the issue. We didn't even have a name at that stage, but those present would go on to form the nucleus of a campaign group that would ultimately help to defeat the Taoiseach's referendum.

From that moment on, our group reconvened roughly every second Monday, in anticipation of an announcement from the Government as to when the referendum would be held.

From day one of our campaign, we were aware that another former Attorney General, Peter Sutherland, had played a key role in defeating a 2011 referendum to give the Oireachtas enhanced powers of investigation.

One of the key interventions in that campaign had been when nine former Attorneys General signed their names to a letter to the *Irish Times* opposing the move. Given their legal experience and authority, this very public contribution helped to swing the vote against the proposals.

We wondered if we could do something similar with our fledgling campaign. First we had to see who would come on board. I was the only one who knew the eminent former Senator and civil servant Dr T.K. Whitaker: we have been friends for many years, and he is someone I have always held in huge regard.

I asked T.K. to write a letter supporting reform of the Seanad rather than abolition, and I was delighted when he agreed to do so, alongside a number of other well-known former Senators. One misstep was that we may have published the letter a little too early in the campaign, a year ahead of the referendum. But it was worthwhile and opened the debate.

In September 2012 we launched a discussion document: *Open It, Don't Close It.*

Among other things, this document proposed a reformed Seanad, which would include universal suffrage on an all-Ireland basis, votes for the diaspora, gender equality, and an enhanced role for the Seanad in scrutiny of EU legislation.

In essence, if implemented this would be the biggest transformation of the role of the Seanad in the history of the State. I was convinced that such a proposition was far more worthwhile than simply abolishing the Seanad.

On foot of this, we adopted a twin-track approach. In addition to attempting to convince people of the need for a reformed Seanad, we decided to produce a Bill and to introduce it into the Seanad. We all get turns to introduce Private Members' Bills should we so wish.

Katherine said she could introduce it in her slot. So in May 2013, we launched a draft version of the Zappone Quinn Bill, written for us by the legal expert Dr Brian Hunt, who drafted many of my Bills over the years. It encapsulated the proposals from *Open It, Don't Close It*.

Our Bill proposed that every person over eighteen eligible for an Irish passport on the island of Ireland would have a vote in Seanad elections on the basis of 'one person, one vote'. Also it would extend the right to vote in Seanad elections to Irish passport holders abroad and to all graduates of the other third-level colleges, and would confer a range of additional powers on the Seanad in areas such as scrutiny of legislation, the examination of public appointments and the holding of inquiries. Finally, the Bill would allow citizens to nominate candidates in a Seanad election.

Enda Kenny, now Taoiseach, had yet to formally announce the date of the referendum, but we knew it was coming.

When we launched the initial discussion document, many Senators volunteered to play an active role in any campaign against the referendum. But we realised early on that if the group of six became much larger, it would be like everything in Ireland: there was bound to be a split!

So the six of us agreed we would limit it to just us.

At this stage, I realised we might need funds. A few of us were happy to say 'I'll pay for that document' by writing a cheque to cover the cost of getting a few thousand copies printed up.

But Noel Whelan rightly pointed out that we needed to be very careful to avoid any suggestion that we were financing the campaign. He volunteered to liaise with the Standards in Public Office body to see we did everything correctly.

We knew we were hamstrung financially compared with the monies available to the Government parties who were supporting abolition.

This was because once we set up our campaign organisation, 'Democracy Matters', there was a limit of €2,500 on how much any individual could contribute.

In comparison, as political parties Fine Gael and Labour received significant sums of money from the Exchequer. This money couldn't on paper be used for campaigning purposes, but it freed them up to use other monies that they received from their supporters to help fund the campaign, should they need to do so.

As the campaign got into its stride, we realised that Fine Gael probably had a 'war chest' of about €200,000 and Labour probably had about €100,000.

In an attempt to address this deficit, Katherine and I wrote to various contacts. Eventually we pulled together €44,180. It was a tiny amount compared to the deep pockets of the Government, our opposition. Unfortunately, the rules seem to be stacked in favour of the Government of the day, and against groups, such as our own, who are trying to argue against them.

The inherent unfairness of this situation served only to reinforce our determination to succeed.

* * *

The Government campaign got under way in earnest when Taoiseach Kenny announced in June 2013 that the referendum would be held the following October.

We were surprised early on to hear relatively recent Fine Gael Seanad members such as Paschal Donohoe saying there was no point in having a Seanad. Our sense, although they would vehemently deny such a claim, was that they were simply doing what they were told.

Others within Government ranks were completely opposed to what they were being asked to do. In fact, a number of fellow Senators from Fine Gael and Labour made it very clear to me in private that they disagreed with their own Government, but had to abide by the ludicrous party whip system.

One Fine Gael and one Labour TD even contributed financially to our campaign, on the understanding that they would remain anonymous (a commitment I will honour here)! Their attitude was very much one of fear. The approach was 'I'm an active member of the party; please don't mention my name; I can't go out knocking on doors or distributing documentation. But I support what you are doing.'

Others went a step further and disobeyed their own party line by actively canvassing against abolition.

A few months before the referendum date was confirmed, in March 2013, we met with the two main opposition parties, Fianna Fáil and Sinn Féin, to gauge their views on whether the Seanad should be saved.

As a party that had been in Government for much of the previous two decades, Fianna Fáil had never done anything much to reform the Seanad. So we were relieved to hear that under the leadership of Micheál Martin, they were in favour of reform rather than abolition.

We met Sinn Féin leader Gerry Adams with his colleague Senator David Cullinane. We got the firm impression that our *Open It, Don't Close It* policy document was acceptable to Sinn Féin. Part of the reason for our confidence in this regard was that we were proposing that everybody eligible for an Irish passport on the island of Ireland should have a vote. We realised this was right up Sinn Féin's alley. Therefore we expected that Sinn Féin would be on board.

When the Sinn Féin Ard Chomhairle met to discuss the party's position, I felt quite confident that they would support us, based on what Gerry Adams and David Cullinane had told us. So it was a disappointment when it emerged that Sinn Féin had reversed its position, and had decided that abolition was the best option.

I learned that Pearse Doherty had come out in favour of abolition. I bumped into Pearse in the car park and he told me that 'We would probably support it if there was an option for reform, but we are not being given that option.'

We were determined to keep our independent campaign going, regardless of what the various political parties were doing. In the run-up to polling day, the Government certainly did its best to ramp up its populist anti-Seanad message.

We found some aspects of its arguments particularly frustrating. The Taoiseach and others from the Government side repeatedly claimed that the Seanad had been around for seventy-five years and yet had only rejected two Bills. This was an utterly flawed argument from our perspective. We made the point that it was not the Seanad's primary function to reject Bills. It was not set up in this way, as the Dáil is the prime democratic House.

Instead, the role of the Seanad was to scrutinise and amend Bills in order to improve them, as well as to introduce its own legislation on occasion. My own record in the House showed just what can be done by individual Senators.

We knew we had to counter this argument with facts, so we analysed the previous two and a half years of the current Seanad and found that over 500 amendments to legislation were proposed during that time alone.

These amendments came from all sides of the House, including the Government parties. They included direct input into Bills covering areas such as personal insolvency, childcare, credit union regulation and the protection of temporary workers.

So we had over 500 quite recent examples whereby legislation that had already gone through the Dáil had come into the Seanad and had been amended. Put another way, it was improved because the Seanad acted as another 'pair of eyes' to scrutinise its content.

This supported our contention that the primary role of the Seanad is not to reject legislation but to improve it.

The second argument put forward by the Government was that numerous efforts had been made down through the years to reform the Seanad, and nothing had come of them. Again, we found this more than a little spurious as an argument for abolition of the Seanad. There was a definite element of 'throwing out the baby with the bathwater' thinking going on here!

Our point was that such reform was in the hands not of the Seanad but of the Government parties of the day. Fine Gael seemed to be saying 'We were not in power: Fianna Fáil were in power for most of that time and nothing happened', when in fact Fine Gael had also been in power on several occasions and had not seized the opportunity for real reform.

Moreover, a previous referendum to allow voting in the Seanad election to be extended to all third-level graduates had been passed by the Irish people in 1979. But no Government of any persuasion in the thirty-plus years since then had taken it upon itself to enact the legislation!

In this context, the Government's claim that there had been numerous failed attempts at reform of the Seanad simply beggared belief.

Despite our enthusiasm during the campaign, the polls were consistently showing widespread public support for abolition. We were acutely aware that the Government were ploughing not just money but political capital into the campaign. They had their 'big hitters' out, including Minister Richard Bruton in addition to Paschal Donohoe and Regina Doherty. We were really up against it.

Maybe it is the natural optimist in me, but I was always confident that we could turn it around. I believed that if we could just make the case for reform of the Seanad, we would be able to convince voters not to abolish it.

We always felt it was hugely unfair to simply present people with a choice between abolition and retention, rather than offering a 'third way' – retention with reform. So as a group we set about getting our message across in earnest. Meanwhile, other independent Senators and Labour Party Senators were equally vocal in their support of retention and reform. Senator John Crown wrote a Bill proposing Seanad reform.

From my perspective, I was most anxious to outline a vision for a Seanad that could represent independent voices of all political persuasions.

I fully agreed with some of the criticisms of the Seanad system as it currently operates. For too long it has been seen as a nursery for future TDs or a retirement home for those who have lost their seats. That was the charge being made by Government, and to a certain extent they were correct because there are a number of people in both lobbies who fit that bill: they didn't get elected to the Dáil for whatever reason, so they decided to take 'second best' – the Seanad.

The logic was 'It gives me a seat and allows me to raise my profile so I stand a chance to get elected to the Dáil next time around', or 'It allows me to ease myself out of politics.'

My own experience after two decades inside Seanad Éireann was that this only applied to those involved in party politics. What's more, this was a 'feudal' system that had been allowed to prosper under successive Governments. My suspicion was that it suited all of the major parties to maintain this status quo.

It was by no means unusual for me to see all five independently university elected Senators present at every Seanad meeting. By comparison, engagement among party political members was often very poor. Sometimes only two or three each from Fianna Fáil, Fine Gael and Labour were present, yet all five independent university Senators were active in the Chamber.

These included Father of the House David Norris, who played a very active role on many disparate subjects over the years; Sean Barrett, who has expertise on the economy and financial matters; the eminent oncologist John Crown, with valuable insight into health and other matters; Rónán Mullen, a lawyer, whose different perspective is not otherwise represented in the Seanad; and then there's me! I saw real value in having these five very different viewpoints and perspectives in the national parliament. Very often you would see the five of us there, chomping at the bit to make a contribution.

I witnessed first-hand what individual Senators could achieve if given the chance. I was convinced by my own experiences that a reformed Seanad could offer a much better way forward, if only the political will existed to make it happen.

In truth, the Taoiseach could have decided to reform the Seanad. But he chose the populist option, to my mind.

The Government came out with yet another reason to abolish the Seanad. On posters and in advertisements they told the public that abolition would lead to fewer politicians and savings of €20m a year.

We got very upset when we saw that figure being bandied about, as we knew it was quite simply untrue. We fought back by checking the actual figures with Kieran Coughlan, the Clerk of the Dáil, who was also Accounting Officer of the Oireachtas.

It was a big moment for us in the campaign when Mr Coughlan publicly testified that the gross annual saving from the abolition of the Vote of the Seanad would be less than €10 million. The net savings would be very much less if we take account of the fact that 30% of it goes back to the Exchequer in taxes, levies and VAT. So the real annual cost of the Seanad is probably in the region of €6 million.

* * *

The referendum campaign was a huge commitment in terms of our time. In the face of the Government's extensive networks and resources, we really were starting from scratch. But we were confident that what we were doing was right. The challenge was to ensure that we got the message out there.

In the run-up to polling day, our group met weekly to strategise how best to get our message across. Also we extended our group to include other voices.

It was non-stop, and certainly we were on the phone to one another or emailing every day. We constantly monitored and counteracted developments in the campaign.

We held public meetings and encouraged others to become involved in our 'Democracy Matters' campaign. We contacted former Seanad members and asked them to get involved. And we set about upping our public and media appearances around the country.

Most of those helping us were volunteers, and I found it genuinely exciting to see the energy and enthusiasm with which they threw themselves into the fray.

Throughout the campaign Fine Gael and Labour TDs came to us saying, 'We support you but we can't say it.' I felt that that spoke volumes about the way the party whip system works in the Oireachtas.

To this day Senators regularly stand up in the Seanad and say 'I agree entirely with you but unfortunately I am going to have to vote with the Government.' Also it was fairly clear that there were Labour Ministers saying 'Well, I'm not going out to canvass; I don't support it. But it's party policy and it's in the Programme for Government so I can't go out publicly against it.'

When I was canvassing for the retention of the Seanad a man said to me, 'I don't need that leaflet; I'm going to vote no to the abolition.' I said 'Tell me why' and he said 'Out of spite … to give the Government a thrashing!' So the protest vote was definitely a factor.

Meanwhile the Taoiseach wasn't really playing any role in the campaign. Despite entreaties from Micheál Martin, he was refusing to engage in debate.

Opinion polls were seldom wrong, and they were consistently showing that we would lose, but my gut was telling me differently. I went canvassing in Dublin city and also went to Wexford, Drogheda and elsewhere. The vast majority of the people we met were supporting us, so I was constantly surprised at the opinion polls that were coming out. We were getting eight out of ten on the street saying 'I'm with you', yet the polls were showing that we had only 30% support! The Irish people, as it turned out, were telling porkies when responding to the pollsters!

At one stage Paddy Power bookmakers were offering odds of 11/1 against us, so as far as some people were concerned it was finished. I didn't listen to the naysayers.

During the last week of the campaign, Enda Kenny's refusal to debate upset people. There was a noticeable turn in public sentiment. If the Taoiseach of the day, and the man whose big idea it was to hold the referendum, was refusing to debate the issues then it definitely sent out a conflicting message.

If you commit yourself to something, even if it's only a football match, the fact that you are told you haven't a chance doesn't matter. One of my favourite quotes is Masatoshi Ito's 'Whether you believe you can or whether you believe you can't, you're right!'

Certainly I got the impression that everyone on the team, the 'Gang of Six' and all the other volunteers, were committed to it right to the end. We simply didn't allow ourselves to contemplate losing.

I woke up on the morning of the results, 5 October 2013, expecting to head into the count centre in the RDS later that day. Then I got a call from Anne to tell me that the early results were suggesting we had won it!

In all honesty, I didn't quite realise that the result would become clear so early on. I began to hear different reports on the radio. Some polling stations were reporting it to be neck and neck. Then we began to hear that in some parts of the country it wasn't neck and neck at all. We were getting some very strong indications that we were ahead, while the reports from more rural areas were less sure.

By lunchtime, we knew we were winning and so Katherine, Noel, Joe, Michael and I went in as a group for the announcement. Unfortunately Anne was down the country, but she was on the phone throughout.

I got a taxi to Dublin Castle – Denise stays away from these things. The TV cameras were there. I was anxious to make sure that we did not seem triumphalist. Also I wanted to reinforce the message that reform of the Seanad – a choice not given to the Irish people in this referendum – should remain firmly on the table.

This all took place on 5 October. Those of you who have been paying close attention in the earlier chapters will realise that this date marked the eve of our 51st wedding anniversary! I could hardly think of a nicer way to celebrate that evening.

* * *

When the result of the referendum was announced, Taoiseach Kenny spoke in Dublin Castle. While acknowledging that he had received a 'wallop' from the electorate, he spoke frankly of how he recognised the will of the people and that he would 'reflect upon the best way' in which the Seanad 'could make a contribution to change in politics'.

Many of us who had opposed the abolition of Seanad Éireann were happy to take the Taoiseach at his word. Our fervent hope was that real and substantial reform could be achieved quickly.

I think everyone gathered in Dublin Castle on results day knew that Seanad Éireann could not continue to function with any credibility based on the old way of doing things, where most of its members are elected only by Councillors, outgoing Senators and incoming TDs.

If anything, our victory in the referendum campaign had served to highlight the fact that this way of doing things was not 'fit for purpose'.

We were also keenly aware, as was the Taoiseach, that real reform of the Seanad and how it is elected could be achieved relatively easily by legislation, rather than by constitutional change. It just requires political will.

So we were somewhat disappointed when it emerged that the Taoiseach's initial proposals for Seanad reform were quite limited. A few weeks after the referendum, in November 2013, he announced his intention to replace the existing arrangement whereby there are two third-level constituencies in the Seanad – one for graduates from the National University of Ireland and the other for

Trinity College graduates – with a single constituency in which all third-level graduates could vote and elect six Senators.

This change would have been welcome, even though it was only really implementing a reform that had been endorsed by the Irish people in a constitutional referendum on 5 July 1979. Indeed, as I have mentioned above, it beggars belief that more than a third of a century on, this change still has not been implemented.

But expanding the basis for third-level representation in the Seanad would not of itself amount to real reform. That is why, in 2013, I asked Enda Kenny to set up an all-party commission to explore wider reform.

After a delay of a year, the Taoiseach finally set up this working group. Chaired by the Chancellor of the National University, Maurice Manning – himself a former leader of the Seanad – the group was charged with proposing changes in how Senators could be elected.

It included former Senators from across the political spectrum, together with some academic experts and Tom Arnold, the former chairman of the Constitutional Convention.

When it published its report in April 2015, it recommended that all citizens, including emigrants and Irish citizens in Northern Ireland, have a vote in Seanad elections. Although it also recommended one thirteen-member panel to be elected by Councillors, TDs and Senators, its proposals were quite dramatic and far-reaching, including enhanced Seanad scrutiny of EU legislation, thirty Senators to be elected by popular vote, etc. If implemented, they would represent the biggest transformation in the make-up of the Seanad since the foundation of the Irish State.

Initially, it looked as if the process for real reform was back on track. Early in May, Maurice Manning and former Senator Joe O'Toole came to Seanad

Éireann to present the working group report as part of a Seanad debate. The group also published a draft Bill to help speed up the process of implementing its recommendations.

But very little, if anything, has happened since. This leaves many of us seriously doubting whether there is any real commitment within Government circles to bring about such sorely needed Seanad reform.

As an independent member of the Seanad, who was never faced with the pressure of 'toeing the line' by agreeing to a party whip, it subsequently made sense for me to join the Independent Alliance and to accept an invitation to act as its Chairman.

Founded in January 2015 by a group of five like-minded independent TDs, it includes significant reform of the existing political structures in Ireland among its key aims. Importantly for me, members will not be subject to a party whip, instead choosing to unite behind a core set of principles. It is a fresh way of thinking which intrigues me, and something that I firmly believe can work given time.

On 3 February 2016, I attended my last formal session of the 24th Seanad, after Taoiseach Enda Kenny announced his intention to dissolve the Dáil and call a general election. This also marked the culmination of my twenty-three years' service as a Senator, since I will not be running for election again (Denise says she will divorce me if I do ... and I don't doubt her!).

As I reflect on that time, I would love to say that our collective effort to save the Seanad has brought about real change, and the kind of reform necessary to reinforce and strengthen its role in Irish society.

I know that if Superquinn received a resounding message from our customers that we needed to change things, we would not hesitate to react. But unfortunately, it seems, the Irish political system does not work that way.

EPILOGUE

As I looked around at the three generations of my family gathered for a photo beneath the Superquinn sign in Sutton, I could not help but smile. Valentine's Day 2014 was a truly bittersweet day for me.

It was perhaps unspoken, but all twenty-eight of us gathered in the supermarket car park sensed that something very significant was taking place that day.

Some of my children and grandchildren had travelled from France just to be there as the current owners of the Superquinn chain, Musgraves, prepared to take down the Superquinn sign from Sutton forever.

This change would mark the disappearance of the Superquinn brand from everyday use, after more than forty years. While some innovations such as our famous Superquinn sausages would retain the brand name, it had been decided that all of the stores and merchandise would be changed to SuperValu.

Over the course of the previous few months, I had been genuinely touched at the amount of goodwill the announcement of the owners' plans to dispense with the Superquinn name had generated, on the airwaves, online and in print.

People rushed to share their stories of Superquinn over the years, and the many traditions it had established.

When Musgraves acquired Superquinn out of receivership in 2011, thereby securing its future after a very difficult period, I was more than a little relieved that my old company was going to an Irish family business rather than some anonymous multinational company.

On paper, at least, it should not have mattered. We had sold Superquinn almost a decade earlier. The days when my family and I were involved in its day-to-day running had long since disappeared.

But I was never that kind of retailer, and the staff who made Superquinn just what it became were never only my employees.

I described it at the time as being like when your daughter is getting married: 'You don't want to lose her but you are pleased with the partner she has chosen.'

Tim Kenny of Musgraves came to see me in Leinster House before the name change was announced publicly in August 2013. I immediately wished him well, before rather cheekily suggesting that he instead change the name of all 200-plus SuperValu stores to Superquinn!

I find the number of people still approaching me, particularly in the Sutton Superquinn (I have never felt right calling it SuperValu Sutton!), quite astonishing.

People regularly come to me on the street too, or stop to talk to me at traffic lights. Often, they tell me about their memories of me, my colleagues, and a time in Irish retailing that is rapidly disappearing.

I will never lose the thrill of chatting to them and hearing their stories.

I have always believed that there is no such thing as a stranger, only a friend you haven't yet met. Nowhere is this more true than in my relationship with the customers and staff of Superquinn.

Simply listening to their stories has helped me to generate a lifetime of wonderful memories.

I'm listening, still.

MY FATHER'S WILL

To be opened only in the case of the death of
Eamonn Eugene Quinn
of "Roscaoin", Newtownpark Avenue, Blackrock, Co. Dublin
June 3rd 1933

My last will and testament.

1. Everything, real, personal or otherwise, of which I die possessed, I bequeath absolutely to my wife Maureen.

2. My desire is that my executors be:
(a) my wife Maureen
(b) my father, John Quinn
(c) my friend, John Lavelle

3. I place no obligations on my wife, Maureen, as to what use she may make of my property, but it is my wish that she be guided in this respect by the other executors in seeing that the business, which I have helped to build up, will be helped as far as possible, while at the same time I believe she will find it a good investment.

Above: My parents, Eamonn and Maureen, on their wedding day in 1931.

4. If my wife, Maureen, desires to remarry she has my whole-hearted approval. She has been a wonderful wife, friend, pal and counsellor to me. She has smoothed out the ruts which at times came in my path and by her sweet personality has cheered me when I most needed cheering. I thank God for placing me in her way and for keeping us both single until we met. It was she in her own persuasive good-natured way, who taught me self-control and to be master of my own body. Any success or good I have done in life, I owe to her. If she remarries and is only one half as good a wife to him as she was and is to me, he will be a lucky man and will have a lot to be thankful for.

5. I also want to thank my father, for suffering me so long and I hope before he or I die to repay him a fraction of what I owe to him for his goodness and kindness. A father in a million.

6. My mother, I can never repay, for the mother's love she has given me unstinted from my childhood is not measurable in terms of repayment.

7. My aunt Ibby, my godmother, I thank from the bottom of my heart for the comradeship and guidance she has given me.

Signed,

Eamonn Quinn

June 8th 1933

In the presence of:

Margaret Heron,

25 Upper George's St,

Dun Laoghaire

'TRADING PLACES', *SUNDAY INDEPENDENT*, 23 JUNE 1996

Leading investigative journalist swaps places with supermarket chief.
Great idea, if it had worked! Veronica Guerin and Feargal Quinn report on
what happened when they tried to trade places.

The idea was great. I was to shadow Feargal Quinn for a week, attend his meetings, watch him in the Seanad; wherever he went I was to follow. In turn he would work with me for a few days. He would help research stories, meet the people I was meeting and generally work his ass off to file a story.

The reality of course differed from the theory and the problems arose when Feargal was due to accompany me on my bout of duty. He never chickened out but both of us agreed it would be inappropriate for him to meet drug dealers and convicted criminals. It was just our misfortune that during the period we were shadowing each other, the stories I was working on involved such meetings.

Realising from the outset therefore that a lot depended on my stint with Feargal, I was determined to meet his demanding schedule. Initially I thought that there was only so much one could listen to about supermarkets.

Customers are Feargal's buzz: what they want, how they feel, what motivates them, their choice of bloody vegetables for God's sake. One of the first meetings I attended with him was a Customer Panel at one of his Southside stores. After ten minutes I was worn out listening to well informed views of the problems in the shop.

Two women explained why they went to Quinnsworth for their vegetables – "the quality is better" and "the choice is greater". I looked across at Feargal expecting to see agitation etched on his face. Not a sign of it, he wanted to hear more and succeeded in drawing further criticisms from his assembled customers. At the end of the meeting I frankly expressed my view that "that was a real pain, you must be bored." "Not at all," he replied sincerely, "we got to know what we've got to do to keep our customers happy."

At the same meeting we heard many kind comments about the staff in the store. All of those mentioned got a personal thank you from the Boss before he left. This wasn't done just for the benefit of the visiting reporter. I attended a function in the Berkeley Court Hotel for long-standing Superquinn staff. They were given the most expensive meal available and had an open bar for the night. Each employee and their partner were personally welcomed by Feargal and Denise and had a photograph taken with them. Before leaving they were presented with a framed shot to mark the occasion. I mingled with the guests as they drank champagne. All claimed Superquinn was a great place to work,

Trading . . .

Leading investigative journalist swaps places with supermarket chief. Great idea, if it had worked! Veronica Guerin and **Feargal Quinn** report on what happened when they tried to trade places.

WHAT'S it like to be followed around by a renowned journalist, looking over your shoulder as you go through your daily work? The answer is that, amazingly quickly, you forget the journalist is there at all. Within minutes of getting involved in any meeting that Veronica attended with me, I was totally oblivious of her being there. You become so wrapped up in doing what you are there to do that the fact there's an audience slips out of your consciousness.

To be honest, this came as little surprise to me. There have been 'fly-on-the-wall' television documentaries where an entire film crew moved in on a family and followed their doings for months. After a while, they stopped noticing — and went on behaving the way families always do behind closed doors. I had my own experience of that some years ago; we had a fire in one of our shops, and we commissioned a video crew to record our response as an exercise in crisis management. Again, we found that we soon forgot about the existence of the camera and got on with the job.

I think most people are more open to being watched than journalists might think. I brought Veronica with me to a wide variety of meetings, and of course before each one I had to ask the permission of the people I was meeting with. Invariably, the reaction was one of interest and welcome.

She sat in with me, for instance, on a judging session of the IFEX food-industry awards, and on a committee meeting of the Grocers Benevolent Fund. Both meetings were exactly the same, as if she hadn't been there. I have, however, to confess one little piece of subterfuge. When Veronica attended one of our customer panel meetings at our Knocklyon shop, I did not warn the customers in advance. Until the end of the meeting, when I came clean, I passed her off as another customer.

The reason I did this was that

I feel it's very important in our customer panel meetings that the customers greatly outnumber the others. It is their show, and I usually am there with just one other person who writes up the report of the meeting. If customers come into a room stuffed with observers, they may be less likely to tell me off — which is exactly what I want them to do.

So on this occasion Veronica travelled incognito — not a difficult task for a crime reporter, even if she isn't the one who does the family shopping! When it came to accompanying me on my Thursday morning tour around a Superquinn shop with the previous week's sales and profit figures, she had — like me — to put on a white coat to go behind the shop counters. No doubt there, however, I told our staff exactly who she was.

But that visit demonstrated one of the hazards for the journalist as shoulder-looker-over: Veronica had to endure tour and over again my telling the exact same anecdote which I used to make a point about the week's figures, as I worked my way around the shop. I try to make my jokes good, but perhaps they don't bear hearing six or seven times in quick succession! Boredom aside, I have generally found it business that being open pays off. We share an enormous amount of information with our staff, information that in other companies might be considered commercially sensitive. In fact, I believe there is very little information in business that has to be kept truly confidential. I work on the premise that most information about the business is not confiden-

tial at all, and indeed that there is a positive benefit in sharing it.

Mind you, I got the impression from Veronica that many of the people she writes about in the crime world have a somewhat different attitude! At the beginning she expressed some surprise that I would trust her to the extent of letting her see anything about my business life that she wanted to. But, as I explained, my instinct is to trust people — and my experience is that people can be trusted. And sure enough, it proved so in this case. You will scour her article about me in vain for a word about one of the greatest fast-as I have made in a very long time. It happened on the very first day she followed me around. I should explain that one of the things I have to work very hard at is getting people's names right. You can't chair a meeting, for instance, if you don't remember the names of the people around the table.

The first function Veronica attended with me was our Superquinn long-service dinner, where people who have been with the company for 10, 15 or 20 years get recognition for their service. I would, of course, have to trouble with the award-winners themselves — not remembering the names of each of their spouses took a good deal of homework in advance. I was feeling very pleased with myself on that occasion, I had managed to get everybody's name right, greeting them as they came into the function. Then Veronica arrived, and I introduced her to my wife Denise.

Then, I said, is Orla Guerin.

THE idea was great. I was to shadow Feargal Quinn for a week, attend his meetings, watch him in the Seanad; wherever he went I was to follow. In turn he would work with me for a few days. He would help research stories, meet the people I was meeting and generally work his ass off to file a story.

The reality of course differed from the theory and the problems arose when Feargal was due to accompany me on my bout of duty. He never clickened out but both of us agreed it would be inappropriate for him to meet drug dealers and convicted criminals. It was just our misfortune that during the period we were shadowing each other, the stories I was working on involved such meetings.

Realising from the outset therefore that a lot depended on my stint with Feargal, I was determined to meet his demanding schedule. Initially I thought that there was only so much one could listen to about supermarkets.

Customers are Feargal's buzz: what they want, how they feel, what motivates them, their choice of bloody vegetables for God's sake. One of the first meetings I attended with him was a Customer Panel at one of his Southside stores. After ten minutes I was worn out listening to well informed views of the problems in the shop.

Two women explained why they went to Quinnsworth for their vegetables — "the quality is better" and "the choice is greater". I looked across at Feargal expecting to see agitation etched on his face. Not a sign of it, he wanted to hear more and succeeded in drawing

further criticisms from his assembled customers. At the end of the meeting I frankly expressed my view that "that was a real pain, you must be bored." "Not at all," he replied sincerely, "we know now what we've got to do to keep our customers happy."

At the same meeting we heard many kind comments about the staff in the store. All of them mentioned got a personal thank you from the Boss before he left. This wasn't done just for the benefit of the visiting reporter. I attended a function in the Berkeley Court Hotel for long-serving Superquinn staff. They were given the most expansive meal available and had an open bar for the night. Each employer and their partner were personally welcomed by Feargal and Denise and had a photograph taken with them. Before leaving they were presented framed shots to mark the occasion. I mingled with the guests as they drank champagne. All claimed Superquinn was a great place to work citing opportunities and conditions. A shop steward told me that in his experience Quinn was the fairest of the supermarket employers.

Part of Feargal's success is due to his ability to manage his time properly. A meticulously planned schedule enables him to work in the shop and attend the Seanad regularly. His diary and timetable is controlled with military precision by his personal assistant, Anne Ó Broin. He tells her what he wants to do, whom he wants to meet, and she does the rest. I thought she'd only let me attend boring shop visits and consumer panels and I mentally prepared myself

as I argued to attend the really sexy business meetings. But I was wrong.

I was handed Feargal's diary and told, "just tell me where you want to go." I was astonished at the openness and cynically enquired about a second chair in angel. "There isn't one," I was told. A careful study confirmed this as every hour of every day was taken up with something. I settled for various business meetings and a visit to the Seanad.

It really did frustrate me that all Feargal's work was done with a smile. During all the

> I was handed Feargal's diary and told, 'just tell me where you want to go'. I was astonished at the openness

hours I spent with him, he never lost his cool. His p.a. insists she has only ever seen him lose his temper once. On that occasion, she says, he lifted out of his chair in anger and went in search of an errant employee. "Luckily for all of us, the employee was on a day off, and Feargal had calmed down by the time the he was back at work."

Feargal and his management team have a good working relationship with staff. Every

employees in each store are briefed on the previous week's trading. I accompanied Feargal on one such briefing to the Finglas store where I was convinced I'll see "an exercise in public relations." I was astonished when Feargal produced a lengthy printout itemising each sections' respective trading figures. Employees saw for themselves the company's overall trading position and heard what stores were performing well and what stores weren't.

The butchers in Finglas asked intelligent questions about profit margins, ratios, percentages of profit against turnover and sounded more like accountants. Their suggestions for higher sales and more customers were noted by Quinn and has a wonderful sense of humour but his work load is boring.

And, given that's he put up with my low boredom threshold and impatience firsthand, I doubt he'd trust me to do his job for a day.

A vital characteristic for Feargal's job is patience and he has it in abundance. His easy going demeanour belies a hardworking, thoughtful individual. Every day for him presents new each fresh challenges, he takes them on and inevitably they succeed. We didn't carry out the exercise as originally intended, but we had great craic together.

He will excuse me a lunch and I'll remind Chief of Staff Ó Broin to fit me in soon.

— FQ

citing opportunities and conditions. A shop steward told me that in his experience Quinn was the fairest of the supermarket employers.

Part of Feargal's success is due to his ability to manage his time properly. A meticulously planned schedule enables him to work in the shop and attend the Seanad regularly. His diary and timetable is controlled with military precision by his personal assistant, Anne Ó Broin. He tells her what he wants to do, whom he wants to meet, and she does the rest. I thought she'd only let me attend boring shop visits and consumer panels and I mentally prepared myself for the row which would ensue as I argued to attend the really sexy business meetings. But I was wrong.

I was handed Feargal's diary and told, "just tell me where you want to go." I was astonished at the openness and cynically enquired about a second diary. "There isn't one," I was told. A careful study confirmed this as every hour of every day was taken up with something. I settled for various business meetings and a visit to the Seanad.

It really did frustrate me that all Feargal's work was done with a smile. During all the hours I spent with him, he never lost his cool. His p.a. insists she has only ever seen him lose his temper once. On that occasion, she says, he lifted out of his chair in anger and went in search of an errant employee. "Luckily for all of us, the employee was on a day off, and Feargal had calmed down by the time he was back at work."

Feargal and his management team have a good working relationship with the staff. Every Thursday morning at 8.00am employees in each store are briefed on the previous week's trading. I accompanied Feargal on one such briefing to the Finglas store where I was convinced I'd see "an exercise in public relations." I was astonished when Feargal produced a lengthy printout item-ising each section's respective trading figures. Employees saw for themselves the company's overall trading position and heard what stores were performing well and what stores weren't.

The butchers in Finglas asked intelligent questions about profit margins, ratios, percentages of profit against turnover and sounded more like account-ants. Their suggestions for higher sales and more customers were noted by Quinn and, I learned, subsequently introduced.

Despite the variety of the roles Feargal has, I could never be persuaded to trade places with him. He's great company and has a wonderful sense of humour but his work load is boring.

And, given that he's put up with my low boredom threshold and impatience firsthand, I doubt he'd trust me to do his job for a day.

A vital characteristic for Feargal's job is patience and he has it in abundance. His easy going demeanour belies a hard-working, thoughtful individual. Every day for him presents new and fresh challenges, he takes them on and inevitably they succeed. We didn't carry out the exercise as originally intended, but we had great craic together.

He still owed me lunch and I'll remind Chief of Staff Ó Broin to fit me in soon.

VERONICA GUERIN

What's it like to be followed around by a renowned journalist, looking over your shoulder as you go through your daily work? The answer is that, amazingly quickly, you forget the journalist is there at all. Within minutes of getting involved in any meeting that Veronica attended with me, I was totally oblivious of her being there. You become so wrapped up in doing what you are there to do that the fact there's an audience slips out of your consciousness.

To be honest, this came as little surprise to me. There have been fly-on-the-wall television documentaries where an entire film crew moved in on a family and followed their doings for months. After a while, they stopped noticing – and went on behaving the way families always do behind closed doors. I had my own experience of that some years ago: we had a fire in one of our shops, and we commissioned a video crew to record our response as an exercise in crisis management. Again, we found that we soon forgot about the existence of the camera and got on with the job.

I think most people are more open to being watched than journalists might think. I brought Veronica with me to a wide variety of meetings, and of course before each one I had to ask the permission of the people I was meeting with. Invariably, the reaction was one of interest and welcome.

She sat in with me, for instance, on a judging session of the IFEX food industry awards, and on a committee meeting of the Grocers Benevolent Fund. Both meetings were exactly the same as if she hadn't been there. I have, however, to confess one little piece of subterfuge. When Veronica attended one of our customer panel meetings at our Knocklyon shop, I did not warn the customers in advance. Until the end of the meeting, when I came clean, I passed her off as another customer.

The reason I did this was that I feel it's very important in our customer panel meetings that the customers greatly outnumber the others. It is their show, and I usually am there with just one other person who writes up the report of the meeting. If customers come into a room stuffed with observers, they may be less likely to tell me off – which is exactly what I want them to do.

So on this occasion Veronica travelled incognito – not a difficult task for a crime reporter, even if she isn't the one who does the family shopping! When it came to accompanying me on my Thursday morning tour around a Superquinn shop with the previous week's sales and profit figures, she had – like me – to put on a white coat and go behind the shop counters. No deceit there, however: I told our staff exactly who she was.

But that visit demonstrated one of the hazards for the journalist as shoulder-looker-over: Veronica had to endure over and over again my telling the exact same anecdote which I used to make a point about the week's figures, as I worked my way around the shop. I try to make my jokes good, but perhaps they don't bear hearing six or seven times in quick succession! Boredom aside, I have generally found in business that being open pays off. We share an enormous amount of information with our staff, information that in other companies might be considered commercially sensitive. In fact, I believe there is very little information in business that has to be kept truly confidential. I work on the premise that most information about the business is not confidential at all, and indeed that there is a positive benefit in sharing it.

Mind you, I got the impression from Veronica that many of the people she writes about in the crime world have a somewhat different attitude! At the beginning she expressed some surprise that I would trust her to the extent of letting her see anything about my business life that she wanted to. But, as I explained, my instinct is to trust people – and my experience is that people can be trusted.

And sure enough, it proved so in this case. You will scour her article about me in vain for a word about one of the greatest faux pas I have made in a very long time. It happened on the very first day she followed me around. I should explain that one of the things I have to work very hard at is getting people's names right. You can't chair a meeting, for instance, if you don't remember the names of the people around the table.

The first function Veronica attended with me was our Superquinn long-service dinner, where people who have been with the company for 10, 15 or 20 years get recognition for their service. I would, of course, have no trouble with the award-winners themselves – but remembering the names of each of their spouses took a good deal of homework in advance. I was feeling very pleased with myself on that occasion. I had managed to get everybody's name right, greeting them as they came into the function. Then Veronica arrived, and I introduced her to my wife Denise.

This, I said, is Orla Guerin.

FEARGAL QUINN